WOMEN AND SOCIETY
An Anthropological Reader

Editor:
Sharon W. Tiffany

Eden Press
Women's Publications

WOMEN AND SOCIETY
An Anthropological Reader

Editor:

Sharon W. Tiffany

Published by:
Eden Press Women's Publications
Montreal, Canada

and

Eden Press Women's Publications
Box 51, St. Albans, Vermont 05478, U.S.A.

ISBN: 0-920792-01-4

Printed in Great Britain by A. Wheaton & Co. Ltd. Exeter.

To the memory of my mother

LIST OF ILLUSTRATIONS

LIST OF TABLES

CONTENTS

PREFACE

This volume has its origins in my teaching and research in anthropology and women's studies. The papers were compiled with two goals in mind: to bring together previously published essays addressed to important questions in the cross-cultural study of women; and to provide an accessible work to students and professionals in both anthropology and women's studies. These papers, written over a twenty year period, consider several topics, with emphasis on female-male relations in the spheres of economics, politics, law, and marriage in societies of differing complexity. Within this institutional framework, the volume attempts to integrate the comparative perspective of anthropology with feminist issues.

To enhance the usefulness of this work, each essay ends with annotated suggestions selected from the anthropological and women's studies literature, in addition to inclusion of a general bibliography and glossary. Suggestions from readers for improving the format or content are welcomed.

This volume owes much to the co-operation and assistance of many persons. I wish to thank the individual contributors and their publishers for permission to reprint their papers. The authors' encouragement and prompt responses to my inquiries are much appreciated. I have learned a great deal about the anthropology of women and the feminist perspective from my colleagues, Kathleen Adams, Ivan Brady, Agate Krouse, and Denise O'Brien. Their stimulating conversations and constructive criticisms of my various manuscripts have been invaluable.

I am indebted to Russell F. Moratz, Reference and Interlibrary Loan Librarian at the University of Wisconsin-Whitewater; and Esther

Stineman, Women's Studies Librarian-At-Large for the University of Wisconsin System, for their prompt assistance with innumerable bibliographic details.

I gratefully acknowledge the help of my assistant, Marilyn Enstad, whose efficient typing and library research enabled me to complete the volume on schedule despite a broken wrist.

Finally, I thank my editor, Sherri Clarkson, for her support and help with numerous publication and editorial tasks.

To all who have shared their time and thoughts with me, my deepest gratitude.

ACKNOWLEDGMENTS

American Anthropological Association: "Women in Modernizing Societies," by Laurel Bossen, *American Ethnologist* 2 (4): 587-601, 1975; "A Note on the Division of Labor by Sex," by Judith K. Brown, *American Anthropologist* 72 (5): 1074-1078, 1970; "The Role of Women in a Changing Navaho Society," by Laila Shukry Hamamsy, *American Anthropologist* 59(1): 101-111, 1957; and "Going Home to Mother: Traditional Marriage among the Irigwe of Benue-Plateau State, Nigeria," by Walter H. Sangree, *American Anthropologist* 71(6): 1046-1057, 1969. Reprinted by permission of the authors and publisher.

American Society for Ethnohistory: "Economic Organization and the Position of Women among the Iroquois," by Judith K. Brown, *Ethnohistory* 17(3-4): 151-167. Reprinted by permission of the author and publisher.

Canadian Journal of African Studies: " 'Sitting on a Man:' Colonialism and the Lost Political Institutions of Igbo Women," by Judith Van Allen, *Canadian Journal of African Studies* 6(2): 165-181, 1972. Reprinted by permission of the author and publisher.

Ethnology: "Sex Differences in the Incidence of *Susto* in Two Zapotec Pueblos: An Analysis of the Relationships between Sex Role Expectations and a Folk Illness," by Carl W. O'Nell and Henry A. Selby, *Ethnology* 7(1): 95-105, 1968. Reprinted by permission of the authors and publisher.

Holt, Rinehart and Winston, Inc.: Excerpts from *The Barabaig: East African Cattle-Herders* by George J. Klima, Holt, Rinehart and Winston, 1970. Reprinted by permission of the author and publisher.

INTRODUCTION: THEORETICAL ISSUES IN THE ANTHROPOLOGICAL STUDY OF WOMEN

Sharon W. Tiffany

Woman, Simone de Beauvoir writes, is "the Other," the second sex. Woman is characterized by her secondary relationship to man and her invisibility--both statuses are fundamental and universal. In the introduction to her classic work, *The Second Sex*, de Beauvoir wonders if there is such a thing as a woman "problem." "And if so, what is it? Are there women, really?" She states that "One wonders if women still exist, if they will always exist, whether or not it is desirable that they should, what place they occupy in this world, what their place should be" (de Beauvoir 1952: xv). Her questions highlight two important issues in the anthropological study of women: Do women everywhere occupy statuses subordinant to those of men? And why do women seem invisible or, at best, marginal?

These questions are entangled in a web of differing concepts and definitions resulting in contradictory conclusions. Some anthropologists state that male dominance is a cultural universal (e.g., Divale and Harris 1976; Rosaldo 1974). Others (e.g., Leacock 1975, 1977, 1978; Sacks 1976) disagree, claiming that sexual equality exists but is overlooked by researchers who assume, based on relations of sexual inequality found in western industrialized societies, that asymmetry is present everywhere else in the world as well. When examining different perspectives concerning male-female relationships, we must ask

This paper was written especially for this volume.

1

what the concepts of dominance, subordination, and women's status mean. Are statements like, "women are subordinant to men in society" or "women's status is low (or high)," meaningful for cross-cultural comparisons?

WOMEN, MEN, AND STATUS

Sexual subordination and dominance imply an asymmetrical relationship in which members of one sex control, directly or indirectly, the activities and life opportunities of the other. Some anthropologists claim that women are subordinant to men in most, if not all, known societies. The reasons are varied. For some, male dominance is linked to differences in biological and reproductive roles. Reproductive and childbearing functions, it is argued, preclude women's active involvement in the social arena of politics and other prestige-enhancing activities associated with the "broader," nondomestic world of men. In this view, femaleness and women's roles are associated with nature and life giving forces, whereas men are equated with culture and intellectual activity (Ortner 1974). Others assert that female preoccupation with childbearing and rearing and the formation of tightly knit male bonds for group defense are adaptive responses to conditions of endemic hostility and warfare. Men are dominant because they are essential for defense and protection; they monopolize power through superior physical strength and by controlling weaponry. Male power is further enhanced by a cultural ideology of male superiority which legitimizes the authority of men to enforce their decisions (Divale and Harris 1976; Tiger 1969). In short, sexual inequality is a fundamental aspect of human existence.

Other authors question assertions of universal female subordination. Asymmetrical relations between the sexes can be interpreted instead as products of specific sociocultural conditions. According to this perspective, dominance is linked to control over the production and distribution of valued goods and wealth. Friedl (1975, 1978), for example, relates male dominance to control over the distribution of scarce resources, which constitute animal protein in economies based on gathering-hunting and land in agricultural societies. Male dominance increases as men enhance their control over valuables. Controlling access to resources and the distribution of wealth are critical in assessing the

2

extent to which women acquire political power that is both socially recognized and approved (e.g., see Engels 1972; Leacock 1975; Sacks 1974; Sanday 1974; Schlegel 1977a). In other words, economic power can, under certain conditions, be translated into political power. Why do women exercise political and economic power in some societies and not in others? The answer, according to this view, lies in determining the conditions under which women do or do not control access to and the distribution of resources. That is, who controls labor and the ways in which goods and wealth are used to form social relations which extend beyond the domestic sphere?

Much of the difficulty in assessing observed similarities and differences in female-male relations stems from using terms like dominance and subordination. Dominance is based on hierarchic relations involving differential control of power and economic resources; subordination implies a relative lack of autonomy over one's own activities and the inability to control the behavior of others. Dominance, as recent writings on women's status illustrate (Quinn 1977; Schlegel 1977a), refers to a wide range of social relations, such as male control of political offices, spatial segregation of the sexes in men's club houses and menstrual huts, exchanging women in marriage for bridewealth (payment of goods or money by the prospective husband to his bride's kin prior to marriage), and physical aggression (e.g., gang rape and wife abuse). Given the variable meanings of dominance, then, it is possible for women in a society to be "dominant" in some spheres of activity and "subordinant" in others. Writers often emphasize either the disadvantaged or (more rarely) the high over-all status of women to confirm or disprove universal sexual inequality (Quinn 1977: 182). But social reality is rarely so simple that it can be neatly categorized without distortion. For example, women in West Africa are given in marriage by their male kin, who in turn receive bridewealth from the husband and his male relatives. This may be considered an indication of female subordination, but these same women exert considerable economic independence from their husbands and relatives through extensive trading and petty entrepreneurial activities (see Ogbu 1978; Robertson 1976; Sudarkasa 1973, 1977). Interrelations of wifely status, domestic relations, and economic roles of West African women cannot be meaningfully summarized or compared with women's roles in other social systems by simply concluding that the over-all position of women in West Africa is "subordinant" or "dominant." Such terminology obscures rather than clarifies.

Similarly, the concept of status has variable referents. To talk of *the* status of women distorts the complex reality of social relations and institutions that are cross-cut by gender distinctions and by other factors such as age, status, and in some societies, by class or caste (Schlegel 1977a: 20-31). For instance, menopausal women may be highly regarded as repositories of sacred knowledge (Jones 1972) or viewed as undergoing a crisis transition from middle to old age involving emotional and physical stress which may require medical or psychiatric treatment (Berger and Norsigian 1976; Weideger 1977: 58-81). Widows may be feared or disparaged as sorceresses and agents of ritual pollution (Harper 1969) or considered marginal ''nonpersons'' who have lost social identity previously provided by their husbands and are therefore to be avoided if possible (Caine 1974). Samoan women of rank have greater access to sources of political power and economic resources than lower status persons of either sex, whereas Moroccan women of all social backgrounds are systematically excluded from public office holding (Dwyer 1978a). In short, gender is only one means by which members of a society are categorized; other variables, including age, marital and reproductive status, political rank, and a multitude of institutional arrangements add to the diversity of female-male relations in all societies.

Status, then, is multidimensional and continuously changing as women move through the life cycle. Quinn (1977: 183) suggests

> . . . that it may be more accurate, and more helpful to future research, to treat women's status as a composite of many different variables, often causally independent one from another. Thus in any given society, this status may be very 'low' in some domains of behavior, approach equality in others, achieve equality with men's status in others, and even, in some domains, surpass the status of men.

Our task is to examine the diversity of social contexts in which female-male roles and relationships occur. In other words, we must observe particular domains of behavior and institutional arrangements in specific societies before generalizations concerning ''women's status'' can be drawn.

4

THE INVISIBILITY OF WOMEN

A second issue in the anthropological study of women concerns their invisible or marginal statuses. In speaking of earlier anthropological accounts of women beginning around 1900, Schlegel (1977a:2) remarks:

One gets the impression from many ethnographies that culture is created by and for men between the ages of puberty and late middle age, with children, women, and the aged as residual categories; women are frequently portrayed, at best, as providing support for the activities of men.

Unfortunately, androcentric depictions of culture and society have not significantly changed. Ethnographies (detailed descriptions of specific societies), as well as introductory textbooks written in the 1970s, frequently omit discussion of women as significant members of society beyond the contexts of reproduction, childrearing, and domestic roles. [1] On the basis of reading a considerable body of anthropological literature, one could easily conclude that women in most societies are marginal breeders.

There are three major reasons for this state of affairs: (1) fieldwork conditions and the nature of researcher-informant relationships; (2) the use of ethnocentric and androcentric models based on western societies and experiences; and (3) disregard for the processes of social change. These factors are interrelated.

Simply stated, male anthropologists do not, as a rule, spend much time with nor talk with women, depending upon field conditions, and if they do, discussions tend to be biased towards topics assumed to be the primary concerns of women—namely, childrearing and other domestic responsibilities. This point does not apply exclusively to male researchers. Women, who are also products of male-oriented thinking in anthropology and influenced by their overwhelmingly male professors and mentors in graduate schools, do not necessarily associate much with women either when doing fieldwork. The results are descriptions and analyses of men's activities that tend to ignore the women of society. Fortunately, this trend is being reversed, as the recent anthropological literature on women attests (e.g., Chiñas 1973; Dwyer 1978a; Elmendorf 1976; Strathern 1972; Weiner 1976; Wolf 1972).

Second, many anthropological studies assume both androcentric and ethnocentric perspectives towards the roles of men and women in other societies. Researchers are oriented towards male informants and often accept male views about both sexes. This is evident, for instance, in studies of the Middle East where foreign male researchers have limited contact with women. Distortion is introduced as anthropologists accept androcentric views about femaleness from men (Nelson 1974: 553). The problem of whether women's perceptions differ from men's is not explored, since both sexes are thought to share similar beliefs. This assumption must be questioned. Moroccan views of adult sexuality, for example, are not homogeneous. Dwyer (1978b: 230) states that "Women are called 'cows' [by men] because of their putative animality." Women also subscribe to the male view of insatiable female sexuality; however, women claim that "If women are animal and so must be denigrated, men also are animal and so merit condemnation, although it must be expressed with guardedness." (Dwyer 1978b: 230). Since few researchers have bothered to ask women about *their* perspectives, we can assume that most studies present a narrow, if not distorted, picture of men and women in different societies.

Ethnocentric models based upon the experience of western capitalist countries have also biased anthropological studies of nonindustrial societies. These models frequently assume that sexual inequality, based on relations of asymmetry in the industrialized West, exist elsewhere as well. Assuming the presence of asymmetrical relations where none may exist is referred to as "state bias" (Sacks 1976).

Anthropological literature on hunting and gathering societies clearly illustrates presumptions of state bias and male dominance. Foraging economies, characterized by the use of simple tools for collecting and hunting wild foods and animals, are often depicted from the perspective of "Man the Hunter." This androcentric view emphasizes male aggression and dominance, the importance of male bonding for organizing hunting and group defense, and the primary significance of men's hunting over plant collecting by women (Ember 1978; Martin and Voorhies 1975: 158-170; Tiger 1969). "Man the Hunter" has been criticized in recent years as our understanding of foraging economies has increased, leading to an alternative model based on "Woman the Gatherer." This approach considers the contributions of collecting to total subsistence, female control over reproduction, and the political

6

and ritual participation of women in society (Hiatt 1974; Slocum 1975). In effect, relations of sexual equality and balance characterize this model of foragers, in contrast to the "Man the Hunter" assumption of male superiority and dominance in important social activities.

Until recently, most research on Australian Aboriginal societies was written from the perspective of "Man the Hunter." The Tiwi of Melville Island, located off the coast of North Australia, are of particular interest to students of women's roles because the Tiwi have been studied from both "Man the Hunter" and "Woman the Gatherer" perspectives. Comparison of Hart and Pilling's (1960) and Goodale's (1971) works illustrates how applying different models to the same society can result in differing interpretations and emphases. Hart and Pilling (1960: 52), for instance, depict Tiwi women as ". . . the main currency of the influence struggle, the main 'trumps' in the endless bridge game [of men]." They describe older females as "ancient crones" and "toothless old hags," in contrast to references to older males as "powerful old men." This terminology illustrates how some researchers ". . . project on the aboriginal women the contempt and disrespect to which the older woman is subject in Western society" (Rohrlich-Leavitt 1976: 199). According to Goodale (1971), the "toothless old hags" depicted by Hart and Pilling are far from being passive pawns in the political chess games of men. Tiwi women are economically self-sufficient, and they exert considerable independence of mind and action in manipulating the politics of bethrothal and marriage. Other reassessments of Australian Aboriginal societies (e.g., Gale 1974; Rohrlich-Leavitt et. al. 1975) provide new insights into the dynamics of female-male relations. They also have general significance for the anthropological study of human societies. Androcentric frameworks that ignore, denigrate, or misinterpret women's roles bias men's roles as well; a distorted picture of male-female relations is the result.

A third factor that has rendered women either marginal or invisible in anthropological studies is the assumption that nonindustrial societies have not significantly changed since western contact and that women in these systems were traditionally subordinant to men. This view, however, ignores the social consequences *for women* of colonial policies, missionization, trade, the introduction of a cash economy, and industrialization. In many instances, these forces have undermined or destroyed historically important political and economic roles held by

7

nonwestern women. Female contributions to subsistence and production were ignored by colonial policy makers and continue to be disregarded by contemporary development planners and researchers as well. The productive roles of women have been altered, often to their detriment, by the introduction of plow agriculture, cash cropping, migrant and wage labor, and development projects sponsored by local governments and international agencies (see Boserup 1970; Brain 1976; Pala 1976; Remy 1975; Rubbo 1975). Women's traditional participation in the political sphere, a domain considered to be the preserve of men, was similarly disregarded or suppressed. The existence of female chiefs who exercised formal power and authority, or the presence of women's political groups which made community-wide decisions acknowledged and respected by men, were incomprehensible to colonial administrators, traders, missionaries, anthropologists, and other westerners who assumed that woman's place was, or ought to be, in the home (see Lebeuf 1963; Tiffany 1978b; Van Allen 1976). In sum, the disadvantaged political and economic status of women in many contemporary Third World societies does not reflect the precontact past, but processes of introduced (and often forced) changes over which women, as well as men, have had little or no control.

REINTRODUCING WOMEN INTO THE STUDY OF SOCIETY

The papers in this volume suggest the assumptions of universal male dominance and the seemingly marginal status of women are problematic. Written by both male and female anthropologists over a period of twenty years, these essays illustrate the wide range of male-female relations in societies of different economic and political complexity. The concept of status, when applied to the position of women in society, is comprised of several interdependent variables. By examining many dimensions of women's roles in specific domains of behavior and institutional contexts, we shall be able to make meaningful cross-cultural comparisons. Each author addresses a specific issue in the anthropological study of women considered earlier in this discussion. And as the following essays suggest, the diversity of women's roles in economic, political, domestic, and religious institutions, as well as the variable ideologies of femaleness and maleness to which both sexes subscribe, show the hazards of premature generalizations concerning the over-all status of women in different societies.

Women and the Division of Labor

The universal division of labor by sex is fundamental to the anthropological understanding of women. In all societies, women's roles are to varying degrees associated with reproductive and childcare functions. There is no known society in which men are primarily responsible for childcare, although in many social systems men are actively involved in childtending. The nature of women's subsistence activities vary considerably in different societies; however, some women must be available at all times to watch infants and children.

Judith Brown's essay in this volume suggests that women's work must be compatible with the demands of nursing and childcare in societies where schools, child nurses, and other care substitutes are absent. In these societies, women's work must be repetitive, require little concentration, be easily interrupted and resumed, safe, and require little travel. The restrictions of childcare account for why women are excluded from large game hunting, herding large animals, deep sea fishing, and plow agriculture. Other anthropologists suggest, however, that women have greater flexibility in their work roles than Brown allows. Mothers in many societies are not exclusive childtenders, and supplemental feeding at an early age is widely practiced (Nerlove 1974). According to this view, the spacing and rearing of children must be accommodated to the requirements of women's subsistence roles, and not the other way around (Friedl 1975, 1978; Nerlove 1974). Despite differences in emphasis, these writers acknowledge the relationship between women's productive and reproductive roles--an association that many feminists view as the basis for female subordination in western industrialized societies.

Political power is related to economic power; the latter is associated with control over valued resources and the right to determine the distribution of goods to persons and groups beyond the domestic unit. The extent to which political power is linked to control over economic production and distribution is illustrated by the Iroquois Indians. According to Judith Brown, Iroquois women enjoyed high political and ritual status as a result of their economic power.

Iroquois society was traditionally (i.e., prior to intensive western influence) organized on the basis of matrilineal descent in which ancestry is traced exclusively through the maternal (female) line. The Iroquois claimed membership in matrilineages, kin groups in which descent is reckoned from a common female ancestor through known female links, and matriclans. (Clans consist of a number of lineages whose members believe they are descendents of a common ancestor, even though they may not be able to demonstrate exact genealogical relationships). 2 Clans provided the basis for tribal organization, with tribes organized into higher levels of political integration known as confederacies. Clan elders or *sachems* were the highest ranking chiefs and represented their clans on tribal and confederacy councils. Women apparently were not elected to chiefships at any level of political organization, although eligibility for office passed through the female line. The political power and influence of women were nonetheless considerable. Iroquois matrons who headed households and work groups could select and remove elders, influence council decisions, and participate in decisions concerning warfare and treaties. Gardening was organized by women, who grew the socially valued staples of corn, beans, and squash on land collectively controlled by related groups of females. Women also supplied (or withheld) food and provisions for male activities, such as hunting and war expeditions and council meetings.

Brown contrasts the Iroquois with the Bemba of Rhodesia; both societies were matrilineal and depended upon horticulture, a simple form of cultivation using hand held tools without the assistance of plows, draft animals, and irrigation. However, the roles of Iroquois and Bemba women were not identical. There was no role counterpart to the Iroquois matron in Bemba society. Most importantly, the economic and political statuses of Bemba women were low in contrast to the Iroquois because men controlled the production and distribution of food in Bemba society. Land was held by male chiefs, and use rights belonged to the man who cleared it. Women contributed to the economy by growing finger millet, the major staple, but men controlled the right to distribute stored and cooked food within and outside the household. According to Brown, status differences between Iroquois and Bemba women were linked to rights over resources. Controlling factors of production necessary to grow, cultivate, and store food for distribution and exchange translated into the ability to exercise political power and authority in the home and society at large.

Women's Work and Social Change

Anthropological studies of women in nonindustrial and western capitalist states reflect opposing views concerning the effect of social change on female-male relations. This controversy is linked to debate over the universal subordination of women (Tiffany 1978a: 40-41). One approach (e.g., Hammond and Jablow 1973) assumes that sexual inequality characterizes nonindustrial societies, whereas women in the West are rapidly achieving equality with men as new role opportunities become available. Others (e.g., Leacock 1975) claim that women in western industrialized societies are economically and politically subordinate to men; moreover, the traditionally high statuses of women in many areas of the preindustrial world have deteriorated as a result of colonialism, industrialization, and other externally imposed changes.

There are a few studies supporting the contention that women's political and economic statuses were enhanced by the imposition of colonial rule and a commercial economy. The introduction of cassava among the Afikpo Ibo of Nigeria resulted in profitable trading activity for women, who subsequently achieved economic independence from their husbands and male kin (Ottenberg 1959). Colonially instituted courts increased the political and jural (legal) status of Toro women in Uganda by granting them property rights and by allowing them to initiate divorce proceedings against their husbands (Perlman 1966).

There is growing evidence, however, that women's roles in many non-western societies have declined as a consequence of colonial policies and economic change. The essays by Hamamsy and Bossen illustrate the wide ranging effects of imposed change on Navaho and Guatemalan women. In both cases women have suffered a notable decrease in economic and political power.

The matrilineal Navaho traditionally lived in extended family groups composed of a woman, her husband, her unmarried children, her married daughters, and the daughters' husbands and children. These stable groups of related females provided women with economic and emotional security. Women exercised considerable domestic authority and retained rights to property and their children in the event of divorce. Women were often wealthier than men because they owned land and sheep which enabled them to earn cash from blanket weaving.

11

Government sponsored irrigation and livestock reduction projects initiated in the early 1930s altered women's productive roles by restricting their sources of livelihood. These programs, which allowed married men only to be eligible for land tracts, disenfranchised women from owning valuable irrigated land and reduced sheep herding, a source of wool for weaving. In addition, increasing need for cash as farming declined has forced both men and women off the reservation to seek wage work. Women are poorly paid in comparison to men and work in lower status, unskilled jobs. Women who remain home work harder as they assume the farm chores previously done by men who are currently employed off the reservation. The economic power of women has steadily declined as men regard their wages as personal property; wives have little or no voice in household decisions. The tendency to live in isolated nuclear families (composed of a husband, wife, and children) has increased the economic independence of men at the expense of women, who are removed from supportive networks of female kin. Divorce therefore results in severe economic liability for women. Hamamsy concludes that Navaho women ". . . are losing their economic independence, the satisfactions and rewards that accompany their functioning, and their security and power within the family" (p. 90).

Bossen's paper questions the view that women's position in pre-industrial and traditional societies improves with social changes associated with increased participation in a world market economy. She documents changes in women's productive roles in a Highland Guatemalan town by focusing on the range of modern training and technology available to both sexes. Women and men do not automatically share new economic opportunities made available through development programs and introduced technology. In comparing occupations by sex, men are found in positions requiring greater capital investment; whereas, women's labor is generally devalued as a result of concentration in unskilled, low paying occupations and high female underemployment. Bossen concludes that the introduction of technological innovations and capital intensive occupations into traditional social systems replicates patterns of sexual differentiation in the West, where the majority of women are clustered in marginal, low paying, and unskilled economic positions. Thus, "In the context of male and female participation in modern national society, it becomes clear that development for one sex may simultaneously lead to underdevelopment for the other" (p. 114).

12

Women and Politics

Most of the anthropological literature suggests that women rarely, if ever, engage in what is assumed to be the male domain of politics. Since women are frequently considered to be socially marginal, their political roles are ignored, especially if they do not participate in formal politico-legal institutions. The general conclusion, shared by both anthropology and political science, is that women are nonpolitical. The low participation of American women in voting and holding public office, for example, is frequently taken as an index of female disinterest in politics (Jaquette 1974: xv-xx). This "state bias" is frequently superimposed on the political organizations of nonwestern societies, where it is also assumed by the anthropologist that women are apolitical. The basis for this view is that women participate indirectly in the political process through their husbands and/or other male representatives. This perspective is further reinforced by the notion that politics take place beyond the home, and since childrearing and domestic tasks are thought to constitute the primary sphere of concern, women have little time or thought for the world of politics (Tiffany 1978b).

The prevailing view of women's lack of political participation and subordination to men is questionable, as reassessments of earlier studies and new research focusing on women's roles illustrate. Anthropologists are criticizing traditional conceptions of power that emphasize formal expressions of political behavior such as office holding but exclude informal relations, the latter often involving women (see, for example, Nelson 1974; Rogers 1975). The view of women as passive pawns in men's political schemes may be more myth than reality. Informal behaviors, such as "behind the scenes" manipulation and maneuvering, bluff, gossip, nagging, spirit possession, threats of ritual pollution or suicide, and other strategies are important components of political activity neglected in earlier studies. These strategies are often utilized by individuals, groups, or categories denied access to formal, socially legitimated avenues for expressing their interests and grievances. Thus, students of women are especially interested in nonformalized actions in societies where females do not participate directly in political and legal institutions.

The papers by Gomm, Klima, and Van Allen discuss the diversity of sex role differentiation in the political and legal spheres of social relations.

13

Their studies show that women are neither politically quiescent nor marginal.

Roger Gomm examines spirit possession as a strategy available to women excluded from formal political participation. The Coastal Digo women of southern Kenya, who occupy subordinate legal, political, and economic roles, depend upon the largess of their fathers and husbands for subsistence and support. Divorce is difficult for a woman unless her kin are willing to take her back; thus, possession represents a woman's only means of escaping an unhappy marriage when relatives refuse assistance and pressure her to remain with her husband. According to Gomm, spirit possession is a type of mendicant or "begging" behavior, which implies an asymmetrical relationship between the supplicant and the person of privilege who grants favors. However, possession strategy is limited in its effectiveness. A chronically possessed woman stands to lose the support of her husband and eventually her kin; if this should happen, she must resort to prostitution and performing part time services for professional exorcists. In sum, chronic spirit possession and prostitution constitute the only means available to Digo women who wish to avoid male dominance. Notably, both positions are held in low esteem; they result in downward mobility for women and pose little threat to male control.

In contrast to the limited political and jural rights of Digo women, the Barabaig cattle herders of Tanzania, East Africa illustrate a "dual-sex system" in which women's political groups are structurally analogous to those of men (Okonjo 1976: 45). The men's local political unit is the neighborhood council; the complementary female institution is a council with judicial, legislative, and executive functions comprised of married neighborhood women. Men recognize women's legal right to hold moots (judicial councils), to make judgements, and to impose sanctions against male offenders. Klima links the high political and legal status of Barabaig women to their important ritual and economic roles. Men acknowledge women's special "ritual competence" and knowledge, which are considered necessary for the general welfare of society. Moreover, married women control wealth in the form of cattle given to them as dowry by their kin. It is not unusual for a wife to own more cattle than her husband, and since cattle constitute the primary source of wealth, women exercise considerable bargaining power over their husbands.

14

Judith Van Allen's discussion of Igbo political institutions in Nigeria shows how the traditional power base of women was undermined by indifferent colonial policies. Igbo women belonged to village level political groups known as *mikiri*, consisting of resident adult women. Legislative and judicial functions of the *mikiri* primarily involved marketing, the most important female activity. Male offenders were punished by strikes, boycotts, insults, or " 'sitting on a man' " organized by the *mikiri*. "Sitting on a man" involved surrounding the offender's house, shouting insults, singing songs listing the women's grievances, ". . . banging on his hut with the pestles women used for pounding yams, and perhaps demolishing his hut or plastering it with mud and roughing him up a bit" (p. 169). These sanctions continued until the offender relented and promised to change his behavior.

Changes in British administrative policies during the 1930s following the 1929 Women's War weakened the village *mikiri*. Feminine self-help and sanctions such as "sitting on a man" were outlawed; women became dependent upon the courts (which were run by males and considered the only legitimate legal institution in British eyes) and upon the assistance of men for seeking redress against other males. Missionary education reinforced colonial notions of appropriate sexual spheres by emphasizing domestic instead of academic skills for girls. Thus, women have been systematically excluded from important avenues of political power and knowledge, a pattern reflected today in the male domination of national politics in Nigeria (Van Allen 1976).

Women and the Structure of Marriage

Marriage, a socially recognized relationship between two or more persons of the same or opposite sex, assumes many forms in various societies. Marriage is generally approached in terms of its sexual, reproductive, socializing, and economic functions. It may perform all these in some societies, but in others these tasks may be assumed by different institutional arrangements (see Gough 1959).

Anthropological studies of marriage are male-oriented; indeed, the androcentric view is so pervasive that males are frequently depicted as the focus of concern in marital relationships, even though it is presumed that women's lives revolve around marriage, family, and home. Marital relations are often described in legalistic terminology that defines men's conjugal rights; for example, rights *in uxorem* refer to a husband's sexual and domestic claims over his wife, and rights *in genetricem* are acquired by the husband over children his wife may bear (Bohannan 1963: 77-80; Radcliffe-Brown 1950: 11-13). By contrast, little or no mention is made of women's conjugal rights in marriage (Ogbu 1978: 248). The male bias in describing marital rights is one component of a broader theoretical tradition that views marriage as the exchange of women. According to this perspective, women are valuable objects with which men seek to initiate and solidify relationships with each other. Women, in other words, are commodities that men use to enhance their political and economic interests through adroit marital alliances (Lévi-Strauss 1969: 480-481).

The unusual system of marriage discussed by Sangree for the Irigwe of Nigeria is of particular interest because women are depicted as active participants in marital relationships. Irigwe marriage, from a woman's perspective, is characterized by geographical mobility, a succession of husbands, repeated separations from one's children, and the propensity for spirit possession. The Irigwe recognize primary and secondary types of marriages. A girl's primary or first marriage is ". . .a marital debut whence she usually leaps into a round of secondary alliances" (p. 199). Since the Irigwe do not recognize divorce, a woman's prior marriages are never terminated; however, these relationships are useful to a woman in later life when she seeks economic support from a grown son or surviving spouse. In contrast to many societies, Irigwe marriage does not guarantee a husband's exclusive sexual access to his wife and custodial rights to her children. Women initiate and terminate liaisons at will, and men must compete with each other in order to claim paternity of a woman's children.

Sangree relates the high incidence of spirit possession among Irigwe women to the stresses and rigors of the continual cycle of marriage and remarriage, which is coupled with repeated maternal separations from children upon assuming another union. Interestingly, possession may become a source of divinatory and curative power for women in their later years, and some women build up large clienteles and are exceptionally wealthy. Sangree suggests this elevated ritual status may be a form of compensation to older women for the stresses of married life.

Eileen Jensen Krige presents a comprehensive overview of the institution of woman-marriage, defined as a socially recognized relationship whereby a woman marries another female and acquires rights over the latter's offspring. This form of marriage is important in the anthropological study of women for two reasons.

First, woman-marriage highlights several misconceptions about the nature of marriage. Anthropologists have traditionally viewed woman-marriage as a bizarre practice that contravenes standard definitions of marriage as a sexual and economic union between persons of the opposite sex; some have even interpreted woman-marriage as a lesbian relationship. Most anthropologists have ignored the active political and economic roles assumed by women who undertake these marriages.

Women acquire wives in several ways. For example, if a son refuses to marry a woman promised to him, she may opt to stay with his mother. In some cases, a woman may inherit her father's wives upon his death, or she can acquire a female originally betrothed to a brother who has died. Woman-marriage is a flexible institution associated with patrilineal (or agnatic) descent (i.e., a system of reckoning ancestry exclusively through the male line), bridewealth, and opportunities for women to control important resources. Women exercise political and economic power by using the brideprice (bridewealth) received for their own daughters as a means of acquiring wives, who represent an additional source of labor and wealth and are also important for creating political alliances with men. Occasionally, woman-marriage is established as a "last resort" for acquiring a male heir to perpetuate the name and inherit the property of a patrilineal descent group. This form of marriage serves to reduce the economic dislocation of women left at home as a result of male migration to towns and mines in search of wage work.

Woman-marriage also illustrates how gender distinctions based on social conceptions of sexually appropriate behavior can be manipulated. Enterprising women may circumvent social rules and a cultural ideology that emphasizes the centrality of men by converting into sociological males. In other words, woman-marriage can provide a socially acceptable role alternative for women who wish to enter a man's world. "Manly-hearted" Piegan women of the Blackfoot tribe in North America illustrate one avenue for acquiring maleness. By publicly expressing masculine attributes of aggression and boldness, manly-

17

hearts could assume ritual and political roles ordinarily reserved for men (Lewis 1941). Gender conversion also occurs to a limited extent in the United States when women who wish to succeed in business or politics, considered male domains, must "act like a man" by de-emphasizing femininity expressed through clothes, speech, and behavior (see, for example, Molloy 1977).

Sex Roles and Illness

Sex differences in illness behavior is of major interest to feminists. Although women in the western world live longer than men, females report more physical and mental illness and utilize health services at substantially higher rates (Nathanson 1975). The apparent contradiction between favorable mortality rates and frequent illness experiences of American women has encouraged researchers to seek relationships between sex differentials of sickness and social roles (see, for example, Bart 1971; Chesler 1972, 1975; Gove and Tudor 1973). In contrast to men, women are more likely to experience certain types of disorders, including ". . . depression, feelings of inadequacy and inferiority, and excessive guilt. Anorexia, a disorder involving self-starvation, is exclusively a female disorder" (Frieze et. al. 1978: 260). Moreover, suicide attempts are six to ten times higher for women than men (Frieze et. al. 1978: 260). Psychological and psychiatric disorders are sex-typed, and incarceration in mental institutions is higher for females than males (Broverman et. al. 1972; Chesler 1972: 32-57).

Conceptions of illness and health change as institutions, social roles, and medical knowledge change. During the 19th century, female disorders in Great Britain and America were interpreted as malfunctions of the reproductive system (Barker-Benfield 1976; Duffin 1978; Ehrenreich and English 1973; Wood 1974). Today, female illnesses tend to be seen as psychological or psychiatric "diseases," although the high incidence of hysterectomies and ovarectomies suggest that female disorders continue to be associated with the reproductive system (Delaney et. al. 1976: 168-170; Norsigian and Swenson 1976; 147-151; Weideger 1977: 59-61).

Anthropological interest in sex differences in illness behavior has been largely confined to the cross-cultural study of spirit possession. I.M. Lewis (1971) relates the high incidence of female spirit possession in certain societies to low social status. He suggests that spirit possession is "an oblique aggressive strategy" used by subordinate persons to express their grievances to those in power in a socially acceptable and nonthreatening manner (Lewis 1971: 32). There are striking parallels between Digo spirit possession described by Gomm in this volume and the "cult of female invalidism" which characterized illness behavior of economically well to do British and American women during the middle 19th century. Both possession and invalidism are behavioral options available to women unable or unwilling to cope with the restricted roles open to them. Spirit possession, hysteria, nervous prostration, and other illness behaviors are socially approved, subordinate, and non-threatening roles. They are also strategies for removing or blunting male control. In some societies, chronic possession enables women to enter possession cults where they receive emotional support and manipulate social relations to their advantage through the intercession of *zar* spirits (Young 1975). Assuming a sick role may confer some immediate advantages to women by avoiding unwanted pregnancies or burdensome tasks, but it generally does not confer higher over-all status. Illness is a respite for the powerless that does not challenge the social structure of inequality.

O'Nell's and Selby's paper describes illness behavior and differential stress in sex roles in a nonwestern setting. *Susto* is a folk illness that is widely distributed throughout Hispanic America and exhibits many local variations. The higher incidence of *susto* among females in two Zapotec communities near Oaxaca, Mexico is linked to differences in sex role performance and expectations. Women's roles are more restricted than men's, and women have fewer mechanisms for reducing stress. According to the authors, *susto* represents a culturally accept-able means of escape from role responsibilities. "The disease condition provides a psychological respite—a moratorium in normal role perform-ance" (p. 241). Similarly, contemporary and 19th century American women have avoided role responsibilities with hysterical, menstrual, or menopausal disorders.

Sex, Ideology, and Symbolism

Peoples' conceptions of self, others, and sexually appropriate role behavior are variously expressed in ritual and symbolism. Cultural ideologies may exalt either or both sexes (Schlegel 1977b), denigrate

19

women (Dwyer 1978a), or picture females as threats to male autonomy or control (Ahern 1975). An important issue in the anthropological study of women concerns the relationship of sexual ideology and symbolism to behavior. To what extent does ideology reflect (and by implication, reinforce) social relations between women and men in society? Cultural conceptions about women are not necessarily directly translated into behavior, but neither is sexual ideology completely divorced from social relationships. For example, the stereotype of the "merry widow" who enjoys seducing other women's husbands does not reflect the reality of loneliness and poverty that many American women confront upon loss of their spouses (see Barrett 1977). This stereotype does, however, reflect the ambivalent attitude many Americans have about older women, particularly those who are alone (i.e., those without males to provide them with social legitimacy).

A male perspective characterizes much of the anthropological work on sexual ideology and symbolism. Cultural derogation of females tends to be emphasized, along with the unquestioned assumption that men's beliefs and perceptions of humanity are also shared by women. Among the Mundurucú Indians of South America, men perceive women as unpredictable, ungovernable, and threatening. Mundurucú men jokingly refer to the vagina as " 'the alligator's mouth,' " and claim that men dominate women by sex (" 'We tame them with the banana' ") (Murphy and Murphy 1974: 94). However, Mundurucú women do not subscribe to similar beliefs about men, and they seem disinterested in establishing counter rites and myths, even though they dislike male stereotypes of femaleness. Women's disinterest in male myths about females may be related to the pattern of same-sex relationships. Mundurucú women have a strong sense of individual and group identity resulting from residence patterns that encourage groups of related females to live and work together (Murphy and Murphy 1974: 87, 139-141).

Research emphasis on cultural ideologies stressing misogynist stereotypes may obscure the actual participation of women in important spheres of social activity. In his work with the Tombema Enga of the New Guinea Highlands, Feil (1978: 263-265) questions whether Enga ideology of the polluting and threatening woman is helpful in understanding male-female relationships. He argues that presumptions of sexual segregation and intersex hostility based on ideological concep-

20

tions have prevented anthropologists from acknowledging the important public roles of women in ceremonial exchanges of wealth hitherto considered an exclusively male activity.

The Bena Bena of Highland New Guinea and the Tokelau Islanders of the South Pacific illustrate the complex interplay between ideology and relations of sexual opposition and complementarity. Patterns of sexual opposition and hostility, particularly among husbands and wives, are widespread among peoples of the New Guinea Highlands and Lowland South America. Sex antagonism is associated with several cultural features, including concepts of female pollution, preoccupation with depletion of male sexual prowess, secret male knowledge, and spatial arrangements that maintain social distance between the sexes.

Langness associates relations of sex antagonism among the Bena Bena to the necessity of maintaining male solidarity in a situation of endemic warfare. The male ideology of male superiority and female pollution is portrayed during dramatic male initiation rites and reinforced throughout the life cycle by spatial and social segregation of the sexes. Men have mixed feelings about women:

> They [men] tell you that women are no good, are unclean, are less intelligent, untrustworthy in certain ways, and so on. But simultaneously they recognize their dependence. 'Women are our tractors,' one of my more preceptive informants remarked one day [p. 269].

Recognition of the interplay between an ideology of male superiority and the social importance of women in men's lives underlies the ambivalent attitudes of Bena Bena men.

Tokelauan concepts of male and female provide an interesting contrast to Bena Bena sexual ideology which devalues women. Tokelauans, like Samoans who are also Polynesians, value both female and male. Sexual differences are conceptualized ideologically and in the realm of social relationships, but there is no implication of the superiority of one sex over the other. Rather, complementarity and balance are stressed by both Tokelauans and Samoans. Tokelauan men, by virtue of their " 'strength,' " exercise formal control and authority. Male strength is counterposed to feminine " 'weakness,' " which ". . . implies that women are emotional, vulnerable and erratic, that they are unable to

21

control their feelings and are prone to express themselves without caution" (p. 285). But these qualities of women are not denigrated. The balance between male-female relationships is dramatically displayed in public when escalating disagreements among men at council meetings are deflected by the humor and antics of female clowns who highlight the foibles of men. It is the women's actions that help to restore social order. Indeed, Tokelauan women are referred to as " 'sacred beings,' " a recognition of their important mediating roles among men.

CONCLUSION

Woman as the "second sex" reflects a male orientation that has profoundly affected anthropological theory and methodology. Assuming universal male dominance says relatively little about relations between the sexes in different societies, but it does reflect an androcentric perspective that many anthropologists have carried to the field as part of their cultural "baggage."

In 1915 Bronislaw Malinowski, considered one of the major "fathers" of the discipline, began his two years of fieldwork in the Trobriand Islands in the western Pacific. His voluminous and detailed writings have become anthropological classics, and his research is often cited as a model for how fieldwork should be conducted. Every introductory textbook contains references to Malinowski's work, especially the famous Trobriand *kula* exchange cycle which he brilliantly documented. In short, the Trobriand Islands occupy a special status in the annals of anthropological history and research.

Malinowski's writings, however, say little about women, except to note in general terms their relatively high social status (e.g., Malinowski 1922 [1961]: 54-55). In 1971 Annette Weiner arrived in the Trobriands, and on her first day in the village she

> . . . *saw women performing a mortuary ceremony in which they distributed thousands of bundles of strips of dried banana leaves and hundreds of beautifully decorated fibrous skirts. Bundles of banana leaves and skirts are objects of female wealth with explicit economic value* [*Weiner 1976: xvii*].

22

Weiner observed ten such ceremonies during her fieldwork. She describes one scene in which

> Women were throwing fibrous skirts and bundles of dried banana leaves into the central clearing while other women waited to hurry into the center and gather up a pile for themselves. It was hot as the morning wore on, but the throwing of bundles and skirts continued for five hours. . . . Later I was to learn that it is not unusual for thirty thousand bundles to be distributed in one day and that each bundle is equivalent to one cent Australian [Weiner 1976: 7].

These important economic events were neither described by Malinowski nor subsequent researchers. In other words, a major area of social organization involving women's participation in large scale exchanges of valuables had been ignored by previous anthropologists. The events of the day altered Weiner's original research topic. She states:

> A critical difference between myself and my male predecessors is that I took seemingly insignificant bundles of banana leaves as seriously as any kind of male wealth. I saw Kiriwina [Trobriand] women as active participants in the exchange system, and thus I accord them an equal place beside Kiriwina men [Weiner 1976: 11].

Trobriand Island ethnography is a classic example of how women have been rendered invisible in anthropology. Disregarding the economic, ritual, and symbolic significance of women has produced an incomplete picture which distorts the complex dynamics of both male and female relationships in this island society. *Women of Value, Men of Reknown* (Weiner 1976) vividly illustrates the perils of ignoring half the human population in any study of society.

Anthropological studies of women are beginning to produce a reassessment of concepts, theoretical models, and methodology, which will eventually yield additional insights into traditional concerns and open new directions of research. The exclusion of women from earlier studies of social organization requires continuing fieldwork that focuses on women's institutional roles, social change, as well as ideology and language. At present, the subject of women is in its descriptive or "natural history" phase of development in anthropology (Brown 1975). Thus, generalizations must first await detailed studies of female-male relations in societies of differing economic and political complexity. It is premature, given the overwhelmingly androcentric perspective of most anthropological work, to assert the universality of male dominance or to discuss the notion of "women's status." Terms such as dominance, subordination, and status must be described within specific sociocultural contexts before meaningful comparisons of women's and men's roles in different societies can be drawn.

The essays in this volume help to counterbalance the male bias in anthropology by illustrating the diversity of female-male relations involving production, reproduction, power, marriage, ritual, and ideology. Bringing women back into the anthropological study of humanity is a challenging task and long overdue.

NOTES

Acknowledgments. References to Samoan women refer to my fieldwork in the Samoan Islands conducted during 1969-71 and the summers of 1973, 1977, and 1978. I wish to thank the Wenner-Gren Foundation for Anthropological Research, the American Philosophical Society, the UCLA Department of Anthropology, and the Government of Western Samoa for their support.

[1] One introductory textbook published in the early 1970s does not even mention women in the index (Hoebel 1972); another discusses the position of women in four pages, however, most examples illustrate male dominance (Beals and Hoijer 1971: 111, 121, 401-402). Marvin Harris' (1975) text, first published in 1971 as *Culture, Man and Nature*, discusses women, but he presents an androcentric perspective that generally depicts women as culturally devalued and subordinate to men. More recent textbooks, however, are now including specific references to women (e.g., Kottak 1978: 395-411).

[2] Matriliny should not be confused with matriarchy. The former refers to a recruitment principle for distinguishing members of kin groups who reckon descent through females from a common female ancestor. Matriarchy refers to the exercise of political power and authority by women and is commonly contrasted in feminist writings with patriarchy, the rule by men. There is no matriarchal society known to anthropologists in which women politically dominated men. For further discussions of matrilineal descent systems, see Schlegel (1972) and Schneider and Gough (1961). Martin and Voorhies (1975: 144-162) examine 19th century evolutionary schemes based on the sequential development of universal cultural stages from matriarchy to patriarchy.

REFERENCES CITED

Ahern, Emily M.
1975 The Power and Pollution of Chinese Women. *In* Women
in Chinese Society. Margery Wolf and Roxanne Witke, eds.
Pp. 193-214. Stanford: Stanford University Press.
Barker-Benfield, G.J.
1976 The Horrors of the Half-Known Life: Male Attitudes
toward Women and Sexuality in Nineteenth-Century America.
New York: Harper and Row, Colophon Books.
Barrett, Carol J.
1977 Women in Widowhood. Signs: Journal of Women in
Culture and Society 2(4): 856-868.
Bart, Pauline B.
1971 Depression in Middle-Aged Women. *In* Woman in Sexist
Society: Studies in Power and Powerlessness. Vivian Gornick
and Barbara K. Moran, eds. Pp. 99-117. New York: Basic Books.
Beals, Ralph L., and Harry Hoijer.
1971 An Introduction to Anthropology. 4th ed. New York:
Macmillan.
Berger, Pamela Chernoff, and Judy Norsigian
1976 Menopause. *In* Our Bodies, Ourselves: A Book by and for
Women. The Boston Women's Health Book Collective. Pp. 327-
336. 2nd ed. New York: Simon and Schuster.
Bohannan, Paul
1963 Social Anthropology. New York: Holt, Rinehart and
Winston.
Boserup, Ester
1970 Woman's Role in Economic Development. New York: St.
Martin's Press.
Brain, James L.
1976 Less Than Second-Class: Women in Rural Settlement
Schemes in Tanzania. *In* Women in Africa: Studies in Social and
Economic Change. Nancy J. Hafkin and Edna G. Bay, eds.
Pp. 265-282. Stanford: Stanford University Press.
Broverman, Inge K., Donald M. Broverman, Frank E. Clarkson, Paul
S. Rosenkrantz, and Susan R. Vogel
1972 Sex-Role Stereotypes and Clinical Judgements of Mental

Health. *In* Readings on the Psychology of Women. Judith M. Bardwick, ed. Pp. 320-324. New York: Harper and Row.

Brown, Judith K.
1975 Anthropology of Women: The Natural History Stage. Reviews in Anthropology 2: 526-532.

Caine, Lynn
1974 Widow. New York: Bantam Books.

Chesler, Phyllis
1972 Women and Madness. New York: Avon Books.
1975 Marriage and Psychotherapy. *In* Women: A Feminist Perspective. Jo Freeman, ed. Pp. 386-390. 1st ed. Palo Alto, California: Mayfield.

Chiñas, Beverly L.
1973 The Isthmus Zapotecs: Women's Roles in Cultural Context. New York: Holt, Rinehart and Winston.

de Beauvoir, Simone
1952 The Second Sex. New York: Vintage Books.

Delaney, Janice, Mary Jane Lupton, and Emily Toth
1976 The Curse: A Cultural History of Menstruation. New York: New American Library.

Divale, William Tulio, and Marvin Harris
1976 Population, Warfare, and the Male Supremacist Complex. American Anthropologist 78: 521-538.

Duffin, Lorna
1978 The Conspicuous Consumptive: Woman as an Invalid. *In* The Nineteenth-Century Woman: Her Cultural and Physical World. Sara Delamont and Lorna Duffin, eds. Pp. 26-56. London: Croom Helm.

Dwyer, Daisy Hilse
1978a Images and Self-Images: Male and Female in Morocco. New York: Columbia University Press.
1978b Ideologies of Sexual Inequality and Strategies for Change in Male-Female Relations. American Ethnologist 5: 227-240.

Ehrenreich, Barbara, and Deirdre English
1973 Complaints and Disorders: The Sexual Politics of Sickness. Old Westbury, New York: The Feminist Press.

Elmendorf, Mary Lindsay
1976 Nine Mayan Women: A Village Faces Change. New York: Schenkman.

Ember, Carol R.
    1978 Myths about Hunter-Gatherers. Ethnology 17: 439-448.
Engels, Frederick
    1972 The Origin of the Family, Private Property and the State.
    New York: International Publishers. (First ed., 1884.)
Feil, D.K.
    1978 Women and Men in the Enga *Tee*. American Ethnologist
    5: 263-279.
Friedl, Ernestine
    1975 Women and Men: An Anthropologist's View. New York:
    Holt, Rinehart and Winston.
    1978 Society and Sex Roles. Human Nature 1(4): 68-75.
Frieze, Irene H., Jacquelynne E. Parsons, Paula B. Johnson, Diane N.
    Ruble, and Gail L. Zellman
    1978 Women and Sex Roles: A Social Psychological Perspec-
    tive. New York: W.W. Norton.
Gale, Fay, ed.
    1974 Woman's Role in Aboriginal Society. Australian Aborig-
    inal Studies, No. 36. Social Anthropology Series, No. 6. 2nd ed.
    Canberra: Australian Institute of Aboriginal Studies.
Goodale, Jane C.
    1971 Tiwi Wives: A Study of the Women of Melville Island,
    North Australia. Seattle: University of Washington Press.
Gough, E. Kathleen
    1959 The Nayars and the Definition of Marriage. The Journal
    of the Royal Anthropological Institute of Great Britain and
    Ireland 89: 23-34.
Gove, Walter R., and Jeannette F. Tudor
    1973 Adult Sex Roles and Mental Illness. American Journal of
    Sociology 78: 50-73.
Hammond, Dorothy, and Alta Jablow
    1973 Women: Their Economic Role in Traditional Societies.
    Addison-Wesley Module in Anthropology, No. 35. Reading,
    Massachusetts: Addison-Wesley.
Harper, Edward B.
    1969 Fear and the Status of Women. Southwestern Journal of
    Anthropology 25: 81-95.
Harris, Marvin
    1975 Culture, People, Nature: An Introduction to General
    Anthropology. 2nd ed. New York: Thomas Y. Crowell.

Hart, C.W.M., and Arnold R. Pilling
       1960   The Tiwi of North Australia. New York: Holt, Rinehart
       and Winston.
Hiatt, Betty
       1974   Woman the Gatherer. *In* Woman's Role in Aboriginal
       Society. Fay Gale, ed. Pp. 4-15. Australian Aboriginal Studies,
       No. 36. Social Anthropology Series, No. 6. 2nd ed. Canberra:
       Australian Institute of Aboriginal Studies.
Hoebel, E. Adamson
       1972   Anthropology: The Study of Man. 4th ed. New York:
       Mc-Graw Hill.
Jaquette, Jane S.
       1974   Introduction: Women in American Politics. *In* Women in
       Politics. Jane S. Jaquette, ed. Pp. xiii-xxxvii. New York: John
       Wiley.
Jones, David E.
       1972   Sanapia: Comanche Medicine Woman. New York: Holt,
       Rinehart and Winston.
Kottak, Conrad Phillip
       1978   Anthropology: The Exploration of Human Diversity. 2nd
       ed. New York: Random House.
Leacock, Eleanor
       1975   Class, Commodity, and the Status of Women. *In* Women
       Cross-Culturally: Change and Challenge. Ruby Rohrlich-Leavitt,
       ed. Pp. 601-616. The Hague: Mouton.
       1977   Women in Egalitarian Societies. *In* Becoming Visible:
       Women in European History. Renate Bridenthal and Claudia
       Koonz, eds. Pp. 11-35. Boston: Houghton Mifflin.
       1978   Women's Status in Egalitarian Society: Implications for
       Social Evolution. Current Anthropology 19(2): 247-275.
Lebeuf, Annie M.D.
       1963   The Role of Women in the Political Organization of
       African Societies. *In* Women of Tropical Africa. Denise Paulme,
       ed. H.M. Wright, trans. Pp. 93-119. London: Routledge and
       Kegan Paul.
Lévi-Strauss, Claude
       1969   The Elementary Structures of Kinship. Rodney
       Needham, ed. James Harle Bell and John Richard Von Sturmer,
       trans. Revised ed. Boston: Beacon Press. (Originally published
       as Les Structures Élémentaires de la Parenté, 1949.)

Lewis, I.M.
1971   Ecstatic Religion: An Anthropological Study of Spirit
Possession and Shamanism. Middlesex, England: Penguin
Books.

Lewis, Oscar
1941   Manly-Hearted Women among the North Piegan.
American Anthropologist 43: 173-187.

Malinowski, Bronislaw
1922   Argonauts of the Western Pacific. (Reprinted New York:
E.P. Dutton, 1961.)

Martin, M. Kay, and Barbara Voorhies
1975   Female of the Species. New York: Columbia University
Press.

Molloy, John T.
1977   The Woman's Dress for Success Book. New York:
Warner Books.

Murphy, Yolanda, and Robert F. Murphy
1974   Women of the Forest. New York: Columbia University
Press.

Nathanson, Constance A.
1975   Illness and the Feminine Role: A Theoretical Review.
Social Science and Medicine 9: 57-62.

Nelson, Cynthia
1974   Public and Private Politics: Women in the Middle Eastern
World. American Ethnologist 1: 551-563.

Nerlove, Sara B.
1974   Women's Workload and Infant Feeding Practices: A
Relationship with Demographic Implications. Ethnology 13:
207-214.

Norsigian, Judy, and Norma Meras Swenson
1976   Common Medical and Health Problems—Traditional and
Alternative Treatments. In Our Bodies, Ourselves: A Book by
and for Women. The Boston Women's Health Book Collective.
Pp. 123-154. 2nd ed. New York: Simon and Schuster.

Ogbu, John U.
1978   African Bridewealth and Women's Status. American
Ethnologist 5: 241-262.

Okonjo, Kamene
1976   The Dual-Sex Political System in Operation: Igbo Women
and Community Politics in Midwestern Nigeria. In Women in

Africa: Studies in Social and Economic Change. Nancy J. Hafkin and Edna G. Bay, eds. Pp. 45-58. Stanford: Stanford University Press.

Ortner, Sherry B.
1974   Is Female to Male as Nature is to Culture? *In* Woman, Culture, and Society. Michelle Zimbalist Rosaldo and Louise Lamphere, eds. Pp. 67-87. Stanford: Stanford University Press.

Ottenberg, Phoebe V.
1959   The Changing Economic Position of Women among the Afikpo Ibo. *In* Continuity and Change in African Cultures. William R. Bascom and Melville J. Herskovits, eds. Pp. 205-223. Chicago: University of Chicago Press.

Pala, Achola O.
1976   African Women in Rural Development: Research Trends and Priorities. Overseas Liaison Committee Paper, No. 12. Washington, D.C.: American Council on Education.

Perlman, Melvin L.
1966   The Changing Status and Role of Women in Toro (Western Uganda). Cahiers d'Études Africaines 6: 564-591.

Quinn, Naomi
1977   Anthropological Studies on Women's Status. Annual Review of Anthropology 6: 181-225.

Radcliffe-Brown, A.R.
1950   Introduction. *In* African Systems of Kinship and Marriage. A.R. Radcliffe-Brown and Daryl Forde, eds. Pp. 1-85. London: Oxford University Press, for the International African Institute.

Remy, Dorothy
1975   Underdevelopment and the Experience of Women: A Nigerian Case Study. *In* Toward an Anthropology of Women. Rayna R. Reiter, ed. Pp. 358-371. New York: Monthly Review Press.

Robertson, Claire
1976   Ga Women and Socioeconomic Change in Accra, Ghana. *In* Women in Africa: Studies in Social and Economic Change. Nancy J. Hafkin and Edna G. Bay, eds. Pp. 111-133. Stanford: Stanford University Press.

Rogers, Susan Carol
1975   Female Forms of Power and the Myth of Male Dominance: A Model of Female/Male Interaction in Peasant Society. American Ethnologist 2: 727-756.

Rohrlich-Leavitt, Ruby

1976   Peaceable Primates and Gentle People: An Anthropological Approach to Women's Studies. *In* Women's Studies: The Social Realities. Barbara Bellow Watson, ed. Pp. 165-202. New York: Harper's College Press.

Rohrlich-Leavitt, Ruby, Barbara Sykes, and Elizabeth Weatherford

1975   Aboriginal Woman: Male and Female Anthropological Perspectives. *In* Toward an Anthropology of Women. Rayna R. Reiter, ed. Pp. 110-126. New York: Monthly Review Press.

Rosaldo, Michelle Zimbalist

1974   Woman, Culture, and Society: A Theoretical Overview. *In* Woman, Culture, and Society. Michelle Zimbalist Rosaldo and Louise Lamphere, eds. Pp. 17-42. Stanford: Stanford University Press.

Rubbo, Anna

1975   The Spread of Capitalism in Rural Columbia: Effects on Poor Women. *In* Toward an Anthropology of Women. Rayna R. Reiter, ed. Pp. 333-357. New York: Monthly Review Press.

Sacks, Karen

1974   Engels Revisited: Women, the Organization of Production, and Private Property. *In* Woman, Culture, and Society. Michelle Zimbalist Rosaldo and Louise Lamphere, eds. Pp. 207-222. Stanford: Stanford University Press.

1976   State Bias and Women's Status. American Anthropologist 78: 565-569.

Sanday, Peggy R.

1974   Female Status in the Public Domain. *In* Woman, Culture, and Society. Michelle Zimbalist Rosaldo and Louise Lamphere, eds. Pp. 189-206. Stanford: Stanford University Press.

Schlegel, Alice

1972   Male Dominance and Female Autonomy: Domestic Authority in Matrilineal Societies. New Haven: Human Relations Area Files Press.

1977a   Toward a Theory of Sexual Stratification. *In* Sexual Stratification: A Cross-Cultural View. Alice Schlegel, ed. Pp. 1-40. New York: Columbia University Press.

1977b   Male and Female in Hopi Thought and Action. *In* Sexual Stratification: A Cross-Cultural View. Alice Schlegel, ed. Pp. 245-269. New York: Columbia University Press.

Schneider, David, and Kathleen Gough, eds.

1961 Matrilineal Kinship. Berkeley: University of California Press.

Slocum, Sally
1975 Woman the Gatherer: Male Bias in Anthropology. *In* Toward an Anthropology of Women. Rayna R. Reiter, ed. Pp. 36-50. New York: Monthly Review Press.

Strathern, Marilyn
1972 Women in Between. Female Roles in a Male World: Mount Hagen, New Guinea. London: Seminar Press.

Sudarkasa, Niara
1973 Where Women Work: A Study of Yoruba Women in the Marketplace and in the Home. Anthropological Papers, No. 53. Museum of Anthropology, University of Michigan. Ann Arbor: The University of Michigan.
1977 Women and Migration in Contemporary West Africa. Signs: Journal of Women in Culture and Society 3(1): 178-189.

Tiffany, Sharon W.
1978a Models and the Social Anthropology of Women: A Preliminary Assessment. Man (n.s.) 13: 34-51.
1978b Women, Power, and the Anthropology of Politics. Unpublished manuscript.

Tiger, Lionel
1969 Men in Groups. New York: Vintage Books.

Van Allen, Judith
1976 "Aba Riots" or Igbo "Women's War?" Ideology, Stratification, and the Invisibility of Women. *In* Women in Africa: Studies in Social and Economic Change. Nancy J. Hafkin and Edna G. Bay, eds. Pp. 59-85. Stanford: Stanford University Press.

Weideger, Paula
1977 Menstruation and Menopause: The Physiology and Psychology, the Myth and the Reality. New York: Dell.

Weiner, Annette B.
1976 Women of Value, Men of Renown: New Perspectives in Trobriand Exchange. Austin: University of Texas Press.

Wolf, Margery
1972 Women and the Family in Rural Taiwan. Stanford: Stanford University Press.

Wood, Ann Douglas
1974 "The Fashionable Diseases:" Women's Complaints and

their Treatment in Nineteenth-Century America. *In* Clio's Consciousness Raised: New Perspectives on the History of Women. Mary Hartman and Lois W. Banner, eds. Pp. 1-22. New York: Harper and Row, Colophon Books.

Young, Allan
1975   Why Amhara Get *Kureynya:* Sickness and Possession in an Ethiopian *Zar* Cult. American Ethnologist 2: 567-584.

SUGGESTIONS FOR FURTHER READING

Leacock, Eleanor
1978   Women's Status in Egalitarian Society: Implications for Social Evolution. Current Anthropology 19(2): 247-275.
Discusses the theoretical and methodological implications of "state bias" in anthropological studies of women's status. The author aruges that traditional anthropological research has imposed models of sexual hierarchy, a characteristic feature of capitalist states, on egalitarian societies based on foraging and horticultural economies.

Mitchell, Juliet
1971   Woman's Estate. New York: Vintage Books.
Identifies production, reproduction, sexuality, and the socialization of children as four ". . . key structures of woman's situation" (1971: 101). Discusses why the liberation of women in industrialized societies rests upon transforming these relationships.

Rosaldo, Michelle Zimbalist
1974   Woman, Culture, and Society: A Theoretical Overview. *In* Woman, Culture, and Society. Michelle Zimbalist Rosaldo and Louise Lamphere, eds. Pp. 17-42. Stanford: Stanford University Press.
Asserts that ". . . women everywhere lack generally recognized and culturally valued authority" (1974: 17). Sexual inequality is linked to the opposition of domestic and public spheres of behavior. According to this view, women can acquire power and positive social value when their activities move beyond the domestic to the public domain.

Schlegel, Alice

    1977   Toward a Theory of Sexual Stratification. *In* Sexual Stratification: A Cross-Cultural View. Alice Schlegel, ed. Pp. 1-40. New York: Columbia University Press.

An important overview of anthropological approaches to the study of women that questions the assumption of universal female subordination. Ideology as well as relations of rewards, prestige, and power are critical dimensions in assessing sex differences in social status.

Tanner, Nancy, and Adrienne Zihlman

    1976   Women in Evolution. Part I: Innovation and Selection in Human Origins. Signs: Journal of Women in Culture and Society 1(3): 585-608, Part 1.

Discusses the importance of female production, reproduction, and socialization in reconstructing early human social life. Criticizes the "Man the Hunter" perspective emphasizing the importance of men and confining women to childbearing roles.

A NOTE ON THE DIVISION OF LABOR BY SEX

Judith K. Brown

In spite of the current interest in the economic aspect of tribal and peasant societies, the division of labor by sex continues to elicit only the most perfunctory consideration. This paper attempts to reassess the scant theoretical literature dealing with this division of labor and to suggest a reinterpretation based on some of the available ethnographic evidence.

I will begin with Durkheim. According to his theory, among the very primitive (both in the distant past and today) men and women are fairly similar in strength and intelligence. Under these circumstances the sexes are economically independent, and therefore "sexual relations [are] preeminently ephemeral" ([1893]1933: 61). With the "progress of morality," women became weaker and their brains became smaller. Their dependence on men increased, and division of labor by sex cemented the conjugal bond. Indeed, Durkheim asserts that the Parisienne of his day probably had the smallest human brain on record. Presumably she was able to console herself with the stability of her marriage, which was the direct result of her underendowment and consequent dependence.

Unlike Durkheim, Murdock does not attempt to reconstruct history, but his explanatory principle is also naïvely physiological. He writes:

Reprinted by permission of the author and the American Anthropological Association from *American Anthropologist* 72(5):1074-1078, 1970.

By virtue of their primary sex differences, a man and a woman make an exceptionally efficient cooperating unit. Man, with his superior physical strength, can better undertake the more strenuous tasks. . . . Not handicapped, as is woman, by the physiological burdens of pregnancy and nursing, he can range farther afield to hunt, to fish, to herd, and to trade. Woman is at no disadvantage, however, in the lighter tasks which can be performed in or near home. . . . All known human societies have developed specialization and cooperation between the sexes roughly along this biologically determined line of cleavage [1949:7].

This overly simple explanation is contradicted by numerous ethnographic accounts of heavy physical labor performed by women. The greater spatial range of male subsistence activities may also not be based on physiology as Murdock suggests. Recently, Munroe and Munroe (1967) have reported sex differences in environmental exploration among Logoli children. According to the authors, the greater geographical range of boys' activities in this society may result from learning, although innate sex-linked factors are suggested as a possible alternative explanation.

Lévi-Strauss also suggests the economic interdependence of the sexes as the basis for the conjugal (or nuclear) family. This interdependence does not so much arise from actual sex differences as from culturally imposed prohibitions that make it impossible for one sex to do the tasks assigned to the other. He writes of the division of labor by sex as ". . . a device to make the sexes mutually dependent on social and economic grounds, thus establishing clearly that marriage is better than celibacy" (1956:277).

Taking their cue from ethnographic descriptions that suggest that women often perform the dull and monotonous subsistence activities (for example, Pospisil 1963), other authors have offered "psychologizing" theories concerning the division of labor by sex. Malinowski suggested that women, owing to their docility, are forced to do such work: "Division of labor is rooted in the brutalization of the weaker sex by the stronger" (1913:287). Others have suggested that women are psychologically better fitted for dull work. Mead summarizes this view,

37

stating, "Women have a capacity for continuous monotonous work that men do not share, while men have a capacity for the mobilization of sudden spurts of energy, followed by a need for rest and reassemblage of resources" (1949:164).

What facts have these theories tried to explain? First, division of labor by sex is a universal. Planned societies such as Israel and Communist China have attempted to implement an ideology that views men and women as interchangeable parts within the economy, but have done so with only mixed success (Spiro 1956; Huang 1961, 1963). Second, in spite of the physiological constants and the possible, but less well-substantiated, psychological ones, women may contribute nothing to subsistence—as among the Rajputs (Minturn and Hitchcock 1963); or they may support the society almost completely—as among the Nsaw (Kaberry 1952). This variation, briefly noted by Mead (1949), has never been fully explained.

I would like to suggest that the degree to which women contribute to the subsistence of a particular society can be predicted with considerable accuracy from a knowledge of the major subsistence activity. It is determined by the compatibility of this pursuit with the demands of childcare. (Female physiology and psychology are only peripheral to this explanation.) This fact has been noted repeatedly by ethnographers, but it has never been articulated in the theoretical literature dealing with the division of labor by sex.

Nowhere in the world is the rearing of children primarily the responsibility of men, and in only a few societies are women exempted from participation in subsistence activities. If the economic role of women is to be maximized, their responsibilities in childcare must be reduced or the economic activity must be such that it can be carried out concurrently with childcare.

The former is the method familiar to us among industrial or industrializing societies. Whether in the United States or in Communist China, the working mother is separated from her child, who is in the care of specialists in the school or the residential nursery while the mother is in her place of employment. In our society, controversy over the presence of mothers in the labor force inevitably centers on the desirability and quality of this substitute care (Maccoby 1960).

Tribal societies also resort to substitute care so that mothers may work. Among the Gusii, women are responsible for the cultivation on which the society depends, and young child nurses (usually girls) are in charge of younger children and infants. However, the mother must periodically supervise the young caretakers. Minturn and Lambert (1964:244, 252) write:

> *This does not mean that the Nyasongo [Gusii] mothers spend a great deal of time actually interacting with their children. They have domestic and agricultural duties that take up most of their time. . . . Older children are often left with no one to look after them directly, but are kept close to home and within earshot of their mothers. . . . The burden of such supervision is clear, for instance, with respect to infant care. Older children chiefly care for infants but mothers must, in turn supervise older children.*

Among the Yoruba (Marshall 1964) an intricate system of reciprocity makes possible the trade activities of the women. During the early years of marriage, when her children are very young, a woman carries on only limited commercial activities. At this time she is likely to take into her home an older child as a helper. When her children are older, they in turn are placed in the homes of women who are still in the previous stage, and the mother's market activities increase in scope.

I have greatly oversimplified both examples. They illustrate two contrasts with the substitute care patterns of our own society. First, the women are not freed as completely for their economic pursuits. Second, the ethnographic accounts suggest that such substitute care is viewed not only as desirable but as an absolute necessity. Finally, the two cases are similar to the cases that are the focus of this paper, in that the work the women perform is not incompatible with child watching, even though the supervision of children may be only sporadic.

My main concern is with those societies that, without the intercession of schools, childcare centers, or child nurses, nevertheless depend on the subsistence activities of working mothers. These societies are able to draw on womanpower because their subsistence activities are compatible with simultaneous child watching. Such activities have the following characteristics: they do not require rapt concentration and are relatively dull and repetitive; they are easily interruptible and easily resumed once interrupted; they do not place the child in potential danger; and they do not require the participant to range very far from home.

Anthropologists have long noted the narrow range of subsistence activities in which women make a substantial contribution: gathering, hoe agriculture, and trade (Lippert 1886/87; Schmidt 1955; Murdock 1957; Aberle 1961). Although men do gather, carry on hoe cultivation, and trade, no society depends on its women for the herding of large animals, the hunting of large game, deep sea fishing, or plow agriculture. That women can be proficient at these activities (Jenness [1923] reports women seal hunters among the Copper Eskimo; Forde [1934] reports that women herd reindeer for parts of the year among the Tungus) is evidence that the division of labor by sex is not based entirely on immutable physiological facts of greater male strength and endurance. However, it is easy to see that all these activities are incompatible with simultaneous child watching. They require rapt concentration, cannot be interrupted and resumed, are potentially dangerous, and require that the participant range far from home.

Bogoras' (1904) report of the summer herding of the reindeer Chukchee provides an especially appropriate illustration of a subsistence activity that is incompatible with child watching. Bogoras suggests that the division of labor is not sexually determined; instead the population is divided according to child-watching and nonchild-watching members. He writes:

With the beginning of summer, when sledges become useless and tents cannot be moved around the country, the Chukchee herdsmen usually leave their families in camp, and move with the herd about twenty miles away, to the summer pastures. Boys and girls of more than ten years, and young women having no small children, usually go along for a time. While moving about with the herd, the herdsmen have to carry on their backs all necessaries, such as extra clothing, rifle and ammunition, kettles, and provisions. . . . The burdens are carried by girls and by men who are not very agile; while the best herdsmen must remain unencumbered for moving swiftly around the herd [1904:83].

The reindeer Chukchee lived by herding and hunting, both very incompatible with simultaneous childcare, and the women of the society made a negligible contribution to subsistence. In contrast, the Azande, as described by De Schlippe, are hoe cultivators, and the contribution of women to subsistence is considerable. De Schlippe (1956) offers a very detailed description of the division of labor by sex. Only a portion will be cited here because it illustrates the compatibility of the women's activities with simultaneous child watching:

> *In all those field types which are grouped around the homestead and to which the common name of garden has been applied, as a rule women work alone or with their children. This may be explained by the proximity to the homestead and accordingly by the nature of this work. It consists of a great variety of different small tasks, many of which can be packed into one single day. A woman, trained in household work, is capable of doing a great deal of minor independent tasks without losing the order of her day's work [1956:140].*

Another account that demonstrates the compatibility of hoe agriculture with simultaneous child watching is offered in the early nineteenth-century biography of the adopted Indian captive Mary Jemison (Seaver 1880). It is the only description of Iroquois agricultural activity given from the point of view of a participant. It runs as follows:

> *Our labor was not severe; and that of one year was exactly similar, in almost every respect, to that of the others. . . . Notwithstanding the Indian women have all the fuel and bread to procure . . . their cares certainly are not half as numerous, nor as great [as those of white women]. In the summer season, we planted, tended and harvested our corn, and generally had all our children with us . . . we could work as leisurely as we pleased [Seaver 1880:55].*

The carefree tone of this account is deceptive. The agricultural activities of the Iroquois women were highly productive. Not only was the tribe well provided with food, but the harvested surplus was carefully preserved and constituted a considerable part of the tribe's wealth.

41

Morgan (1962) had high praise for the industry of the Iroquois women. It is all the more remarkable that such high productivity was possible with simultaneous childcare responsibilities.

The relaxed atmosphere that characterized the agricultural—child-watching activities of the Iroquois women also characterized the gathering—child-watching activities of the Lunga women, inhabitants of the Kimberley District of Western Australia. Phyllis Kaberry writes of the Aborigine women, "If livelihood is sometimes precarious, it is belied by the absence of any feverish haste" (1939:18). Children accompanied the small groups of women gatherers on their daily forays into the bush. Kaberry describes one of these forays in great detail, ending her account as follows:

> *They lie for a while in the shade, gossip, eat some of the fish and roots, sleep, and about three o'clock move homeward. For all their desultory searching, there is little that they miss, or fail to note for a future occasion. . . . In actual quantity, the woman probably provides more over a fixed period than the man, since hunting is not always successful. She always manages to bring home something, and hence the family is dependent on her efforts to a greater extent than on those of the husband [1939:22, 25].*

A more recent study, that by Rose of the Angus Downs Aborigines, focuses on the effects of white contact on Aborigine economic activity and kinship structure. Under precontact conditions, according to Rose, when women gathered nuts and seeds for grinding, they formed themselves into ". . . collectives of co-wives for the purpose of sharing the burdens of caring for children" (1965:99). With the introduction of white flour, the women's economic role became what Rose considers a passive one, "collectives" were no longer necessary, and polygyny decreased markedly.

The final ethnographic example I will offer is that of the Yahgan as described by Gusinde. This tribe was rated by Murdock (1957) as being supported mostly by the subsistence activities of its women. It was the only tribe that depended on fishing, marine hunting, and marine gathering that was so rated in the world sample of 565 societies. Gusinde (1937:538) writes:

42

> *Far beyond the limited participation of the man in procuring food, she makes a considerable, altogether independent contribution to the support of her family by means of an activity that she alone can carry out. This is gathering, for which she is equipped by nature and to which she can devote herself without jeopardizing her more important duties as mother and wife.*

His description of subsistence activities is extremely detailed. Only a small portion will be cited here:

> *Assuming that low tide sets in during the day, one woman will make a date with another. . . . Each of them brings along her baby clinging to her back, and little girls run ahead, each with her own little basket. Sometimes a boy or two will run along out of curiosity and sheer pleasure, and they will watch for a while, but it would never occur to them to help because that is not their work. These women are only short distances apart. Walking slowly, they go from one spot to another, for the entire ocean floor is usually densely strewn with mussels. . . . They stop working only when their little baskets are full [Gusinde 1937:541-542].*

The ethnographers cited here have all addressed themselves to the relationship between women's economic activities and their child-rearing responsibilities. It is obvious that certain subsistence activities are extremely compatible with simultaneous childcare and that societies depending on such subsistence bases invite considerable economic contribution by women. In the past, theoretical considerations of the division of labor by sex have suggested that women do only certain kinds of work for physiological and psychological reasons. On the basis of the ethnographic evidence I have presented here, I would like to suggest a further explanation: in tribal and peasant societies that do not have schools and childcare centers, only certain economic pursuits can accommodate women's simultaneous childcare responsibilities. Repetitive, interruptible, nondangerous tasks that do not require extensive excursions are more appropriate for women when the exigencies of childcare are taken into account.

NOTES

Acknowledgments. I am grateful to the Radcliffe Institute for its generous support of my research, and to Beatrice Whiting, Bonnie Gray, and Patricia Harpending for many stimulating discussions on the subject of women's work.

REFERENCES CITED

Aberle, David
    1961   Matrilineal Descent in Cross-Cultural Perspective. *In*
    Matrilineal Kinship. David M. Schneider and Kathleen Gough,
    eds. Pp. 655-727. Berkeley: University of California Press.
Bogoras, Waldemar
    1904   The Chukchee. The Jesup North Pacific Expedition.
    American Museum of Natural History Memoir. Vol. 7, No. 1.
    New York: Stechert.
De Schlippe, Pierre
    1956   Shifting Cultivation in Africa: The Zande System of
    Agriculture. London: Routledge and Kegan Paul.
Durkheim, Émile
    1893   De la Division du Travail Social. (English translation: The
    Division of Labor in Society. George Simpson, trans. New York:
    Free Press, 1933.)
Forde, C. Daryll
    1934   Habitat, Economy and Society: A Geographical Introduc-
    tion to Ethnology. (Reprinted New York: E.P. Dutton, 1963.)

Gusinde, Martin
1937 Die Yamana, vom Leben und Denken der Wasser-nomaden am Kap Horn. (English translation: The Yamana: The Life and Thought of the Water Nomads of Cape Horn [1937]. Frieda Schütze, trans. New Haven: Human Relations Area Files, 1961.)
Huang, Jen Lucy
1961 Some Changing Patterns in the Communist Chinese Family. Marriage and Family Living 23: 137-146.
1963 A Re-evaluation of the Primary Role of the Communist Chinese Woman: The Homemaker or the Worker. Marriage and Family Living 25: 162-166.
Jenness, Diamond
1923 The Copper Eskimo. Report of the Canadian Arctic Expedition, 1913-18, No. 12. Ottawa: Acland.
Kaberry, Phyllis
1939 Aboriginal Woman: Sacred and Profane. Philadelphia: Blackiston.
1952 Women of the Grass Fields: A Study of the Economic Position of Women in Bamenda, British Cameroons. Colonial Research Publication, No. 14. London: Her Majesty's Stationery Office.
Lévi-Strauss, Claude
1956 The Family. In Man, Culture, and Society. Harry L. Shapiro, ed. Pp. 333-357. New York: Oxford University Press.
Lippert, Julius
1886/87 The Evolution of Culture. (English translation: George P. Murdock, trans. and ed. New York: Macmillan, 1931.)
Maccoby, Eleanor E.
1960 Effects upon Children of their Mothers' Outside Employment. In A Modern Introduction to the Family. Norman W. Bell and Ezra F. Vogel, eds. Pp. 521-537. Glencoe, Illinois: Free Press.
Malinowski, Bronislaw
1913 The Family among the Australian Aborigines: A Socio-logical Study. Monographs on Sociology, Vol. 1. London: University of London Press.
Marshall, Gloria A.
1964 Women, Trade and the Yoruba Family. Ph.D. dissertation, Anthropology Department, Columbia University.

Mead, Margaret
1949   Male and Female: A Study of the Sexes in a Changing
World. New York: William Morrow.
Minturn, Leigh, and John T. Hitchcock
1963   The Rājpūts of Khalapur, India. *In* Six Cultures: Studies
of Child Rearing. Beatrice B. Whiting, ed. New York: John
Wiley.
Minturn, Leigh, and William Lambert
1964   Mothers of Six Cultures: Antecedents of Child Rearing.
New York: John Wiley.
Morgan, Lewis Henry
1962   League of the Iroquois. New York: Corinth Books.
(Originally published, 1851.)
Munroe, Robert L., and Ruth H. Munroe
1967   Maintenance-System Determinants of Child Development among the Logoli of Kenya. Paper presented at the
American Anthropological Association meetings, Washington,
D.C.
Murdock, George Peter
1949   Social Structure. New York: Macmillan.
1957   World Ethnographic Sample. American Anthropologist
59:664-687.
Pospisil, Leopold
1963   Kapauku Papuan Economy. Yale University Publications
in Anthropology, No. 67. New Haven: Department of Anthropology, Yale University.
Rose, Frederick G.G.
1965   The Wind of Change in Central Australia: The Aborigines
at Angas Downs, 1962. Berlin: Akademie-Verlag.
Schmidt, Wilhelm
1955   Das Mutterrecht. Studia Instituti Anthropos, No. 10.
Vienna-Mödlingen: Verlag der Missionsdruckerei St. Gabriel.
Seaver, James E.
1880   Life of Mary Jemison: Deh-He-Wä-Mis. Buffalo:
Matthews Brothers and Bryant. (First ed., 1824.)
Spiro, Melford E.
1956   Kibbutz: Venture in Utopia. Cambridge: Harvard University Press.

SUGGESTIONS FOR FURTHER READING

Blau, Francine B.
   1979   Women in the Labor Force: An Overview. *In* Women: A Feminist Perspective. Jo Freeman, ed. Pp. 265-289. 2nd ed. Palo Alto, California: Mayfield.
   A concise overview of women's work in the home and labor market from the preindustrial economy of the American colonial period to the present.
Johnson, Orna R., and Allen Johnson
   1975   Male/Female Relations and the Organization of Work in a Machiguenga Community. American Ethnologist 2: 634-648.
   Examines the organization of work as a determinant of male-female relations among the Machiguenga of southeastern Peru.
Nerlove, Sara B.
   1974   Women's Workload and Infant Feeding Practices: A Relationship with Demographic Implications. Ethnology 13: 207-214.
   Discusses the relationship between women's productive roles and childcare responsibilities. Based on a sample of eighty-three societies, the author concludes that women who begin supplementary feeding of their infants before the age of one month contribute more to subsistence than those who introduce supplementary foods later.
Sacks, Karen
   1974   Engels Revisited: Women, the Organization of Production, and Private Property. *In* Women, Culture, and Society. Michelle Zimbalist Rosaldo and Louise Lamphere, eds. Pp. 207-222. Stanford: Stanford University Press.
   Compares women's economic roles in four noncapitalist and stateless societies in Africa to illustrate Engels' theory. Concludes that a major precondition for sexual equality in modern capitalist societies requires that women's domestic labor be accorded full social value.

ECONOMIC ORGANIZATION AND THE POSITION OF WOMEN AMONG THE IROQUOIS

Judith K. Brown

INTRODUCTION

My purpose is to investigate the relationship between the position of women and their economic role. Three possibilities are suggested in the literature. Lowie (1961:201) felt that in determining women's status economic considerations could be "offset and even negatived" by historical factors. Malinowski (1913) maintained that the considerable economic contribution of Australian Aborigine women was extorted from them through male "brutalization" and confirmed female subservience. The opposite point of view is expressed by Jenness (1932: 137):

> *If women among the Iroquois enjoyed more privileges and possessed greater freedom than the women of other tribes, this was due . . . to the important place that agriculture held in their economic life, and the distribution of labour . . . [which left] the entire cultivation of the fields and the acquisition of the greater part of the food supply to the women.*

His explanation for the high status of women among the Iroquois is essentially economic, stressing the extent of their economic contribu-

Reprinted by permission of the author and the American Society for Ethnohistory from *Ethnohistory* 17(3-4):151-167, 1970.

tion, but failing to deal with their place in the economic organization. Other authors have suggested that matrilineality, matrilocality, or a combination of the two explain the high status of women among the Iroquois.

That matrilineality and matrilocality are hardly unrelated to economic considerations had been suggested by Stites (1905), and has been again more recently by Gough (1961), Aberle (1961), and D'Andrade (1966).

In the present study, an attempt has been made to hold matrilineality and matrilocality constant by comparing the Iroquois with the Bemba. If the two tribes are far removed from each other in time, location, and tradition, the Bemba were also essentially matrilineal and matrilocal (Richards 1939:17), and Bemba women enjoyed high status. In both tribes women made a considerable contribution to subsistence activities. However, the economic organization underlying these activities differed markedly, and there were important differences in the status of their women.

The relationship between women's status and women's work is more complex than the three points of view above would suggest. An analysis must begin with careful definitions for both "status" and "work." More than the extent of women's economic activities must be known. The economic organization of the subsistence activities must be considered. It is for this reason that no simple relationship exists between the extent of women's economic contribution and women's status. The latter is related to women's place in the economic organization of subsistence activities, not simply to the proportion of the food women produce.

THE POSITION OF WOMEN AMONG THE IROQUOIS

The Iroquois have been treated as if they had been a homogeneous group by most authors, and in the *Ethnographic Atlas* (Murdock 1967), and will be considered as such here. The six member nations of the Iroquois Confederacy do not appear to have differed on the variables under consideration.

The accounts giving fullest information on the relevant variables

49

describe the Iroquois during the 18th and 19th centuries. This was hardly a time of stability for the tribe, and economic organization and the status of women did not remain constant over the period. Cara Richards (1957) has pointed out the increase in the decision-making powers of Iroquois women, and Noon (1949) has noted the increase in their economic responsibilities in the early part of the period under consideration.

In dealing with the status of women, two factors must be clearly differentiated. High status may be inferred from deferential treatment, or may consist of an actual position of power over basic resources and important decisions. The two need not coincide and should be considered separately (D'Andrade 1966).

Among the Iroquois, women were not accorded deferential treatment. Morgan (1962:324) noted with Victorian bias that such amenities signal the advance of civilization. He observed, "The Indian regarded woman as inferior, the dependent, and the servant of man, and from nurture and habit, she actually considered herself to be so."

However, the position of power that Iroquois women held has been pointed out by numerous authors such as Beauchamp (1900), Carr (1887), Goldenweiser (1912), Hewitt (1933), and Randle (1951).[1] Murdock's (1934:302) statement can be taken as a summary: "Indeed of all the people of the earth, the Iroquois approach most closely to that hypothetical form of society known as the matriarchate."

An early, detailed and much-cited appraisal was made by Father Joseph Lafitau of the Society of Jesus. Lafitau's (1724) charmingly illustrated four-volume work carries the inscription *avec approbation et privilege du Roy,* but no doubt helped to promote the revolutionary idea of the noble savage.

Lafitau differs from other early sources in that his account is not anecdotal but descriptive. The tone of the book is scholarly, and the information it contains is based on Lafitau's five-year stay in Canada, material supplied by another missionary who worked in Canada for sixty years, and on material in the *Jesuit Relations.*

According to Lafitau (1724 I: 66-67):

*Nothing, however, is more real than this superiority of
the women. It is of them that the nation really consists;
and it is through them that the nobility of the blood, the
genealogical tree and the families are perpetuated. All
real authority is vested in them. The land, the fields and
their harvest all belong to them. They are the souls of
the Councils, the arbiters of peace and of war. They
have charge of the public treasury. To them are given
the slaves. They arrange marriages.˙ The children are
their domain, and it is through their blood that the order
of succession is transmitted. The men, on the other
hand, are entirely isolated. . . . Their children are
strangers to them [my translation].*

This passage must be interpreted with caution. Lafitau does not specify
in these often-quoted lines exactly which *Ameriquains* he is describing.
It may be the Iroquois, the Huron, or both. The particular section from
which this quotation is taken attempts to establish similarities between
tribal customs and those of antiquity, thus foreshadowing much of late
19th century anthropology. Moreover, a number of the unusual powers
enumerated were not vested in all Iroquois women, but only in the
matrons, the elderly heads of households, and work groups. However,
such a position was achieved and could be aspired to by all women, as
Randle (1951) had noted. Unfortunately, there is no detailed description of how matrons were chosen. Fenton's (1957a:31) statement, which
suggests that women made the selection on the basis of personality
traits, ". . . the mild person who speaks easily and kindly succeeds to
public roles which the women withhold from the over-anxious person,"
does not specify the sex of the would-be officeholder.

The evidence for statements such as those of Murdock and Lafitau must
be evaluated by examining the role of Iroquois women in the political,
the religious, and the domestic life of the tribe. In the political sphere,
Iroquois matrons had the power to raise and depose the ruling elders,
the ability to influence the decisions of the Council, and occasional
power over the conduct of war and the establishment of treaties.
Although women could not serve on the Council of Elders, the highest
ruling body of the League, the hereditary eligibility for office passed
through them, and the elective eligibility for office was also largely
controlled by them. Goldenweiser (1912:468) gives a retrospective

account of the power of the matrons to raise and depose the ruling elders (whom he called chiefs):

> *When a chief died, the women of his tribe and clan held a meeting at which a candidate for the vacant place was decided upon. A woman delegate carried the news to the chiefs of the clans which belonged to the "side" of the deceased chief's clan. They had the power to veto the selection, in which case another women's meeting was called and another candidate selected. . . .*

The actions of the new chief were closely watched, and if his behavior deviated from the accepted norms, he was warned by the woman delegate. If after several warnings he still did not conform, she would initiate impeachment proceedings.

It is surprising that Lewis Morgan, whose *League of the Ho-De'-No-Sau-Nee, Iroquois* stands as a classic to this day, should have taken no particular note of the political power of Iroquois matrons. His account of the raising of the elders in *Ancient Society* (Morgan 1963) differs in some details from the account given by Goldenweiser. Speaking of the election he states, "Each person of adult age was called upon to express his *or her* preference. . ." (Morgan 1963:72; italics mine). The right to depose "was reserved by members of the gens. . ." (Morgan 1963:73). Thus Morgan's observations do not contradict the fact that the matrons had a voice in these important matters. But for some reason, he did not find this remarkable, or did not choose to comment upon it. However, in a later work, Morgan (1965:66) quotes from a letter written by the Rev. Ashur Wright (who had been a missionary among the Iroquois for forty years) as follows:

> *The women were the great power among the clans, as everywhere else. They did not hesitate, when occasion required, to 'knock off the horns,' as it was technically called, from the head of a chief and send him back to the ranks of the warriors. The original nomination of the chiefs also always rested with them.* [2]

Morgan's (1965:66) next paragraph begins, "The mother-right and gyneocracy among the Iroquois here plainly indicated is not over-

52

drawn." He ends his paragraph with a footnote to Bachofen. It is therefore surprising when twenty-odd pages later he states:

> But this influence of the woman did not reach outward to the affairs of the gens, phratry, or tribe, but seems to have commenced and ended with the household. This view is quite consistent with the life of patient drudgery and of general subordination to the husband which the Iroquois wife cheerfully accepted as the portion of her sex [Morgan 1965:128].

In his earlier work, however, Morgan (1962) noted that women had the power of life or death over prisoners of war, which must certainly be regarded as an influence reaching beyond the household. Furthermore, the women could participate in the deliberations of the Council through their male speakers, such as the Council of 1791 (Snyderman 1951), the Council of 1804 (Beauchamp 1900), and the Council of 1839 (Parker 1916), and had a voice concerning warfare and treaties. Schoolcraft (1860 III: 195-196) sums up these powers as follows:

> They are the only tribes in America, north and south, so far as we have any accounts, who gave a woman a conservative power in their political deliberations. The Iroquois matrons had their representative in the public councils; and they exercised a negative, or what we call a veto power, in the important question of the declaration of war. They had the right also to interpose in bringing about a peace.

It appears from the evidence (some of it Morgan's), that the political influence of the Iroquois matron was considerable. The nation was not a matriarchy, as claimed by some, but the matrons were an *eminence grise*. In this respect the Iroquois were probably not unique. What is unusual is the fact that this power was socially recognized and institutionalized.

In addition, Iroquois matrons helped to select the religious practitioners of the tribe. Half of these "keepers of the faith" were women, and according to Morgan (1962:186), "They had an equal voice in the general management of the festivals and of all their religious concern-

53

ments." Furthermore, as Randle (1951) has pointed out, women's activities were celebrated in the ceremonial cycle, and female virtues of food-providing and natural fertility were respected and revered.

Kin group membership was transmitted through the mother, and since there were rules of exogamy, the father belonged to a kinship group other than that of his wife and children. Morgan (1962:84, 326-327) describes the rules of inheritance and succession as follows:

> *Not least remarkable among their institutions, was that which confined transmission of all titles, rights and property in the female line to the exclusion of the male. . . .*
>
> *If the wife, either before or after marriage, inherited orchards, or planting lots, or reduced land to cultivation, she could dispose of them at her pleasure, and in case of her death, they were inherited, together with her other effects, by her children.*

Marriages were arranged by the mothers of the prospective couple, and they also took responsibility for the success of the union thus created. Both marriage and divorce involved little ceremony. The latter could be instigated by either the wife or the husband. In the case of a separation, the children usually remained with the mother (Morgan 1962). Parker (1926) mentions that spacing the births of children was in the hands of the mother and there was greater delight at the birth of a daughter than at that of a son (Stites 1905). The mother often had the power to confer a name on her child (Goldenweiser 1912, 1914).

Crucial in consolidating the power of the women was the family long house. Traditionally this was a large structure of bark and wood containing many compartments and several fires all connected by a central aisle. Each family occupied a compartment and shared a fire with several other families (Bartram 1895:40-41). Wright is quoted by Morgan (1965:65-66) concerning the domestic arrangements of the tribe:

> *As to their family system, when occupying the old long-houses, it is probable that some one clan predominated, the women taking husbands, however, from the other*

54

clans; and sometimes, for a novelty, some of their sons bringing in their young wives until they felt brave enough to leave their mothers. Usually, the female portion ruled the house, and were doubtless clannish enough about it. The stores were in common; but woe to the luckless husband or lover who was too shiftless to do his share of the providing. No matter how many children, or whatever goods he might have in the house, he might at any time be ordered to pick up his blanket and budge; and after such an order it would not be healthful for him to disobey; the house would be too hot for him; and unless saved by the intercession of some aunt or grandmother, he must retreat to his own clan, or as was often done, go and start a new matrimonial alliance. . . .

Two features of Iroquois domestic life deserve special mention. First, as noted by Murdock (1934), the authority over the household resided in the matron and not in one of her male relatives. Second, as Randle (1951) has pointed out, the long house was the analogy on which the League was built. The Iroquois referred to themselves as the people of the long house. The figurative long house of the League was divided into geographical compartments, each occupied by a tribe. It is probable that this analogy helped to consolidate the considerable political power of the Iroquois matrons.

In sum, Iroquois matrons enjoyed unusual authority in their society, perhaps more than women have ever enjoyed anywhere at any time. The position of matron was open to all women who qualified. The matrons were socially recognized and institutionalized powers behind the throne (though one can hardly term the supremely democratic Council of Elders as a "throne"). Women were able to serve as religious practitioners, and the matrons helped to select all "keepers of the faith." Finally, the matron ruled supreme within the long house and domestic arrangements were such that all women had dominant power within the household.

THE POSITION OF WOMEN AMONG THE BEMBA

The Bemba, with whom the Iroquois will be compared, were the largest and the most highly organized tribe in Northeastern Rhodesia at the time they were studied by Audrey Richards (1939). Unlike the Iroquois, they had a highly centralized government under an autocratic chief. However, they resembled the Iroquois in their strong military tradition, in their complex political organization, and in their relatively simple economic organization based on agriculture.

Among the Bemba, a few of the princesses (sisters and maternal nieces of the chiefs) enjoyed considerable political and religious power, as did the wives of senior chiefs and the mother of the supreme ruler. However, such roles were comparatively few, were ascribed, and could not be aspired to by all Bemba women. Bemba women were free to contract their second marriages and were able to initiate divorce, unlike the women among their patrilineal neighbors. However, in the domestic sphere, women were ultimately subservient to men, in spite of the considerable prestige a matron could acquire. Richards (1956:50, 159) writes:

> *Menfolk are dominant in Bemba society. Women used to greet men kneeling, and they still do so on formal occasions today. Men receive the best of the food and take precedence at beer drinks and on other social occasions. They speak first in family matters . . . . Girls are taught to please their husbands . . . . Women calmly accept the fact that their husbands will beat them . . . .*
>
> *. . . Fathers are respected autocrats in the home, but are dethroned as their children grow up and realize that ultimate power lies with their mothers' brothers.*

Thus although Bemba women enjoyed a higher status than women in many societies, it was not nearly as high as that of Iroquois women, in spite of the similarities in the rules of descent and marital residence between the two tribes.

Status has here been defined as power over basic resources and important decisions in the political, the religious, and the domestic spheres.

In agricultural societies such as the Iroquois and the Bemba, such power does not exist independently from the control of food and the essential elements used in its production. It is to economic organization of the subsistence activities of the two tribes that we now turn.

ECONOMIC ORGANIZATION OF SUBSISTENCE ACTIVITIES

Agricultural Activities

Both the Iroquois and the Bemba depended upon garden agriculture for the major portion of their food supply. Both tribes supplemented cultivated foods with foods gathered by the women, with meat hunted by the men, and with fish obtained by both men and women. Among the Iroquois, women occasionally joined the hunting expeditions. Both tribes practiced shifting agriculture which consisted of four stages: clearing the ground, planting, cultivating, and harvesting. Among the Iroquois, men were in charge of preparing the fields, although Waugh (1916) claims that the women helped. Trees were girdled and allowed to die. The following spring, the underbrush was burned off (Parker 1910). The remaining agricultural activities were conducted by the women in organized work groups. For men to do this work was considered demeaning. As Stites (1905) has pointed out, the warrior in the field was always an assistant, never an owner or director.

The economic organization of the Iroquois was remarkable (and far from unique) for the great separateness of the sexes which it fostered. Men were often away on war parties for years at a time. Although wives or temporary wives, appointed especially for the purpose, occasionally accompanied men on the hunt, it was more usual for this to be a male pursuit. Even at the daily meal, the sexes ate separately. It is no wonder that Morgan (1962:323) wrote:

> *Indian habits and modes of life divided the people socially into two great classes, male and female. The male sought the conversation and society of the male, and they went forth together for amusement, or for the severer duties of life. In the same manner the female sought the companionship of her own sex. Between the sexes there was but little sociality, as this term is understood in polished society.*

This separateness of the sexes applied also to the childrearing methods of the tribe. In the words of Morgan (1962:325), "The care of their infancy and childhood was intrusted to the watchful affection of the mothers alone." This must have afforded the growing girl a reassuring continuity, but it contained inherent problems for the young boy. Eventually he would have to move from the agricultural world under female authority to the life of the hunter and warrior under the authority of older men.

Mary Jemison, a white woman adopted into the Seneca tribe, gave the following description of the women's work group and the tasks it performed:

Our labor was not severe; and that of one year was exactly similar in almost every respect to that of the others . . . . Notwithstanding the Indian women have all the fuel and bread to procure, and the cooking to perform, their task is probably not harder than that of white women, who have those articles provided for them; and their cares certainly are not half as numerous, nor as great. In the summer season, we planted, tended, and harvested our corn, and generally had all of our children with us; but had no master to oversee or drive us, so that we could work as leisurely as we pleased. . . .

We pursued our farming business according to the general custom of Indian women, which is as follows: In order to expedite their business, and at the same time enjoy each other's company, they all work together in one field, or at whatever job they may have on hand. In the spring, they choose an old active squaw to be their driver and overseer, when at labor, for the ensuing year. She accepts the honor, and they consider themselves bound to obey her.

When the time for planting arrives, and the soil is prepared, the squaws are assembled in the morning, and conducted into a field, where each plants one row. [Note: The seeds were first soaked, and then planted in prepared hills.]

58

*They then go into the next field and plant once across,
and so on till they have gone through the tribe. If any
remains to be planted, they again commence where
they did at first, (in the same field,) and so keep on till
the whole is finished. By this rule, they perform their
labor of every kind, and every jealousy of one having
done more or less than another is effectually avoided*
[*Seaver 1880:69-71*]. [3]

Loskiel (1794:16, part 1) emphasized the toil of the women, adding
". . . nothing but hunger and want can rouse the men from their
drowsiness, and give them activity." Parker (1910) tends to agree with
Mary Jemison that the work of the women was not hard.

The division of agricultural work by sex among the Bemba was essentially as follows: the land was cleared by the men with the help of the
women, men and women planted, and women alone cultivated and
harvested. Their method of clearing land was unique and is described
by Richards (1939) as follows:

*The method of shearing the trees of their branches is
exceedingly skilled. It is the man's task* par excellence
*in the whole economic routine. The Bemba are daring
climbers . . .* [*1939:289*]. *Every year two or three deaths
occur during tree-cutting. Other men are disabled
through falls* [*1939:290*]. *It will be seen that in this form
of cultivation the people's emotions seem entirely
centered round one process - a particular method of
tree-cutting which is their pride and delight, and closely
associated with an elaborate form of ritual...* [*1939:300*].

*Next comes the business of stacking the branches . . . .
The aim of the native is plainly not to clear the bush of
obstructions, but to collect the maximum amount of
brushwood to burn. It is the ash which he considers
valuable, and the burning of the soil. The woman who
piles the branches carries them as high as possible from
the ground, so that twigs and leaves should not snap off
in transit, and thus waste valuable fuel.*

59

Piling the branches is the hardest work a Bemba woman does . . . . The women lift boughs, often fifteen or twenty feet long . . . [1939:293].

The millet seed was sown broadcast, usually by a man, while a woman walked behind him covering the seeds with earth. Richards (1939) considered the sowing a quick, light task, but one that required skill. The men also built fences for the gardens as they were needed. The little cultivation that was required was performed by the women. They also did the reaping.

In sum, the agricultural work of Iroquois women appears to have been lighter but more highly organized than that of the Bemba women. Although the work of the Bemba women was more arduous, their total contribution to economic activities was not as great. Furthermore, the pollarding of trees by Bemba men was unique to their tribe, a daring and celebrated enterprise which established the man as the owner of the fields he cleared. There was no cultural emphasis on the ground-clearing activities of the Iroquois men. Thus the actual agricultural activities reveal little that is relevant to the status of women in the two tribes.

Factors of Production

In agricultural production, land constitutes the natural resource; seeds constitute the raw materials; and agricultural implements constitute the tools. The ownership of these factors of production—the land, the seeds, and the implements—among the Iroquois is difficult to establish from existing evidence. Goldenweiser (1912:469) offers the following information: ". . . The husband, in ancient times, could regard as his own only his weapons, tools, and wearing apparel, his wife owned the objects of the household, the house itself, and the land."

It seems possible to infer that the women owned the seeds, and the rake, hoe, and digging stick, the agricultural implements enumerated by Stites (1905). Possibly they were owned by the household or by the women's work group. Male ownership is nowhere recorded.

It is also not entirely clear who owned the land. The importance of the fields can be deduced from the fact that village sites were chosen largely for the fertility of the surrounding land. As Randle (1951) has pointed out, these sites were changed as land became depleted, and not when an area had been hunted out. The extent of the corn fields can be estimated from the various accounts of their destruction at the hands of white war parties. In one such foray mentioned by Stites (1905), it took the French forces about a week to destroy the fields of four Iroquois villages.

Morgan (1965) stressed that land was communally owned and that its individual ownership was unknown. Snyderman (1951) mentions the belief that land belonged to future generations as well as to the present generation. However, according to Randle (1951), land was often registered in female names. Hewitt (1933) states that women owned the lands, the village sites, and the burial grounds. Nominal female owner-ship is indicated in the following statement by Red Jacket, speaker for the women at the Council of 1791: "You ought to hear and listen to what we women shall speak . . . for we are the owners of the land and it is ours . . ." (Snyderman 1951:20).

In contrast, land ownership among the Bemba is described by Richards (1939) as follows:

> . . . *Any chief will reply quite simply that the whole territory belongs to him, together with the food that is produced in it, its game and fish, and the labour of its people [1939:245].*

> . . . *Bemba rights to the use of land are a part of a reciprocal series of obligations between subject and chief. The former accepts the political status of subject and membership of a village group. He gives respect, labour, and tribute to his chief, and in return he is able to cultivate as much land as he pleases and to occupy it for as long as he needs. The latter prays to the tribal spirits in order to make the land productive, initiates economic effort, feeds the hungry, and maintains his court and tribal councillors . . . [1939:266].*

> *The millet garden is commonly spoken of as belonging to the man, because it is he who originally cleared the*

ground for it. But the married man is described as
making a garden for his wife . . . [1939:189]. Hence the
millet garden is the man's, although the use of the crop
is given to the wife. But her rights are not absolute.
They depend strictly on the continuance of the mar-
riage, and are forfeited by divorce or death, and are
subject to the claims of the husband's relatives, who,
since they live in another village, are constantly appre-
hensive lest they do not get their due [1939:190].

In short, the lands of the Iroquois appear to have been communally owned, but held by the women; whereas, among the Bemba, all lands nominally belong to the chief, but were held by the men who cleared them.

The Food Produced

Among the Iroquois, a great variety of corn was raised. Speck (1945) estimates from fifteen to seventeen varieties, and it was prepared in numerous ways. Murdock (1934) suggests as many as fifty. Even the husks, silk, cobs, and leaves were used to make a number of useful articles (Parker 1910). Beans were also a popular food. Speck (1945) estimates there were sixty varieties, as were squashes, of which there were eight varieties according to Speck (1945). All three of these foods were provided by the women and held in high esteem by the Iroquois. The foods were represented in their pantheon as "The Three Sisters," "Our Life," and "Our Supporters" (Morgan 1962).

These staples were supplemented by goods gathered by the women: maple sugar, berries, wild fruit, nuts, roots, mushrooms, leaf foods, and by other cultivated foods such as melons. Schoolcraft (1847) refer- red to the apple as "the Iroquois banana." The fruit was one of several introduced by the Dutch and the French. According to Parker (1910:94), during the Revolutionary War "General Sullivan in his famous raid against the hostile Iroquois cut down a single orchard of 1500 trees." Thus an impressive commissariat was supplied by the women of the tribe. The diet of the Iroquois was ample, varied, and nutritious. One is forced to agree with Morgan (1962) who considered the indigenous diet of the Iroquois far superior to that typical of the Europeans of pre- contact times.

The Bemba diet, like that of the Iroquois, contained one basic cereal staple: finger millet. Richards (1939:37) writes:

> The bulk of each meal consists of a porridge made of this flour, and the subsidiary foods, meat or vegetable, are eaten with it in small quantities only (about half a pound of the latter to five pounds of the former). For their nutrition the Bemba depend almost entirely on the amount of millet they are able to get, and the seasonal variations from hunger and plenty consist in effect of the shortage or absence of this particular grain.

In distinct contrast to the Iroquois, the Bemba regularly experienced periods of food shortage. Richards (1939:35) observes:

> The most pronounced feature of this dietary is its alternation between hunger and plenty. . . . In this territory the existence of a definite scarcity is noticed at once by the most casual observer. The Bemba constantly talk about 'hunger months' as distinguished from food months.

A number of other foods besides the finger millet were available to the Bemba, but the list seems a short one indeed when compared with the foods available to the Iroquois. There were mushrooms and gourds, wild fruits, green leaves, cultivated groundnuts, and assorted pulses. Game and fish were very scarce, but caterpillars and wood-lice were eaten.

The two societies present a distinct contrast. The Iroquois women provided a varied, nutritious, and dependable diet. The Bemba women provided a monotonous, marginal diet which was interrupted by periods of near famine. These facts are significant for the way food was distributed, as will be shown below.

Distributing and Dispensing Food

The generous hospitality which was customary among the Iroquois was probably the most salient feature of their food distribution. The rule of hospitality was perpetuated and its protocol codified by Handsome

Lake, the early nineteenth century prophet (Parker 1913). Hospitality was extended to all strangers, and the stranger was to be fed before he was questioned about his mission (Lafitau 1724). Hospitality was also extended to other members of the village, to the extent that no one went hungry (Parker 1910). It is of interest to note Morgan's (1962:329) comment: "It [hospitality] rested chiefly upon the industry, and therefore upon the natural kindness of the Indian woman. . . ." This statement demonstrates that the hospitality of the household reflected favorably on its women, not on its men. Furthermore, hospitality was motivated by generosity, which was valued in and of itself (Fenton 1957a).

There is conflicting evidence concerning the distribution of the fruit of the chase. Beauchamp (1900) says that the meat was given to the hunter's wife. Carr (1887) claims it was given to the hunter's mother-in-law. Lafitau (1724) mentions that the legitimate wife had a prior claim to that of the temporary hunting wife. Although not a polygynous society like the Bemba, the Iroquois were not rigidly monogamous. Hunting expeditions often lasted as long as a year, and if the hunter's wife refused to go, a special temporary wife might accompany him instead.

Stites (1905) cites one *Jesuit Relation* to the effect that one of women's chief winter tasks was to go into the forest to bring home the deer their husbands had slain. However, citing a different *Jesuit Relation*, she states that women were sometimes not given a share of the meat at all. [4] Wright, quoted by Morgan (1965), seems to suggest that the meat was contributed by the hunter to his wife's household. Morgan (1965:127) makes a similar statement himself, and this is probably the most correct description.

Thus the distribution of the food of the tribe, even the food procured by the men, appears to have been at the discretion of the matrons. By observing the rules of hospitality, the matrons made it possible for every member of the tribe and for visitors to obtain a share of the food supply.

The dispensing of food within the household also rested with the matrons. As Morgan (1962:327) observed, "The care of the appetite was left entirely with the women, as the Indian never asked for food."

No author mentions any specified obligations which the matron had to meet in performing this task.

The Iroquois had one meal a day, which was served in the morning. Lafitau (1724 III:79-80) offers a description of this meal. Morgan's (1965:65) later description is as follows:

> Every household was organized under a matron who supervised the domestic economy. After a single daily meal was cooked at the several fires the matron was summoned, and it was her duty to divide the food, from the kettle, to the several families according to their respective needs. What remained was placed in the custody of another person until it was required by the matron. . . . It shows that their domestic economy was not without method, and it displays the care and management of woman. . . .

It was not only in the domestic realm that the matrons controlled the dispensing of food. By supplying the essential provisions for male activities—the hunt, the warpath, and the Council—they were able to control these to some degree. Thus Randle (1951:172) writes, "Indirectly, too, it is stated that the women could hinder or actually prevent a war party which lacked their approval by not giving the supplies of dried corn and the moccasins which the warriors required."

Stites (1905:78) makes a similar assertion: ". . . They also had control of the cultivated land and its produce, and gave support to the warriors only in return for their military services. . . ."

This control was effected by the monopoly that the matrons exercised on the staple food used on both the hunt and the warpath. According to Morgan (1962), this food was prepared while the warriors performed their dance. He gives the recipe for the dried corn-maple syrup provision (see also Bartram 1895:71) and concludes, ". . . The warrior could carry without inconvenience in his bear-skin pocket a sufficient supply for a long and perilous expedition" (Morgan 1962:340). Further on he states, "This [the same recipe] was carried in the bear-skin pocket of the hunter, and upon it alone he subsisted for days together" (Morgan 1962:373).

The importance of these provisions was also mentioned by Loskiel (1794), who observed that hunting was not possible on the warpath for fear of giving warning to the enemy. He also describes the importance of the food provided by the matrons for the Council: "Provisions must always be in plenty in the council-house; for eating and deliberating take their turns" (1794:134, part 1; also see Bartram 1895:58-63).

Iroquois women were in charge of the ingenious methods of preserving and storing the abundant food supplies. Corn, meat, fish, berries, squashes, and even fats were preserved. Some of these foods were buried in specially constructed pits, and some were kept in the long house. Stored food constituted one of the major forms of wealth of the tribe. Stites (1905:72) claims, ". . . It was the women's organization which controlled the surplus and represented the owning class." Hewitt (1933) describes a tribal public treasury which contained wampum belts, quill and feather work, furs, and assorted stored foods. Its contents were scrupulously guarded by the matrons.

In sum, among the Iroquois, the distribution of food within the tribe was the responsibility of the matrons. They also controlled the provisions within the household, as well as those that made the major male activities possible. Some authors claim that the matrons controlled the wealth of the tribe (much of it in stored food) as well.

Like the Iroquois, the Bemba were hospitable and placed the dispensing of the daily meal in the hands of a few matrons. Here the similarity ends. The distribution of food followed a number of institutionalized rules, and far less was left to the discretion and generosity of the matrons. It is possible that these prescribed obligations stemmed from greater scarcity of food, just as it has only been in times of perceived scarcity that our own country has resorted to food rationing.

Concerning the distribution of Bemba grain Richards (1939:188-189) writes:

> *Control over the contents of the Bemba granary are governed by more complex rules. Roughly speaking, the labour given to the production of the crop gives a man ultimate right of disposal, but this is subject to the superior claims of certain older relatives and ultimately*

to that of the chief himself. That is to say, the owner may be the only person able to reap the grain and store it, but he may have to give portions of the crop to others on demand.

Furthermore, the dispensing of cooked food, although conducted by the matrons, reflected the prestige and power of the male household heads, and was analogous to the hospitality extended by the chief, which bestowed obligations on the recipients. Richards (1939:135, 144, 150) observes:

> *. . . The distribution of cooked food is an attribute of authority, and therefore prestige, and that its reception puts a man under an obligation to return respect, service, or reciprocal hospitality. . . . It is on these reciprocal obligations to serve and to feed that the whole political and economic system of the tribe is based.*

> *The whole institution of the* kamitembo *(sacred kitchen and storehouse of the chief) illustrates to my mind that close association between authority and the power to distribute provisions on which the tribal organization depends. The chief owns the food and receives tribute, and the chief provides for his subjects and distributes cooked food to them.*

SUMMARY

The role of women in the economic organization of the Bemba and the Iroquois have been compared. Unlike Bemba women, Iroquois women controlled the factors of agricultural production, for they had rights in the land which they cultivated and in the implements and the seeds. Iroquois agricultural activities, which yielded bountiful harvests, were highly organized under elected female leadership. The male ground-clearing activities were not culturally emphasized unlike the pollarding of trees among the Bemba. Most important, Iroquois women maintained the right to distribute and to dispense all food, even that procured by the men. This was especially significant as stored food constituted one of the major forms of wealth for the tribe. Through their

67

control of the economic organization of the tribe, Iroquois matrons were able to make available or to withhold food for meetings of the Council and for war parties, for the observance of religious festivals, and for the daily meals of the household. These economic realities were institutionalized in the matrons' power to nominate Council Elders and to influence Council decisions. They had a voice in the conduct of war and the establishment of treaties. They elected "keepers of the faith" and served in that capacity. They controlled life in the long house.

The unusual role of Iroquois women in politics, religion, and domestic life cannot be dismissed simply as a historical curiosity. It cannot be explained by Iroquois social structure, nor can it be attributed to the size of their contribution to the Iroquois economy. The high status of Iroquois women was the result of their control of the economic organization of their tribe.

NOTES

Acknowledgments. This study has been made possible by the generous support of the Radcliffe Institute. Hilda Kahne and Ying Ying Yuan have made numerous helpful comments on the manuscript.

[1] Beauchamp (1900), Carr (1887), and Hewitt (1933) published their articles over a span of nearly fifty years, yet all describe Iroquois "matriarchy." Carr's article contains the most documentation. Hewitt's information is somewhat idiosyncratic and contains no documentation. He ends his article with a paraphrase of Lafitau's (1724) famous passage, but does not attribute it to its original source.

[2] The letter was written in May, 1879, and appears in its entirety in Stern (1933). Another interpretation by Wright of the "knocking off of horns" appears in Fenton (1957b).

[3] *Life of Mary Jemison: Deh-he-wä-mis* was originally published in 1824 when Mary Jemison was about eighty. The book, written by James Seaver, is supposed to present Mary Jemison's narrative, but is written in a style that can hardly have been the idiom of a woman who spent most of her life as a Seneca. As it is the only source of its kind, it is quoted here.

The edition used is that published in 1880 and contains chapters by a number of later authors. By 1924, the book had gone through twenty-two editions at the hands of four revisers, one of whom was Lewis Morgan. Any edition of the book is difficult to obtain today. Milliken (1924:87) writes of the first edition:

> *Published before the day of the dime novel, at a time*
> *when tales of adventure and romance were much less*
> *common than now and the thrillers of the silver screen*

69

were entirely unknown, it was circulated and read almost to complete destruction.

[4] This discrepancy demonstrates one of the difficulties in using the *Jesuit Relations*. The *Relations* cover an extended period of time and are anecdotal rather than descriptive. They are the work of many authors, whose prime purpose was to describe not the customs they found, but their own missionary activities.

REFERENCES CITED

Aberle, David
    1961 Matrilineal Descent in Cross-Cultural Perspective. *In* Matrilineal Kinship. David M. Schneider and Kathleen Gough, eds. Pp. 655-727. Berkeley: University of California Press.
Bartram, John
    1895 Observations on the Inhabitants, Climate, Soil, Rivers, Productions, Animals, and Other Matters Worthy of Notice. (Reprinted Geneva, New York: W.F. Humphrey.)
Beauchamp, William M.
    1900 Iroquois Women. Journal of American Folk-Lore 13(49): 81-91.
Carr, Lucien
    1887 On the Social and Political Position of Woman among the Huron-Iroquois Tribes. Annual Report of the Trustees of the Peabody Museum of American Archaeology and Ethnology 3: 207-232.
D'Andrade, Roy G.
    1966 Sex Differences and Cultural Institutions. Stanford Studies in Psychology, No. 5. Pp. 174-204. Stanford: Stanford University Press.
Fenton, William N.
    1957a Long-Term Trends of Change among the Iroquois. Proceedings of the 1957 Annual Spring Meetings of the American Ethnological Society. Pp. 30-35. Seattle: American Ethnological Society.

Fenton, William N., ed.
1957b   Seneca Indians by Asher Wright (1859). Ethnohistory 4(3): 302-321.

Goldenweiser, Alexander A.
1912   On Iroquois Work, 1912. Summary Report of the Geological Survey of Canada, Anthropology Division. Sessional Paper, No. 26. Pp. 464-475. Ottawa: Government Printing Bureau.
1914   On Iroquois Work, 1913-1914. Summary Report of the Geological Survey of Canada, Anthropology Division. Pp. 365-373. Ottawa: Government Printing Bureau.

Gough, Kathleen
1961   The Modern Disintegration of Matrilineal Descent Groups. In Matrilineal Kinship. David M. Schneider and Kathleen Gough, eds. Pp. 631-652. Berkeley: University of California Press.

Hewitt, John N.B.
1933   Status of Woman in Iroquois Polity before 1784. Annual Report of the Board of Regents of the Smithsonian Institution for 1932. Pp. 475-488. Washington: U.S. Government Printing Office.

Jenness, Diamond
1932   The Indians of Canada. Bulletin of the National Museum of Canada, No. 65. Ottawa: F.A. Acland.

Lafitau, Joseph F.
1724   Moeurs des Sauvages Ameriquains, Comparées aux Moeurs des Premiers Temps. Four volumes. Paris: Saugrain l'aîné.

Loskiel, George H.
1794   History of the Mission of the United Brethren among the Indians in North America. Christian LaTrobe, trans. London: The Brethren's Society for the Furtherance of the Gospel.

Lowie, Robert H.
1961   Primitive Society. Fred Eggan, ed. New York: Harper. (Originally published, 1920.)

Malinowski, Bronislaw
1913   The Family among the Australian Aborigines: A Sociological Study. Monographs on Sociology, Vol. 1. London: University of London Press.

Milliken, Charles
1924   A Biographical Sketch of Mary Jemison, the White

Woman of the Genesee. Researches and Transactions of the New York State Archeological Association, Lewis H. Morgan Chapter 4(3): 81-101.

Morgan, Lewis Henry
  1962   League of the Iroquois. New York: Corinth Books. (Originally published, 1851.)
  1963   Ancient Society. Eleanor B. Leacock, ed. Cleveland: World Publishing. (Originally published, 1877.)
  1965   Houses and House-Life of the American Aborigines. Chicago: University of Chicago Press. (Originally published, 1881.)

Murdock, George P.
  1934   Our Primitive Contemporaries. New York: Macmillan.
  1967   Ethnographic Atlas: A Summary. Ethnology 6: 109-236.

Noon, John A.
  1949   Law and Government of the Grand River Iroquois. Viking Fund Publications in Anthropology, No. 12. New York: Viking Fund.

Parker, Arthur C.
  1910   Iroquois Uses of Maize and Other Food Plants. New York State Museum Bulletin, No. 144. Albany: University of the State of New York.
  1913   The Code of Handsome Lake, the Seneca Prophet. New York State Museum Bulletin, No. 163. Albany: University of the State of New York.
  1916   The Constitution of the Five Nations. New York State Museum Bulletin, No. 184. Albany: The University of the State of New York.
  1926   An Analytical History of the Seneca Indians. Researches and Transactions of the New York State Archeological Association, Lewis H. Morgan Chapter 6(1-4): 1-162.

Randle, Martha C.
  1951   Iroquois Women, Then and Now. Bulletin of the Bureau of American Ethnology, No. 149. Pp. 167-180. Washington: U.S. Government Printing Office.

Richards, Audrey I.
  1939   Land, Labour and Diet in Northern Rhodesia: An Economic Study of the Bemba Tribe. London: Oxford University Press, for the International Institute of African Languages and Cultures.

1956 Chisungu: A Girls' Initiation Ceremony among the Bemba of Northern Rhodesia. London: Faber and Faber.

Richards, Cara B.
1957 Matriarchy or Mistake: The Role of Iroquois Women through Time. Proceedings of the 1957 Annual Spring Meeting of the American Ethnological Society. Pp. 36-45. Seattle: American Ethnological Society.

Schoolcraft, Henry R.
1847 Notes on the Iroquois; or, Contributions to American History, Antiquities, and General Ethnology. Albany: Erastus H. Pease. (Originally published, 1842.)
1860 Archives of Aboriginal Knowledge. Six volumes. Philadelphia: J.B. Lippincott.

Seaver, James E.
1880 Life of Mary Jemison: Deh-He-Wä-Mis. Buffalo: Matthews Brothers and Bryant. (First ed., 1824.)

Snyderman, George S.
1951 Concepts of Land Ownership among the Iroquois and their Neighbors. Bulletin of the Bureau of American Ethnology, No. 149. Pp. 13-34. Washington: U.S. Government Printing Office.

Speck, Frank G.
1945 The Iroquois, A Study in Cultural Evolution. Bulletin of the Cranbrook Institute of Science, No. 23. Bloomfield Hills, Michigan.

Stern, Bernhard J., ed.
1933 The Letters of Asher Wright to Lewis Henry Morgan. American Anthropologist 35: 138-145.

Stites, Sara H.
1905 Economics of the Iroquois. Bryn Mawr College Monographs, Vol. 1, No. 3. Bryn Mawr, Pennsylvania.

Waugh, F.W.
1916 Iroquois Foods and Food Preparation. Memoir of the Canada Department of Mines, Geological Survey, No. 86. Anthropological Series, No. 12. Ottawa: Government Printing Bureau.

SUGGESTIONS FOR FURTHER READING

Murphy, Yolanda, and Robert F. Murphy
    1974   Women of the Forest. New York: Columbia University Press.
    Describes the dynamics of female-male relations among the patrilineal Mundurucú Indians of Amazonian Brazil. The organization of women's work and the bases for female solidarity provide interesting comparisons with the Iroquois.

Sanday, Peggy R.
    1974   Female Status in the Public Domain. *In* Woman, Culture, and Society. Michelle Zimbalist Rosaldo and Louise Lamphere, eds. Pp. 189-206. Stanford: Stanford University Press.
    Compares the relationship among female status, political authority, and economic control in twelve societies. Concludes that women develop political and economic power in social systems characterized by a balanced division of labor.

Strathern, Marilyn
    1972   Women in Between. Female Roles in a Male World: Mount Hagen, New Guinea. London: Seminar Press.
    Excellent, detailed analysis of women's productive roles among the patrilineal Melpa speakers of Mount Hagen. Useful for comparing women's economic and political status with the Iroquois.

Weiner, Annette B.
    1976   Women of Value, Men of Reknown: New Perspectives in Trobriand Exchange. Austin: University of Texas Press.
    Focuses on women's important roles in large scale ceremonial exchanges of wealth in a matrilineal Pacific Island society.

THE ROLE OF WOMEN IN A CHANGING NAVAHO SOCIETY

Laila Shukry Hamamsy

INTRODUCTION

Most of the work on which this paper is based was done in 1951-52 in the Fruitland Irrigation Project in San Juan County, at the northwestern corner of New Mexico. The project area has a thirteen-mile boundary along the southern bank of the river, which is settled on the north by Mormons and other white farmers. The area at that time included 2,500 acres of irrigated land divided into 205 farms and assigned to 191 family units (Sasaki 1950). The nearest urban center is the predominantly white town of Farmington, just off the reservation.

Although the area has long been inhabited by Navaho farmers and owners of livestock, the development of the irrigation project dates from 1933 when the land was surveyed for the purpose of establishing farm tracts. These tracts were assigned in ten-acre lots to original residents and to applicants from other parts of the reservation.

Particular aspects of Fruitland's position made it useful for the purposes of this study. There is directed social change in the form of government programs, including the irrigation project itself. Further, Fruitland is on the edge of the reservation and is in continuous interaction with the neighboring white society. It is also a well-defined geographic and social unit. Finally, there was available a great deal of

Reprinted by permission of the author and the American Anthropological Association from *American Anthropologist* 59(1):101-111, 1957.

data gathered by the research team of the Cornell University Southwest Project which had been working in the area since 1948.

Data for the present study were gathered by the author during a seventeen week residence in the Fruitland area in 1951 and 1952, and preceding that, during a three week residence at Navaho Mountain, a more traditional settlement than that represented by Fruitland. Methods of collecting data were primarily those of participant observation and informal open-ended interviews. They were chosen because of the limited time of residence and because the relationship between the author and the residents rapidly became one of friendship, which seemed to make difficult the role of formal interviewer. Additional sources of data were the field notes of other research workers of the Southwest Project, Indian Service reports and documents, and anthropological literature on the Navaho.

TRADITIONAL ECONOMIC AND SOCIAL ORGANIZATION

The economic and social organization here termed traditional is that which developed after 1868 when the Navaho returned to the southwestern location after a four-year forced exile. It is informal and loosely knit in comparison to that of many other Indians, for example, the Pueblo; and there are local variations due to differing degrees of contact with other groups, historical accidents, and geographic conditions. A general pattern, however, is fairly evident, and even today many conform to it. Kluckhohn and Leighton (1946) estimate conformity in live-stock regions at 85 percent.

The Navaho traditionally live in widely scattered matrilocal family groups (extended families). Within each group, each nuclear family lives in a separate hogan. The extended family is usually composed of an older woman, her husband, her unmarried children, her married daughters, and the daughters' husbands and children. Some families have additional but secondary shelters at summer pasture lands.

Raising livestock and subsistence farming are the major economic activities. In these, and in the management of the hogan, there is a division of labor between men and women, each assuming significant functions. Men are generally responsible for the horses and cattle, women for the sheep and goats. Women carry the main burden in the running of the hogan, including the making of clothing, but men are responsible for the leather and silver work. Blanket weaving is a common pursuit of the women, and baskets and pottery are made by a few.

The smallest and most important unit of social and economic co-operation is the nuclear family, but in the frequent times of heightened activity such as harvest and planting, all members of the group in an area may help each other. On the other hand, in some regions the extended family operates as a unit. The sheep of all members of the family will be pooled under the direction of the matron of the household and are herded by the group's young men and women.

The ownership and the use of property and livestock is generally subject to control by the extended family, although individuals and nuclear families may be owners in fact. Only personal property such as jewelry and cash is not under such control. Economically, the women fare equally with or better than the men, since they are the usual owners of sheep, a major property, and since they can earn cash through their weaving. In addition, inheritance is through the women, and daughters and nieces often receive the same as or more than the male relatives.

The father is the formal head of the family, but the mother and children make up its stable core. The man moves frequently between his family of orientation and his family of procreation, since he has obligations to both. In contrast, the woman remains with her family of orientation, in her own extended family group. Within this group, and in her own nuclear family, she usually has as much or more influence than her husband. She often makes the decisions in the family's financial affairs, even if the goods involved were originally the husband's individual property. ''The general tendency, even in spite of the theoretical power of the avunculate, is for sons, brothers and husbands to consult the maternal head of the house and to respect her opinion'' (Reichard 1928: 53). Children count descent through the mother and are considered to belong to her and her clan.

The one social function of the family that is usually left to the men is that of relations with the world outside the group, but here too, women can play a part if they choose.

All members of the extended family participate in the raising and training of children. The mother has the day-to-day responsibility for their care and discipline. Maternal uncles have important teaching and disciplinary functions. The father's relationship to the children, on the other hand, is mainly affectional. As the young grow into adult life, they remain under the social control of the family, since they are dependent on the goodwill of parents and relatives for their economic survival and social acceptance.

Marriages are usually arranged by parents and relatives, most importantly the maternal uncles, and are frequently made for economic and social reasons. The groom provides a bridal gift, often livestock and household utensils, and these become the property of the bride. Newly wed couples live near the wife's family, and there is constant visiting of the young woman and her children with the family matron. The husband is excluded from such contact by a taboo forbidding a man to look upon his mother-in-law. The son-in-law's position is a subordinate one in the extended family household and he is closely supervised by his father-in-law. One groom was told: "Your folks have turned you over to us. You don't belong over there any more. You are here now, to take care of the bride's property" (Dyk 1947:109-110). The young married woman, on the other hand, enjoys security and assistance with her household and family tasks from the close relatives surrounding her. Her family protects her if her husband is abusive, and she retains her property and her children in case the marriage fails.

If the marriage is successful and productive, the husband and wife may establish a more independent hogan and may separate their flocks from the family herd, thus becoming the nucleus of a new extended family group. If the marriage dissolves, as is frequent, it is the husband who suffers dislocation and financial loss. Leighton and Kluckhohn (1947: 83) estimate that only one woman in four reaches old age with her original husband. Desertion is the most common cause of family dissolution, more frequent even than death. The husband is forced out of his home, to return to his family of orientation or to a new wife's hogan, and his property usually remains with his former wife.

Beyond the extended family, the next unit of social organization is the outfit: a group of related extended families who co-operate in large economic, social, and religious functions. Groups of outfits occupying specific localities are organized into bands with recognized leaders. There is also a clan organization which is chiefly important as a regulator of marriage choices. There is no indigenous centralized tribal organization.

NEW ECONOMIC POSITION

The drastic changes introduced into the traditional Navaho economic pattern within the last twenty-odd years have had direct effects on women's economic position and on the value of their work, and are, we suggest, important among the forces that are redefining the role of Navaho women today.

Most Navaho have been subject to a slow economic decline and to the accompanying need for new sources of income, notably wage work. In Fruitland the economic picture is particularly sharp. It is an area in which the greatest changes have been made in traditional agriculture and herding patterns. Being a border community, the residents are nearer to work opportunities and more enticed than Indians in the interior by employment opportunities in the white world "outside." Both of these factors have direct effects on the Navaho woman's economic position.

Two aspects of the land policy initiated in 1933 are relevant. First, only married men were originally eligible for land, and only on the condition that they made proper use of it. Women and children, traditionally important owners of land, were thus barred in the beginning from ownership. They could become owners only through inheritance or other transfer from the male assignees. Further, the threat that the government might take away the land if it were used improperly introduced an uncertainty not existing in traditional ownership patterns.

The second aspect of the changing economy is less direct. It is that few families manage to make a living from farming alone, or even in combined farming and livestock operations. Most of them are forced to seek additional income. The most available source is in the white communities at Fruitland's border. The economic result of this is that the Navaho woman's family may have more cash than formerly, but it is provided by the man of the house. Both of these are elements foreign to traditional organization, and their effect will be discussed in some detail later.

The extent to which this new economic picture applies in Fruitland can be indicated briefly. Crop report estimates obtained from the Farm Management Supervisor of the Fruitland Project reveal that in the summer of 1951 about 69 percent of 191 families had under assignment between six and fifteen acres and earned a generously estimated yearly income of less than $900. Only nine families owned between twenty-five and thirty-three acres (the maximum holding) and averaged $1,774. Livestock holding are limited by government regulation and by the lack of good range vegetation. In 1952, sixty-nine individuals held sheep-permits, but they stocked only 61 percent of the sheep their permits allowed them.

On the other hand, the dependence of the Fruitlanders on wage work has increased. In 1952, the author interviewed thirty-eight families and found that of the thirty-two men in these, all but two had at some time engaged in off-reservation or government work. The two exceptions are men who have large acreages and are successful farmers. There were forty-three able-bodied women in this same group of families, but only eleven of them had ever engaged in wage work. Of these, only four were married women living with their husbands. The others were widowed or divorced.

When the women do find work, they are usually poorly paid in comparison with the men. There are a few openings in government institutions such as schools and hospitals, but the major sources of employment are in such areas as seasonal agricultural work, restaurants, and domestic service. The men, on the other hand, find their major employment opportunities in such relatively better paid fields as railroads, agriculture, lumbering, construction and road work, and oil, military, and mining operations, in that order of importance.

EFFECTS OF NEW ECONOMIC POSITION ON SOCIAL PATTERNS

All of the traditional units of Navaho social organization still function in Fruitland, but significant changes are taking place in the relative importance of family units. The importance of the independent biological family is increasing, while the influence of the extended family and of larger units lessens. There is also a strong tendency away from matrilocality. Some men and women still share farm and home tasks and the responsibility for children, but many men are frequently not at home to do their share. Finally, the economic responsibilities of the family fall less on the family as a unit, and more on the male head of the independent nuclear family.

Fruitland residence patterns in 1952 show a trend away from matrilocality. Of thirty-six families studied, there were only five older families acting as heads of extended family units. There were thirteen younger couples living as part of these extended groups, but twelve of these were in patrilocal residence. The remaining eighteen families lived independently on their own plots; five of them near, but not as part of the husband's family; five near the wife's family, and eight not near families of either spouse. The five families living hear the wife's family were cases in which daughters had married outsiders.

In families where subsistence farming and herding are still major occupations, men and women share the tasks. But many women have been forced by their husbands' absences in wage work to take over many of the farm chores that traditionally belong to men. Thus:

> In the summer time [according to one informant] she comes and stays at Fruitland in order to take care of the farm. Her husband stays at Shiprock and visits on weekends. Her husband helps on the farm, does the carrying of heavy things, while she does all the rest.

Women without husbands and living away from an extended family find it difficult to maintain their farms. One woman told an interviewer:

> My boy has been working outside and I have to irrigate my farm all by myself. Sometimes my neighbors, who belong to the same clan come and help, but most of the time I work it all myself.

Some in this position give up their land:

After her husband's death, she found that she could not take care of the farm, so she gave it to her son and moved next to her daughter.

Women still have major responsibility for housework and the care of children, but housework takes little time. Laundry is meager and cooking had become simplified and less time-consuming as the women adopt processed foods. Care of the children is less demanding since only the preschool children are constantly at home. The older children are in school, some in day schools and some in off-reservation boarding schools. The traditional craft of weaving has become impossible with the decline of sheep flocks.

This changing pattern toward independent families and less housework affects the women in a number of ways. Mothers of preschool children, while usually not over-worked, lack the support that other members of the extended family could provide. They have the continuous care of the children and if they leave home to visit or shop, must either take the children with them or hire a baby-sitter. Many complain that they feel tied down. They also lack the guidance and assistance in training and discipline that older members of the family could provide.

The women who have no children, or only older children, have little to do. Many are bored or restless:

> *Before getting married, Elizabeth worked in a cafe in town. She had stopped 'to have a rest.' She is bored with home, however, and would like to go back to work again. 'I hate to stay at home. There isn't much to do.'*

A few of the women do try to find wage work; many seek diversion in the nearby town, and others in visiting friends and relatives:

> *I asked: 'What does Mary do all day?' Her aunt said, 'Nothing. She just takes care of her baby. She comes to visit me and she goes to visit my mother, that's all.'*

Economically, the wives are generally dependent on their husbands, but the men are often erratic and irresponsible providers. Cash, as was noted above, traditionally the property of an individual owner, is still considered by many men to belong solely to them, with the result that many women are frequently without economic support. One old man told an interviewer:

> The Navaho people who work for wages don't put any money in the bank. They spend everything and at the end, they don't have any money to take care of the needs of other members of the family. They will spend all their money on cars sometimes, but they won't have enough money to eat and buy clothes for the children.

Some women do manage to get part of their husbands' earnings. The following comment by one who does, suggests that she feels her husband to be an exceptionally considerate provider:

> My husband give me money. Sometimes he cash check and give me money. Many times he give me all of it. . . . He is good that way. He don't go and spend all his money like some do.

In a few families interviewed by the author, both husband and wife have wage work. In most of these, however, each pays his own way, even in recreational expenses such as an evening in town.

The poorest women in Fruitland are generally the middle-aged and old women who have no male providers. They frequently have no economic support except the relatively inadequate welfare aid. Under traditional conditions these women would be well off; they might be managers of large extended family units, or at least respected female relatives with secure positions within the family group.

OUTSIDE INFLUENCES ON TRADITIONAL SOCIAL PATTERNS

Through increasing contact with the white world, the Navaho have become familiar with new goods, new ways of doing things, new forms of recreation, and a number of new problems. Many Navaho now own cars, radios, stoves, washing machines, and other modern durable goods. Some build frame or stone houses to replace the traditional and inexpensive hogans. The desire for these new things makes many women urge their men to greater effort in finding wage work, often with the result that the women become still more alone on the farm and in the home. In addition, these new products and ways are rapidly replacing traditional bases for determining prestige and standards of living. The direct effect of this on the women is that they become less important for the family standards and prestige, while the men, as the wage earners, become much more so.

Traditionally, religious ceremonies, dances, fairs, family visiting, and family parties were major forms of recreation. Women, it may be noted, have important functions in most of these. The frequency of these events, particularly the larger and more organized forms, is now diminishing, and no new forms of recreation have developed on the reservation to replace them. Instead, there is an increasing tendency, especially among younger Navahos, to seek amusement in the urban center off the reservation. To get there, however, the women usually have to depend on the men - for the ride to town and the money to spend. Once in town, men and women frequently seek separate entertainment. For the women this may be going to the movies, eating in restaurants, drinking, shopping, meeting friends, and window-shopping. One man described his family's trip to town: "I'm happy, and my family is happy. I take a couple of drinks, and my wife goes shopping."

"Outside" educational patterns are replacing the traditional home education in the skills of home-making, farming, and herding. While this newer education, which is under government direction, is available to both boys and girls, it is frequently the boys of the family who receive the better and longer training. Many girls are taken out of school early to help at home. Since school-learned skills and the ability to speak English are important factors in earning and social abilities, the girls are often disadvantaged. The author found only a few families in which the wife was better educated than her husband, and in some of these families she was a strong member and family spokesman, a position roughly comparable to that of the wife in a traditional family group.

Many of these new ways can be further traced for their effect on family relationships and family harmony. Differences in education, of course, are an important source of conflict between generations of a family, as well as between members of a single generation. The increasing amount of disposable income and the increasing desire for purchased goods means increasing occasions for family conflict over how wages will be used. For example: "M.B. was reported to the police by his wife who is having a difficult time because M.B. does not bring home his checks" (field notes). Drunkenness, wife-beating, infidelity, and jealousy are marked causes of discord in the Fruitland area. Drunkenness is reported to be the most common cause of friction, and it is often a contributing factor in other conflicts: "Suspicion of infidelity of marital partners appears to be especially marked at Fruitland because of easy access to town and liquor. Whenever men or women are away over night they are immediately suspected of having had an affair" (Sasaki 1950:89).

CHANGING SOCIAL ORGANIZATION OF THE FAMILY

Relationships within the family are changing. The father, because of his importance as breadwinner, and because of the change from matrilocal to neolocal or patrilocal residence arrangements, is becoming more indispensable to the family for its economic and social well-being, and at the same time he is frequently away from home. The wife, therefore, still has the daily responsibility for running the house and for the care and training of the younger children.

Both mother and father lose influence, however, as the children grow and undertake school education. Frequently the parents find themselves in an ambivalent position toward these children. Many favor white education, and want their children to embrace white ways:

> *The son told me that his father . . . [felt] the main thing was to get an education, so the white man could not cheat him.*

Another father told an interviewer that:

> *He was anxious for them [the children] to learn a little English and a trade because things were going to get tougher for the Navahos if they don't have a trade.*

At the same time, parents find themselves ineffectual in the face of their children's greater education and rejection of traditional customs. Lacking economic and social control, they have little effect against rebellion. Girls frequently express revolt through sexual adventures, which result in the further problem of illegitimate children. Traditionally such children were absorbed into the large, loose framework of the extended family, but today both the unmarried mother and her children may be without economic or social support.

The growing independence of the young carries over to marriage customs, and increasingly marriages are contracted without parental consent. The author knew twelve Fruitland couples who had married within the last ten years. Eight of these married through personal choice and only four through parental arrangement. All of the women in the first group were educated to the extent that they spoke English, and seven of them had worked for wages before marriage. Of the four in the latter group, only one was sufficiently educated to speak English. Even in traditionally arranged marriages, the groom's gift has undergone a change. Frequently, he no longer gives livestock or household utensils, but instead a cash payment.

The position of the daughter-in-law in a patrilocal extended family unit (and to some extent in an independent nuclear family) needs special mention for the marked contrast it provides with that of the daughter-in-law in the traditional matrilocal residence. In a patrilocal unit, the young married woman has to live closely and interact frequently with people who do not embrace her as one of them. Her mother-in-law, the head of the woman's division of the extended family, exercises authority over her without at the same time offering her protection and emotional security. A possessive mother-in-law is in fact often a rival for the young husband's attention. In such rivalry, the daughter-in-law is in a weak position, and even lacks the protection provided by a mother-in-law taboo. The young woman's main, and possibly only, defense in such rivalry lies in her personal influence over the husband.

Conflicts occur frequently in such situations. When mild, they take the form of verbal battles, with gossip a strong weapon. In more serious cases, the young woman can be forced from her home alone, or with her husband if her influence over him is strong. In either case, she suffers dislocation and the loss of economic security and opportunity that she may have enjoyed as part of the extended family. When there is a marked degree of difference in the education of the older and younger women, there are occasions for additional and serious conflicts. Again, it is a struggle which the daughter-in-law, alone in the family group, is likely to lose. Such conflicts arise over education of the children, health measures, the family's manner of living, recreation, and related matters.

In virtually every kind of family organization today, most conflicts that result in divorce or desertion by the husband mean economic and social disorganization and loss of prestige for the women and children. If the family has been in patrilocal residence, the woman and children are frequently forced to leave their homes. In neolocal residence, deserted wives, while possibly retaining their houses, lose economic support. They sometimes return to the wife's family, but this often imposes an economic burden on her people. Other solutions are the finding of a new husband, or moving to town in search of employment. This move is likely to result in minimal economic security, at best, and more often in unemployment, drunkenness, and sexual promiscuity.

The nine cases of divorce known to the author in Fruitland suggest the extent to which women's position in broken marriages has changed. Six of the nine cases resulted in the woman's leaving home. Only two of these women returned to live with their own relatives; the other four left Fruitland and went to the nearby urban white center. In three cases the men left the family. Two of these were families in matrilocal residence and the wives, although not suffering dislocation, did suffer economic hardship, since they had been economically dependent on their husbands' wages.

CONCLUSION: EVALUATION OF THE NEW POSITION OF NAVAHO WOMEN

The preceding summary of life in Fruitland today suggests that there are three aspects of the woman's role that have been adversely affected by the recent social and economic changes there: her economic position, the significance of her function within the family, and her sense of security and bargaining position in family interaction. The last of these is largely a result of the first two.

Although the Fruitland society, in gross calculation, has gained economically from the recent industrial development in the San Juan Valley, a close examination shows that while the men have been compensated for the loss of their traditional sources of livelihood, the women have not been directly compensated in any way. In wage work most men find an adequate substitute for the declining livestock economy. As far as women are concerned, in losing their sheep, they have lost their economic independence. There are few job opportunities for them, and their duties in the home make it impossible for most of them to seek work outside.

This economic dependence of women is aggravated by the fact that the wants of their families have increased considerably. To obtain the goods and services of white society, the women have to depend upon the industry and good-will of the wage earners—the men. Some women do benefit from what their husbands earn, for there is beginning to develop a definition of the husband's role as economic provider. But there are many instances in which the traditional attitude toward cash is still operative and is applied with a vengeance. Middle age bestows prestige and wealth on the Navaho woman of traditional society, especially if she is fortunate enough to have a large female progeny. In contrast, the poorest category of women in Fruitland are the middle-aged women without male providers.

In assessing the significance of woman's functions in Fruitland today as against those of traditional society, the following questions may be asked: How valuable are her social and economic activities, and how personally rewarding? Can the performance of these be a means for the attainment of status in the prestige hierarchy of society?

Traditionally, every member of the family performs significant tasks that contribute to the survival of the whole unit. The woman, as the central figure in the home, assumes functions there that are indispensable to the economic and social well-being of her family. She is also well equipped to handle most phases of an important economic activity —sheep-raising. The accumulation of wealth is possible for both men and women. As wealth spells prestige among the Navaho, this means that woman's labor and industry are important in determining the status of the family on the prestige ladder of the community.

88

In Fruitland, the division of labor still follows convenience, and convenience decrees that women perform most of the tasks in and around the house. But the home has been shorn of much of its economic and social significance, and has been largely deserted by the men and older children. The importance of women's functions has declined accordingly. Wage employment is for most families the only means for acquiring processed goods and the newer prestige symbols such as cars and modern homes. It is the men who make these acquisitions possible, and who are therefore mainly responsible for determining the social and economic status and the prestige of the family.

Although women no longer have equal economic opportunities and rewards, they still have the traditional functions of childbearing and rearing. Are these personally satisfying? Many younger women express dissatisfaction. Mothers in independent residence complain of being tied down by their children, and school-trained women who worked prior to marriage describe home life as confining and dull. In addition, children are no longer social and economic assets. For women who have no children, homemaking offers unproductive leisure, boredom, and restlessness. Farm work is seasonal, and housekeeping takes little time. Weaving is no longer a possible leisure-time activity.

The woman's sense of security and her position within the family have been affected by these changes. The absence of the support of close relatives and the lack of economic opportunities that traditional organization provides, have threatened her sense of economic and social security. And the very facts of her dependence and the diminished significance of her functions have greatly lowered her bargaining position in family interaction. The pertinent questions here are: Which marriage partner can function more adequately without the other? And, who suffers most in case of disagreement that breaks up the family?

When we compare the traditional economic organization to that which is evolving in Fruitland, we find that the woman has become more dependent on the man for her economic and social well-being, and correspondingly, she is much less indispensable to her husband for his well-being. In case of a disagreement that results in a split of the family, she is the one who suffers most, both economically and socially. Thus, the majority of women find themselves relegated to a very minor position of power in the family arena, unless they manage through some personal influence or advantage to counteract the disadvantages of the weak bargaining position offered by the emerging culture.

We conclude, then, that the changing economic position and social organization of the Navaho today are adversely affecting the women. They are losing their economic independence, the satisfactions and rewards that accompany their functioning, and their security and power within the family.

Navaho men are adjusting to the changing conditions by increasingly adopting the life and culture of the white world, but the women are being left stranded on the reservation. Much that was economically and socially important there has become out-moded and discarded, and little has so far evolved to fill the void resulting in the lives of the women. We cannot assume that this is a final, stable position. What direction the women's lives will take depends on where the women see their opportunities; whether life on the reservation can be revitalized and made more satisfactory, or whether the women will follow their men into the world outside. Many of the forces that have helped to shape the changes outlined in this paper continue to be effective and will continue to influence the role of women: government agricultural and service programs, the continually emerging cash economy, school education, and, not least, the continuing culture of the Navaho, which acts as a sieve through which other forces must pass.

NOTES

Acknowledgments. This paper has its origin in the Cornell Southwest Project, which in turn is part of the Cornell Program for Research and Training in Culture and Applied Science. The total program is directed by Lauriston Sharp. The Southwest Project is under the general supervision of Alexander H. Leighton; John Adair is former Field Director, and Tom T. Sasaki is the current Field Director. The research, supported primarily by the Carnegie Corporation of New York, was done by Hamamsy. This paper was prepared with the assistance of Mrs. Alice Longaker, professional editor.

REFERENCES CITED

Dyk, Walter
    1947   A Navaho Autobiography. New York: Viking Fund Publications in Anthropology, No. 8. New York: Viking Fund.
Kluckhohn, Clyde, and Dorothea Leighton
    1946   The Navaho. Cambridge: Harvard University Press.
Leighton, Dorothea, and Clyde Kluckhohn
    1947   Children of the People: The Navaho Individual and His Development. Cambridge: Harvard University Press.
Reichard, Gladys A.
    1928   Social Life of the Navaho Indians, with Some Attention to Minor Ceremonies. New York: Columbia University Press.
Sasaki, Tom T.
    1950   Technological Change in a Navaho Farming Community:

A Study of Social and Psychological Processes. Ph.D. dissertation, Anthropology Department, Cornell University.

SUGGESTIONS FOR FURTHER READING

Downs, James F.
    1972   The Navaho. New York: Holt, Rinehart and Winston.
    Ethnography of Nez Ch'ii society and culture based on fieldwork conducted during 1960-61 on the Navaho reservation. Discusses matriliny and the importance of women's productive roles in sheep husbandry.
Jopling, Carol F.
    1974   Women's work: A Mexican Case Study of Low Status as a Tactical Advantage. Ethnology 13: 187-195.
    Compares the cottage industry of women's shirt-making, introduced in the early 1960s, with the male occupation of sandal-making in a southern Mexican village. Concludes that economic success in shirt-making derives from women's traditionally low status and the lack of prestige accorded to female work in general.
Schneider, David, and Kathleen Gough, eds.
    1961   Matrilineal Kinship. Berkeley: University of California Press.
    Includes essays on nine matrilineal societies, matrilineal descent in cross-cultural perspective, and social change. A basic reference.

WOMEN IN MODERNIZING SOCIETIES

Laurel Bossen

Many recent studies dealing with women have attempted to explain the degree of sexual equality within a particular society. Some have integrated their data with a general theory of women's role in modern society or in social evolution. But apart from those concerned with revolutionary situations, there have been relatively few attempts to develop a theory to deal with the historical and contemporary changes in women's position in modernizing societies. By modernization, I refer to the technological and sociocultural changes that result from increasing integration into the world market economy. In this paper I will examine some of the theoretical issues involved. This will entail a brief discussion of the inadequacies of a common theoretical approach to modernization as it affects women. An alternative approach will be proposed. To illustrate its application, I will discuss certain studies of women and development that are explicitly concerned with the process of women's incorporation into the modern world. Finally, I will evaluate this approach in terms of some of my own observations of modernization as it affects women in a Guatemalan community.

A general lack of interest in the consequences of modernization for women has meant that much of the theory has remained at the level of assertion. In western social science, these assertions have largely shared the kind of dualistic framework that has characterized certain explanations of national development. In this way, societies are clas-

Reprinted by permission of the author and the American Anthropological Association from *American Ethnologist* 2(4):587-601, 1975.

sified as either traditional or modern. The western industrialized nations are thought to be closest to an ideal of modern egalitarian treatment for women. Legal freedoms, specifically the right to vote, run for office, and own property have been cited as evidence of women's increasing equality in the western world. The spread of these rights is taken as evidence of an improvement in women's position in underdeveloped nations (Goode 1963; Bernard 1971). Also, the growing participation of women in the wage labor force, as an index of modernization, has been taken to imply increasing equality. Goode (1971) and Bernard (1971) apparently associate the spread of female wage labor with a change to the modern conjugal family and female economic independence from traditional family structures. In contrast, the position of women in preindustrial or traditional societies is depicted as servile, dependent, and decidedly inferior to that of men. Hence, modern changes that bring societies closer to the western pattern and standard are presented as advantageous to women.

A typical statement of this view is that of Raphael Patai, editor of *Women in the Modern World* (1967:1), who states:

> *Throughout the world women have moved toward greater freedom and have achieved greater equality with men both within and outside the family, in the legal, sexual, social, occupational, economic, political and cultural realms. The old order, which confined women to the home as servants, and helpers to their menfolk, has been, or is in the process of being, replaced by a new one in which women increasingly undertake to fill many roles within the home, as wives, mothers, and homemakers, and outside it as partners and coworkers of men in all types of enterprises.*

This sweeping pronouncement defines two polar alternatives: traditional bondage or modern emancipation. Note the transformation of women's role as home "servant" to that of "homemaker." Two premises are involved. Historically, it is suggested that the relative position of women has improved with modernization, and prospectively, that it will improve with modernization in areas still underdeveloped. This view is part of a more general identification of progress with our own cultural norms. The ethnocentrism becomes explicit when

Patai asserts that ". . . all women who fight for emancipation fight for modernism and Westernism" (1967:17).

This theoretical approach has a number of weaknesses. It both over-simplifies the problem and fails to resolve the tension between the assertion that equality increases with modernization and the recognition that equality is still a long way off in modern society. For example, Patai's assertions of unilinear progress are paradoxically set against his observation that the change in women's position has been "circular."

> It is a noteworthy fact that the closer women are to equality with men in any given country the less they seem to make use of this achievement by devoting their lives to professional careers. It is as if, having started out from a base line representing the traditional position of legal and social disability and a life confined in its entirety to home and family, the developments in the most advanced Western countries had described a full circle and reached a goal that, at least in its practical connotations, is found to lie very close to the start [Patai 1967:2].

Similarly, the discrepancies between the assertions and the data presented by Goode (1963:54-75) suggest that the global trend toward female equality may be more apparent than real. Goode confesses that the main theoretical issues are not "entirely clear" (1963:369, 374). The reappearance of a women's liberation movement and the growing body of literature demonstrating great inequalities and disabilities for women in western society weakens the argument that modern western civilization encourages emancipation and equality for women. It is increasingly obvious that the theory regarding women in modernizing societies needs to be reformulated using more explicit data on the effect of modern changes.

For our purposes, there are four main criticisms of the general view that women's position improves with modernization:

1. Modernization and westernization do not imply full equality or autonomy for most women in the modern western nations. Therefore,

the likelihood that such processes do more than encourage the formal or legal appearance of such conditions in the rest of the world is in question.

2. Since the modern ideal-type does not describe the reality of women's situation in modern societies, *a priori* the traditional ideal-type seems equally removed from reality as an overly rigid and prejudicial characterization of underdeveloped or nonindustrial societies. In fact, this stereotype of female domesticity and dependency appears to derive more directly from Euro-American traditions than from any global analysis of women's highly varied social and economic roles in nonindustrial societies. I will return to this argument when I consider an alternative theoretical approach.

3. Important differences in women's condition in traditional and modern societies may be the result of differences in the over-all standard of living as well as changes in sexual equality. While women in modern societies may be more fortunate and have more opportunities than they have in traditional societies, it does not follow that the greater wealth and superior technology controlled by modern societies corresponds to greater equality among its members, female or otherwise. The unilinear view is frequently vague as to whether modernization improves women's position *relative to men's,* or whether the improvements cited are unrelated to the issue of sexual equality.

4. The model also tends to obscure important differences in women's position according to class or strata. It does this by confusing dominant ideologies with actual conditions.

This leads to another set of criticisms and some alternatives to this model of development. These are criticisms of development theory in general that have importance for my approach to the specific problems women face when nations attempt to develop. Patai, Goode, and Bernard are hardly unique in their use of the concept of a unilinear transition from traditional to modern society; this idea has been widely accepted by North American social scientists and vigorously attacked by a few (see discussions in Frank 1969, 1971 and Ribeiro 1972). Those who have opposed the unilinear model have argued that traditional societies are largely a fiction, and that they are neither as pristine, unchanging, nor isolated as they have been presented. The implication that nonindustrial societies have been isolated from modern developments and continuously governed by tradition (since some indeterminate time until the present efforts to adopt the western model of development) is challenged with the demonstration that western mercantilist powers have been meddling with much of the world since at least the fifteenth century. This interference has been such that even most of the remote villages in underdeveloped countries have long been significantly affected, and altered, by western economic expansion through a chain of economic relations that ties the small peasant market into the international economic system.

A related objection is directed at the implication that diffusion from the developed nations, or acculturation to western values and technology, will result in a duplication of the benefits of western society. Here the model's critics maintain that, on the contrary, many of the conditions that are attributed to "backward" traditions are, in fact, the historical product of interaction with the economically and militarily more powerful, developing states of the West which developed and continue to develop at the expense of those regions which are now considered underdeveloped. In view of this interaction, an alternative theory has been introduced whereby underdevelopment can be explained and understood only if it is based on an examination of the historical relationship between developed and underdeveloped nations as part of *one* system, where some nations have been forced to fund the economic needs and imperial adventures of others.

In examining the changing status and role of women in modernizing societies, I shall be concerned with how well each of these two theories fits the reality. That is, does the impact of "modernization" tend to foster equality and autonomous development for women, or does it tend to create the very conditions of underdevelopment which limit their potential? The immediate problem, then, is how to compare or evaluate movement toward sexual equality in societies at widely different levels of development.

There are a number of difficulties attendant upon any attempt to establish a cross-culturally valid standard of sexual equality. One of these is that sexual equality can refer to a wide variety of factors separately or collectively. The appearance of sexual equality in some areas, such as sexual permissiveness or marriage forms, need not correspond to equality in the division or rewards of labor, nor in the areas of political, economic, and military decision-making. Brown (1970) and Sanday (1974) make a similar point in arguing that high female status inferred from deferential treatment should not be confused with high female status consisting in actual power over basic resources and important decisions. A common solution to this problem is to choose one index which seems especially significant in itself, or which seems to entail corresponding measures of sexual equality in a wide range of social institutions.

A related problem is that many of the indices used to measure or symbolize sexual status in one culture may lack a comparable significance in other cultures. Historically, this problem has contributed to some major misconceptions about the position of women in other cultures. Well-known examples have been the nineteenth-century European interpretations of polygyny and matrilineality encountered in other cultures as clear evidence of female servility or female dominance, respectively. We now know the problem is much more complex. Even the use of broad standards of social differentiation such as wealth, status, and power may prove misleading as standards of sexual equality, since some societies separate these attributes for men and women and others treat conjugal or other units corporately.

To avoid some of these problems, it seems that a suitable standard should describe the most fundamental factors that determine and limit the participation of women in a variety of social systems, and it should be based on an evaluation of these factors within each context. It is also necessary to evaluate the role of women *relative* to men in each situation so that it will be possible to discover if women in underdeveloped societies are indeed moving toward greater social equality, or if they are merely moving toward the assumption of western or other social patterns.

Given these requirements, I propose to evaluate women's status in terms of an economic standard involving two considerations. The first is the extent to which women participate in the production of socially necessary goods and services. The second is the extent to which surplus labor or labor-saving innovations are available to provide the products and services that are designated as women's work. This second part assumes that if there are certain economic activities that are socially assigned to women, then it is necessary to consider the extent to which the female contribution is a scarce or abundant resource within a society.

Although discussions of sexual equality follow diverse themes, it has been widely accepted that the economic role of women is a fundamental factor in determining their over-all social position. In modern industrial societies, it is common to use the labor force participation of women as an index of their position in society. It is assumed that greater equality is possible when one's labor commands a regular monetary wage; otherwise one easily becomes dependent on (and subordinate to) other wage earners. However, the rate of labor force participation, which really measures wage labor, can be a misleading index of women's economic participation in underdeveloped economies where subsistence activities are still essential. Even in fully modern market economies, a high percentage of women in the labor force need not reflect economic independence which requires not just a wage, but a "living wage."

Cross-cultural comparisons of women's status have also tended to stress the importance of women's economic activity as a basis for equality in a larger social sense. This was essentially Engel's (1948) position when he argued that equality for women would depend on their participation in public production on a large scale. Boserup (1970:31), in an important study comparing women's economic functions across five continents, states that ". . . women always seem to bear a large part of the work burden in the more egalitarian communities." Others point out that this contribution to production is a necessary condition for high female status, but that the problem is more complex (Brown 1970; Sanday 1974; Sacks 1974). Indeed, it is a characteristic of highly stratified or slave-owning societies that a heavy work contribution *per se* does not permit one to share equally in the fruits of society.

It is interesting to consider the situation in which women are not considered economically active or productive. There seem to be two directions from which people can be exempted from society's "productive work:" they can belong to the "idle rich" where the exercise of power can override productive functions, or they can be "idle," poor, and powerless such that their productive functions are devalued or not counted. In the case of women, when they are not fully integrated into the laboring group, they usually fall into the latter group. This does not mean that they have in fact been exempted from the need to produce any socially useful product or service, but rather that for social and historical reasons they have been confined to, or forced to specialize in, the production of one product or a narrow range of products and services only. Typically this means specialization in domestic service, including childbearing and rearing, and other kinds of services. It is by virtue of this specialization that women become an easily exploited surplus labor force. If female labor is in oversupply relative to the needs of society, then the status of all women will be lowered.

For women, this type of specialization is analogous to that imposed on underdeveloped countries. Since the production of, say, babies and bananas are each restricted to certain populations (female, or tropical, respectively), more powerful or external economic interests may attempt to impose a rigid specialization in only this one product as the most profitable way to organize a system for the benefit of these external interests. If women or banana republics are not permitted any other kind of economic production, then by virtue of their extreme specialization in one product they both lose their economic autonomy and become a highly vulnerable surplus labor force that can be bought cheaply and easily recruited to produce their single "export" crop. Therefore, in order to understand women's position in different types of social structures we need to know both what kinds of economic and productive activities they engage in, and if society is structured to make their contributions, as individuals, valuable. That is, it is important to consider not only the relative quantity of women's economic contributions, but also the supply and demand conditions which affect the value of their contribution.

I shall now consider some studies of women's changing roles in terms of the theoretical issues that have been raised.

THE CHANGING ROLES OF WOMEN

As suggested above, one of the ways in which the unilinear model is most inadequate is in its depiction of women's role in nonindustrial or traditional societies as "domestic." Even Evans-Pritchard, who is aware that such societies exhibit "almost every conceivable variety of institution," generalizes that for women in a society with a primitive technology and economy ". . . running the home is a whole-time occupation . . . for the adult primitive woman is above all a wife whose life is centered in her home and family" (1965:45-46). Unless farming and trading are defined as domestic, this type of model completely ignores many traditional societies in which women are highly mobile, productive workers. These societies have been sufficiently numerous and widespread to make it impossible, without great distortion, to dismiss them as exotic exceptions to a universal principle.

Concerning women's roles as farmers, Boserup (1970) defines two patterns of subsistence farming which she calls female and male farming systems, depending on which sex makes the greater contribution to agricultural food production. Female farming systems are typically those involving shifting cultivation using the hoe. According to Boserup, female farming systems (in which women devote significantly more work hours to agriculture than men) can be found in most of sub-Saharan Africa, parts of India and South East Asia, and in some Indian and Afro-American communities of Latin America. She considers Africa "the region of female farming par excellence" (Boserup 1970: 16). Citing a study prepared in 1928 by Baumann, she states:

> It appears that forty years ago female farming with no male help except for the felling of trees predominated in the whole of the Congo region, in large parts of South East and East Africa and in parts of West Africa. Female farming was far more widespread than systems of male farming and it also seems to have been more widespread than systems of predominantly female farming with some help from males in cultivation [Boserup 1970:17].

In these same regions, before the European conquest, male occupations were mainly felling trees, hunting, and warfare.

With a division of labor of this sort, it would be reasonable to conclude that, as long as the economy was largely subsistence based, the productivity of women was at least equal to, if not greater than, that of men. Boserup claims that it is ". . . normal in traditional African marriage for women to support themselves and their children and to cook for their

101

husband often using food they produce themselves'' (1970:42). Similar findings appear in Wheeler's study (1967), which also points out the customary independence of African women's income and property rights.

Let us now consider some of the changes in these systems that have occurred as a result of European contact. These changes have varied according to the particular context and motives of the Europeans and therefore have to be interpreted separately. However, certain broad observations are possible. With respect to the European impact on agriculture, it would be fair to generalize that Europeans have had a strong interest in inducing autonomous subsistence based economies to become participants in the modern international economic system by converting them to commercial production for export. This has meant the introduction of more intensive agricultural production based on modern technology.

In the case of Africa, Europeans, with an agricultural tradition of male farming using plows, have consistently introduced modern agricultural technology and cash crops to males only, ignoring the traditional female role in production (Boserup 1970). In some cases, this technology was rejected because it was associated with activities that were traditionally female, but it was not introduced to females. In cases where men did accept it, it tended to make them more successful than their female counterparts who still used traditional, primitive technology. This one-sided introduction of modern technology tended to introduce a significant gap between the productivity of male and female labor in agriculture, so that female labor became relatively less productive. According to Boserup, ''. . . the transfer of rights from women to men was often felt to be an injustice committed by the Europeans'' (1970:63). In illustration, she reports a revolt of the Kon women of Eastern Nigeria in 1959 where ''Women's resistence to the deterioration of their position as farmers coupled to their fear of losing their land to male farmers led to major upheavals'' (Boserup 1970:63-64). The revolt was a response to fears that the government might sell their land to the Ibo tribe. Accordingly, the traditional women's organization set fire to a neighboring market and made the following resolutions: ''. . . elimination of all foreign institutions, such as courts and schools, and the expulsion from the region of all foreigners, including Ibos, members of other tribes and Europeans'' (Boserup 1970:64).

Obviously, the inroads of modern, international capitalist economy and technology have affected a great deal more than agricultural production. Mining, industry, plantations, and cities have all appeared as products of modern efforts to develop isolated economic systems into exploitable suppliers and markets in the world economy. In Africa, each of these new European-controlled sectors tended to exclude women. Both Boserup (1970) and Wheeler (1967) point out that in many African countries Europeans recruited only males to work on plantations and large foreign-owned farms and in mining towns and sea ports. This produced a pattern of "male towns" in Africa, where the percentage of men greatly exceeded that of women. Men have been concentrated in the modern export sectors of the economy, while women were forced to remain in the rural subsistence economy (Simons 1968; Boserup 1970). As able young men were drawn out of the villages, women's workload in the subsistence sector was increased.

In an attempt to summarize the effects of modernization upon female agriculturalists in Africa, I have identified the following trends:

1. The introduction of a money economy tends to devalue the subsistence-based activities of women by forcing them to compete with more lucrative export production.

2. Men have been recruited in modern occupations and urban centers where they have had greater opportunities to receive technical training and western education, while women have remained in the rural sectors, uneducated, and employing primitive technology.

3. A division of labor in which women were roughly equal to men with respect to productivity has developed into one in which women's productivity is greatly surpassed by that of men.

4. Increasing pressure on the land has tended to require more intensive agricultural techniques and commercial production which, being controlled by and taught principally to males, has the effect that women (with the aid of foreign advisors and progressive government agents) lose their traditional rights to land and their traditional functions as agriculturalists (Boserup 1970; Simons 1968).

In short, women are excluded from productive roles in the modern

103

sector and phased out of traditional productive roles as part of the process of "development."

Parallel changes accompanying modernization can be seen when we consider societies in which women have traditionally been active traders. Such societies can be found in West Africa, the non-Hispanic Caribbean, parts of mainland Latin America, and South East Asia (Mintz 1971; Boserup 1970). In some of these areas, women trade in cash crops or imported goods as well as traditional subsistence goods and are able to amass fortunes as intermediaries. However, Mintz points out that in the cases he has studied, women are largely concerned with internal rather than external markets. Among their functions as traders he notes that they: (1) convey produce from producer or import house to consumer; (2) they bulk produce and break bulk; (3) they process items and food for resale; and (4) they act as credit sources to clients. In order to perform these activities, a woman normally has certain rights such as ". . . the right to travel widely, to consign care of her children to others, and, to a variable extent, to use her profits as she sees fit (Mintz 1971:266). In fact, in societies where women are agriculturalists or traders, there may be a high degree of economic separation or independence between husbands and wives. Both Boserup (1970:64) and Mintz (1971:255) cite examples where husbands and wives require cash payments of each other for goods and services that have an established market value.

If we now consider the trading activities of women in the light of the generally expanding commercial sector that has accompanied western penetration, certain important trends are apparent. According to Mintz, internal market systems, such as those in which women are active, occur commonly in underdeveloped societies. Although increasing commercialization is expected to reduce their relative importance, at times stimulation from commercial agriculture can actually increase their absolute volume while their relative share in the economy is declining. Correspondingly, Mintz shows that on some occasions modernization has been to the short-run benefit of traditional women traders. However, when he analyzes some of the larger trends, another pattern emerges. Although comparable data are not available for many regions, it is reported that among the Ibo and Yoruba, for example, men are replacing women in trade with non-African firms in sectors that had formerly been controlled by women. Mintz (1971:264) suggests that

104

> . . . *the traditional predominance of female traders in much of Nigeria is being threatened by the expansion of men's commercial activities. When this development is added to the virtual exclusion of women from export commodity activity we can see that the expanded market and commercial opportunities in some spheres of West African trade are probably redounding more to the benefit of the male trader.*

A suggested explanation is that representatives of European firms prefer to deal with men. Thus in Haiti, Dakar, and Nigeria, Mintz finds that although women can become wealthy through trade, there are upper limits to the expansion of these activities. For example,

> *The Haitian economy provides such women with scanty space for innovative maneuver, and with little or no opportunity to reinvest in new forms of production. It is the men who control coffee, sisal, and livestock production and sale, for the most part; men and foreign firms who control the licensed purchasing and bulking of export commodities; men who engage in most craft activities and artisanship; and men, of course, who dominate the governmental and military apparatus of Haitian society. Thus it is not surprising that market women often give over much of their earnings to the education of their children, as the major means of 'reinvestment'. As in the Afikpo (Ibo) case, girl children are trained when possible for careers in teaching, nursing and similar jobs . . . and here, as in Dakar, the woman of limited education is trained to the lower-status, non-manual occupations so typical of the western social and economic pattern [Mintz 1971: 259-260].*

Thus it appears that modernization or economic "development" has an impact on women's role in trade that is remarkably similar to its impact on women in agricultural production. That is, it exerts strong pressures to reduce or limit the traditional productive activities of women and severely restricts or prohibits their entry into modern productive occupations. I shall now briefly examine modern changes that have had a similar impact on women in the pastoral economy of the Navajo.

Among the Navajo, women traditionally had an important economic role, principally because they were owners of major property, particularly sheep, and because they could control cash income through blanket weaving (Kluckhohn and Leighton 1946; Downs 1972; Hamamsy 1957 [this volume]). In addition, inheritance was traditionally matrilineal, and residence was matrilocal. Since the 1930s, however, increasing interaction with white society has greatly altered the position of women and the value of their work. Government intervention in the form of a land policy and livestock reduction program transferred land ownership and often livestock rights from women to married men (Hamamsy 1957:104; Aberle 1961:143, 102). This restricted the traditional livelihood of women as sheepowners and, hence, as weavers. The impetus of World War II with the military draft and increased demand for wage labor hastened the transformation from an economy based mainly on livestock, agriculture, and weaving to one in which male wage work on or off the reservation assumed greatest importance in the economy (Downs 1972:131-132; Kluckhohn and Leighton 1946:56). Similar opportunities for wage work were not opened to women. Hamamsy (1957:104) reports:

> *When the women do find work, they are usually poorly paid in comparison with the men. There are a few openings in government institutions such as schools and hospitals, but the major sources of employment are in such areas as seasonal agricultural work, restaurants, and domestic service. The men, on the other hand, find their major employment opportunities in such relatively better paid fields as railroads, agriculture, lumbering, construction and road work, and oil, military, and mining operations, in that order of importance.*

Pointing out the increasing economic dependence of women on male wage earners, she notes that:

> *A close examination shows that while the men have been compensated for the loss of their traditional sources of livelihood, the women have not been directly compensated in any way. In wage work most men find*

106

> an adequate substitute for the declining livestock
> economy. As far as women are concerned, in losing
> their sheep, they have lost their economic independence
> [Hamamsy 1957:109].

Corresponding to this economic change and the influence of white customs, there has been a change toward neolocal and patrilocal residence (Kluckhohn and Leighton 1946:103; Hamamsy 1957:108). Hamamsy observes that women's position within the family has also been adversely affected by these modern changes. She concludes that ". . . the woman has become more dependent on the man for her economic and social well-being, and correspondingly, she is much less indispensable to her husband for his well-being" (Hamamsy 1957:111).

The case of the Navajo is consistent with the examples of women as traditional farmers and traders in that modernization results in a smaller share for women in the total economy due to restrictions against their entry into many modern occupations and a devaluation of traditional subsistence activities. To the extent that women are integrated into the modern capitalist economy, this tends to occur in the low-paid service sector consisting largely of domestics, nurses, secretaries, and elementary school teachers. Although this entry into "modern" occupations is applauded as a sign of development and progress by many social scientists, including women from underdeveloped countries who are proud to possess western education and values, one might very well conclude that such modernization does not increase sexual equality, productivity, or independence for women, but rather that it produces modern inequality, the devaluation of female labor, and economic dependence—in a word, "underdevelopment."

WOMEN IN A HIGHLAND GUATEMALAN TOWN

Having considered some fairly broad studies of women's changing position in modernizing societies, I will now examine the particular case of a Highland Guatemalan town to see if the changes affecting women are consistent with those already observed. I will be especially concerned with women's entry into modern occupations and their access to modern training and technology.

Tecpanaco is a municipality located in the western Highlands of Guatemala.[1] The town itself has a population of around 5,000 and serves as an administrative and political center for a territory with roughly 50,000 people. Due to its administrative status and its market, Tecpanaco serves as a center of modern western technology, institutions, and culture for much of the surrounding rural population. Like most of the towns of the western Highlands, it has a very small percentage of *ladinos* who share the Spanish culture of the national government. The vast majority of the population are Maya-Quiché Indians who have retained their own language and culture to varying degrees.

Being more westernized, the *ladinos* tend to live and work in town in modern occupations where industrial products and technology are available. The Indians are generally more dependent upon subsistence agriculture. While the "traditional" economic activities of the Indian population have been changing since the Spanish conquest, some basic principles of the subsistence economy appear to be relatively stable. These are that men do most of the agricultural labor, women do most of the food preparation, and both sexes actively participate in the local markets. Within this context of traditional subsistence, the basic economic roles of men as maize-growers and women as tortilla-makers appear to have equal importance. Vogt's description of mutual dependency between the sexes for the Maya of Zinacantan seems applicable to the traditional subsistence pattern of Tecpanaco: "The domestic group . . . must contain both men and women, since each sex controls technological skills that are required for the successful operation of any domestic unit" (1969:129). However, in many respects the traditional work patterns have been significantly altered by colonial and modern technology, labor requirements, and market relationships. For instance, in Tecpanaco the traditional method of weaving with a backstrap loom by women has been completely displaced by the large Spanish foot loom which is generally used by men. Much of the clothing is machine made. Food preparation has been simplified by the introduction of power mills for maize, commercial bakeries, and improved water supplies. Modern transport has greatly increased the impact of foreign markets and products. As labor-intensive products have been supplanted by capital-intensive products there has been an increasing dependence on cash income. In addition, the general scarcity of land has meant that no households can subsist without additional income.

108

Household industries (particularly weaving), commercialism, and migratory wage labor are established means of acquiring such income.

In order to assess the impact of the modern economy on women in Tecpanaco, I will compare the occupations of women with those of men. Although many of these occupations do not appear to be modern *per se,* they are all affected at least indirectly by modern market conditions. It should be noted that among traditional Indians, subsistence activities normally continue alongside other cash producing activities. Among acculturated Indians and *ladinos,* subsistence farming is less important.

The Sexual Division of Labor

As already mentioned, women in Tecpanaco are generally responsible for a variety of domestic tasks. These include food preparation, laundering, weekly marketing, and the care of small children, small animals, the house, and garden. Table 1 below presents the occupations of sixty women in Tecpanaco. The sample is not random, having been chosen to encompass the range of occupations encountered. It nevertheless is an approximate guide to their relative frequency.

It is apparent that the range of occupations is narrow. The most common occupation, listed as "spinner," actually represents a whole complex of activities, such as carding and dyeing, that are part of a traditional household weaving industry. The complementary nature of male weaving and female spinning within each domestic unit gives this occupation a greater resemblance to the mutually dependent subsistence economy than to the newer, more individualistic occupations. Most of the occupations involve very little capital investment. Even a number of those that represent recent acculturation, such as embroidery and storekeeping, involve little modern technology or skill. While a few of the storekeepers and the plantation labor contractor have highly profitable enterprises, it is noteworthy that their positions and capital were originally provided by male relatives. In terms of independent capital accumulation by women, the best option appears to be teaching in the national school. With a salary of $100 per month, this far surpasses the income of most women. The rare woman working as a traveling merchant may also accumulate a significant amount of

Table 1. **Occupations among Sixty Women in Tecpanaco.** [1]

Occupation	Number
Spinner	14
Storekeeper/clerk	13
Daily marketer	7
Craft assistant (to butchers, candlemakers, bakers, tailors)	7
Seamstress	5
Restaurant or kitchen operator	5
Embroiderer	4
Servant	3
Midwife	2
Weaver	2
Traveling merchant	2
Teacher	2
Secretary	1
Plantation labor contractor	1

[1] Includes full and part time occupations. As many women practice more than one occupation, the total is greater than sample size. Six women of the sixty had no occupation other than the standard domestic responsibilities.

capital. Most women, however, either work as subordinates in family enterprises, where they do not control the capital or final product, or they work at individual occupations, where income is so low or irregular that it can barely cover subsistence needs. While there are a few women weavers and seamstresses, looms and sewing machines, which are relatively large capital expenditures, are generally owned and operated by men.

It is noteworthy that women are absent from such occupations as carpentry, shoemaking, firecracker manufacture, barbering, construction work, and masonry. Among the occupations employing modern technology, women are absent from occupations such as bus and truck driver, mechanic, electrician, photographer, postal clerk, and telegraph operator. In addition, women are not represented among the town's administrative officials, police, and military personnel. On the other hand, there are men who teach, do office work, and run some of the stores with a valuable inventory, including the pharmacies.

On the basis of these differences in the available occupations by sex, the following generalizations seem justified.

1. Men are generally found in occupations with greater capital investment. This is true in household industries such as weaving, where the footloom costs roughly five times as much as the spinning wheel. It is also true in commercial clothing manufacture, where it is far more common for men to own sewing machines. In commerce itself, men tend to have a larger capital investment and a larger trading circle.

2. Relative to men, few women have special skills. Apart from those who share in family enterprises, most women work in occupations that are paid forms of standard domestic services. Only the women merchants, teachers, clerks, and medical personnel have skills which mark them off from the majority of women. However, these women must compete with male merchants, teachers, clerks, and the doctor. Embroidery of blouses is one exclusively female occupation, but it requires little capital or skill and could be widespread among the female population if the market expanded. In contrast, a number of occupations held by men can be described as individual skills or specialties that are neither generalized among the male population, nor shared by the female population. In particular, many of those occupa-

tions using modern technology fit into this category. The greater specialization of at least some men and their association with the more capital-intensive occupations tend to give their labor a higher market value.

3. Due to advances in technology which reduce the time needed for household tasks, there has been a general decrease in the value of female labor. When women generally lack the training, capital, or cultural permission to enter new occupations, this means that they must accept a condition of partial or disguised unemployment as they engage in occupations where their marginal product approaches zero. Thus, spinning, embroidery, domestic work, and food selling are poorly paid, because there are so many women trying to earn money this way. Even for those women who have a small amount of capital to invest, the restriction of women to such occupations as running a household store means that Tecpanaco is awash with little stores operated mainly by women who are seeking more employment. Disguised unemployment exists among men as well as women in Tecpanaco. Among women it is virtually endemic. Modern cultural proscription limits their occupational opportunities to areas where neither skills nor associated capital can operate to create a labor scarcity. As a result, these areas are glutted with women whose unemployment is disguised by their hard work and submarginal incomes.

Acculturated Men and Traditional Women

While occupational differentiation offers a measure of the present impact of the modern economy on women, the exposure to outside influence and the opportunities for education and occupational training affect future occupational choices for women. Among the Indians, men have had significantly more exposure to other parts of the country through their migratory work on plantations, military service, trading activities, and their political roles. A much smaller proportion of Indian women have traveled outside of Tecpanaco, typically to work as domestics in the city. This differential degree of direct exposure to the national culture is reflected in the fact that fewer Indian women than men are able to speak Spanish, and Indian women continue to wear traditional clothing that sets them apart on sight. Indian men of Tecpanaco have long abandoned their traditional clothing (not necessarily voluntarily) due to their interaction with *ladinos*.

There is a corresponding lag in women's formal education. Indian women are more likely to be illiterate than men and have generally had less schooling. Despite the expansion of the national school system, girls form only one-third of the students in the town's elementary school, and their participation is even less in the higher grades and in the more rural schools. While wealthier families, particularly *ladinos*, are more likely to provide higher education for both sexes, the institutions are often sexually segregated. Domestic arts may be offered to girls, while boys are trained in industrial arts. National data for the highest educational levels indicate that sexual disparities persist both with respect to total enrollment and occupational specialization. Women are concentrated in the humanities, while men are more likely to study economics, law, medicine, and engineering (Dirección General de Estadistica 1970:253-254).

Sexual disparities are equally evident in other local training programs. The Community Development program and the Catholic educational program offer women training in literacy, cooking, and sewing, while they offer training in literacy, agriculture, construction, carpentry, and social organizing to men.

Perhaps a more important factor in education among the Indian population is the obligatory military service required of males (Kelsey and Osborne 1961:66; Adams 1970:248; Roberts 1973:19). Despite a general desire to evade this service, many are nonetheless provided with a number of educational benefits. In addition to learning better Spanish, men are taught to read and write, to use modern technology and military equipment, and they have the opportunity to see other parts of the country. This military experience and training is clearly an asset to many men in their interactions with the modern urban economy. It provides a variety of social contacts and increases their familiarity with and readiness to use the implements of modern technology. It should be noted that this greater degree of adaptation to westernized culture and society is not the result of traditional proclivities of Indian men and women. Men do not volunteer, but are drafted, for military training; women are excluded.

These differences suggest that in Tecpanaco, as in our other examples, modern technology does not make its appearance as a neutral factor; it tends to support the structural interests and priorities of the system that introduces, or imposes, it. This appears to be true despite important differences both in precontact economic systems and in the history of interaction with western capitalism. One of the structural characteristics of western capitalist societies is a priority for males in all productive activities and particularly in capital intensive occupations. There is a corresponding preference to assign women to domestic, dependent, and marginal economic roles. These priorities are transmitted, along with technology, through a host of institutions—educational, economic, military, financial, religious—whose technical and spiritual advisors are imported from the metropolis to pave the way for "development." In the context of male and female participation in modern national society, it becomes clear that development for one sex may simultaneously lead to underdevelopment for the other.

CONCLUSION

In this paper, the extent of women's equality in preindustrial societies is not the fundamental concern. It is sufficient to emphasize that women's role, relative to the role of men, is highly variable. I have been more concerned with the possibility that women will be integrated into the modern world as equals. The orthodox model is one that implies that ancient traditions or differences in physical strength made women unequal in the underdeveloped world. It also implies that the introduction of modern technology and western institutions enables and encourages women to be as fully productive as men. The limited investigations presented in this paper prove this model false. On the contrary, they suggest that the impact of the modern capitalist world economy and modern western institutions may be largely detrimental to sexual equality since, under very diverse circumstances, women appear to be losing their productive functions, as modernization progresses. Although it cannot be argued that women in all underdeveloped areas have previously had highly productive roles that were structurally valued, it is nevertheless clear from this investigation that westernization or "modernization," as defined here, in itself is not the solution to providing them. The "new opportunities" heralded by many observers may be only that—new, but not better.

This is not to argue that women constitute the only sector to be underdeveloped under the influence of modern capitalist penetration, nor that such underdevelopment occurs in a simple unilinear fashion. The point is that women are underdeveloped in special ways that relate as much, if not more, to their participation in economic systems dominated by western capitalist nations as to any previous conditions of isolation and "backwardness."

In trying to assess women's position in terms that do not automatically applaud any cultural changes that appear more like those of the developed, western nations, I have made analogies between the underdevelopment of nations and the underdevelopment of women. The cases considered were selected to show that such underdevelopment occurs in societies with widely differing economic and historical backgrounds. However, the simplistic optimism of the orthodox model should not be replaced with an equally simplistic assertion that women's position inevitably declines with modernization. Such an assertion would be untenable, since it is well known that in many precontact societies women's position was already quite low. Rather, I have attempted to show that it is necessary to examine more carefully the particular historical and economic forces that affect women's position. In so doing, it becomes more difficult to confuse the dominant ideology of the upper classes and international elites with the actual conditions under which sex roles are developed.

On examination of historical and economic factors in the various societies considered, the underdevelopment analogy has proven to be realistic in describing the changes affecting women. While women continue to participate in the various economies cited, they appear to lose control, especially relative to men, of both expertise and capital. Surely the control of capital, or at least expertise in its use, is related to the value placed on various forms of labor. It is here, more than with regard to participation in productive activities *per se*, that modernization appears to be working to reduce the relative status of women in many areas. I hope that future studies of women in modernizing societies will provide further testing of this theoretical approach and help to clarify the extent and conditions of its usefulness.

NOTES

Acknowledgments. This is a revised version of a paper presented at the 14th annual meeting of the Northeastern Anthropological Association, Worcester, Massachusetts, in 1974. I should like to thank Robert Carmack, Samih Farsoun, and Judith K. Brown for their helpful suggestions on an earlier version.

[1] Fieldwork upon which this section is based was undertaken during the summer of 1973, supported, in part, by an assistantship from the Department of Anthropology, State University of New York, Albany. The name of the community studied has been changed to Tecpanaco in order to protect the privacy of its inhabitants.

REFERENCES CITED

Aberle, David
    1961   Navaho. *In* Matrilineal Kinship. David Schneider and Kathleen Gough, eds. Pp. 96-201. Berkeley: University of California Press.
Adams, Richard N.
    1970   Crucifixion by Power: Essays on the Guatemalan National Social Structure, 1944-1966. Austin: University of Texas Press.
Bernard, Jesse
    1971   The Status of Women in Modern Patterns of Culture. *In* The Other Half: Roads to Women's Equality. Cynthia Fuchs Epstein and William J. Goode, eds. Pp. 11-20. Englewood Cliffs, New Jersey: Prentice-Hall.

Boserup, Ester
    1970 Woman's Role in Economic Development. London: Allen
    and Unwin.
Brown, Judith K.
    1970 Economic Organization and the Position of Women
    Among the Iroquois. Ethnohistory 17(3-4): 151-167.
Dirección General de Estadística
    1970 Anuario Estadístico. Guatemala: Ministerio de
    Economía.
Downs, James F.
    1972 The Navajo. New York: Holt, Rinehart and Winston.
Engels, Friedrick
    1948 The Origin of the Family, Private Property, and the State.
    Moscow: Foreign Language Publishing House. (First ed., 1884.)
Evans-Pritchard, E.E.
    1965 The Position of Women in Primitive Societies and Our
    Own. *In* The Position of Women in Primitive Societies and Other
    Essays in Social Anthropology. Pp. 37-58. New York: Free
    Press.
Frank, André G.
    1969 Latin America: Underdevelopment or Revolution. New
    York: Monthly Review Press.
    1971 Capitalism and Underdevelopment in Latin America:
    Historical Studies of Chile and Brazil. Revised ed. Harmonds-
    worth, England: Penguin.
Goode, William J.
    1963 World Revolution and Family Patterns. Glencoe, Illinois:
    Free Press.
    1971 Civil and Social Rights of Women. *In* The Other Half:
    Roads to Women's Equality. Cynthia Fuchs Epstein and William
    J. Goode, eds. Pp. 21-32. Englewood Cliffs, New Jersey:
    Prentice-Hall.
Hamamsy, Laila Shukry
    1957 The Role of Women in a Changing Navaho Society.
    American Anthropologist 59: 101-111.
Kelsey, Vera, and Lilly de Jongh Osborne
    1967 Four Keys to Guatemala. New York: Funk and Wagnalls.
    (Originally published, 1939.)
Kluckhohn, Clyde, and Dorothea Leighton
    1946 The Navaho. Cambridge: Harvard University Press.

Mintz, Sidney W.
　　1971　Men, Women, and Trade. Comparative Studies in Society and History 13(3): 247-269.
Patai, Raphael, ed.
　　1967　Women in the Modern World. New York: Free Press.
Ribeiro, Darcy
　　1972　The Americas and Civilization. Linton Lomas Barrett and Marie McDavid Barrett, trans. London: Allen and Unwin.
Roberts, Bryan R.
　　1973　Organizing Strangers: Poor Families in Guatemala City. Austin: University of Texas Press.
Sacks, Karen
　　1974　Engels Revisited: Women, the Organization of Production, and Private Property. In Woman, Culture, and Society. Michele Zimbalist Rosaldo and Louise Lamphere, eds. Pp. 207-222. Stanford: Stanford University Press.
Sanday, Peggy R.
　　1974　Female Status in the Public Domain. In Woman, Culture, and Society. Michele Zimbalist Rosaldo and Louise Lamphere, eds. Pp. 189-206. Stanford: Stanford University Press.
Simons, Harold J.
　　1968　African Women: Their Legal Status in South Africa. Evanston, Illinois: Northwestern University Press.
Vogt, Evon Z.
　　1969　Zinacantan: A Maya Community in the Highlands of Chiapas. Cambridge: Harvard University Press, Belknap Press.
Wheeler, Elizabeth H.
　　1967　Sub-Saharan Africa. In Women in the Modern World. Raphael Patai, ed. Pp. 317-345. New York: Free Press.

SUGGESTIONS FOR FURTHER READING

Boserup, Ester
　　1970　Woman's Role in Economic Development. New York: St. Martin's Press.
　　Discusses the impact of development policies on women's productive roles in developing countries of Africa, Asia, Latin

America, and the Middle East. An excellent introduction to development issues from a female perspective.

Hartmann, Heidi

1976   Capitalism, Patriarchy, and Job Segregation by Sex. *In* Women and the Workplace: The Implications of Occupational Segregation. Martha Blaxall and Barbara Reagan, eds. Pp. 137-169. Chicago: University of Chicago Press. (Originally published in Signs: Journal of Women in Culture and Society 1[3]: 137-169, Part 2, 1976.)

An historical overview of the sexual division of labor in preindustrial and capitalist societies. Argues that sexual segregation of jobs and the inferior economic status of women in contemporary industrialized societies can be traced to the development of patriarchy, a ". . . system of male oppression of women" based on differential economic control and hierarchic relations between the sexes (1976: 138).

Rubbo, Anna

1975   The Spread of Capitalism in Rural Columbia: Effects on Poor Women. *In* Toward an Anthropology of Women. Rayna R. Reiter, ed. Pp. 333-357. New York: Monthly Review Press.

Examines the impact of modernization on women's roles among black peasants in the Cauca Valley. The author concludes that the transition from peasant subsistence to wage earning has resulted in women's increased economic dependence on men.

Wellesley Editorial Committee

1977   Special Issue. Women and National Development: The Complexities of Change. Signs: Journal of Women in Culture and Society 3(1): 1-338.

A selection of essays presented at a conference on women and development held at Wellesley College in 1976. Topics include models of development, women's labor force participation in the Third World, migration, and political change.

BARGAINING FROM WEAKNESS: SPIRIT POSSESSION ON THE SOUTH KENYA COAST

Roger Gomm

INTRODUCTION

The meaning of this title is aptly explained by a quotation from Lewis (1971:32):

> *In its primary social function, peripheral possession emerges as an oblique aggressive strategy. The possessed person is ill through no fault of his own. The illness requires treatment which his (or her) master has to provide. In his state of possession the patient is a highly privileged person. He is allowed many liberties with those whom in other circumstances he is required to treat with respect. Moreover however costly and inconvenient for those to whom his normal status renders him subservient, his cure is often incomplete. Lapses are likely to occur whenever difficulties develop with his superiors. Clearly, in this context,* possession works to help the interests of the weak and downtrodden who have otherwise few effective means to press their claims for attention and respect [*my emphasis*].

Reprinted by permission of the author and the Royal Anthropological Institute of Great Britain and Ireland from *Man* (new series) 10:530-543, 1975.

Peripheral spirit possession is thus represented as a strategy (consciously adopted or not) which redresses the disadvantages of occupying a lowly status.

The pattern of spirit possession among the peoples of the south Kenya coast [1] is broadly similar to that described for other east and northeast African peoples. [2] The spirits involved are, to use Lewis's words, ". . . not morally charged with powers held to be responsible for upholding public morality by rewarding meritorious acts and punishing evil" (1970:294). Sometimes, however, an exorcism ceremony *is* made an occasion for highlighting the moral delicts of the host and his/her kinsfolk. The biographical details of these spirits are sketchy. Most are regarded as exotic in origin, deriving from other tribes, from Arabia, India, and Europe. Some are nature spirits, known to haunt particular localities, and in very rare cases the possessing spirits involved are those of ancestors who have been subverted from their moral functions for the purposes of sorcery. The generic term most commonly used for all these spirits is *shaitani*.

The idea of influence by a capricious spirit is a common, often half-joking explanation for a wide range of unusual personality traits; unusual greediness, spitefulness, bad-temper, moodiness, lasciviousness, and so on, and is used also to explain unusually good fortune. Used in such circumstances the spirit possession explanation may be a benign alternative to suspicions of witchcraft, for witches are known by their unpleasantness and sudden good fortune. The explanation also competes with a recognition that people are innately different from one another, and that luck, God, and the ancestors play a part in human affairs. Likewise bad fortune may be explained with reference to *shaitani*, witchcraft attack, Allah, luck, or the ancestors. Applied in these ways as an explanation, spirit possession does not usually lead to attempts at exorcism.

Spirits are believed to lie in wait for the unwary in lonely places, to creep into bed beside those sleeping alone, or to take possession of the dancers at weddings or funerals. Although people who dance themselves into a trance are said to be possessed by spirits, the onset of possession in this way is rarely followed by attempts at exorcism. Spirits that attack dancers are described as *shaitani ya wirani* and generally go away of their own accord. "Serious" cases of possession, those which do lead to exorcism, are described as being caused by *shaitani ya kitchwa* and are said to be known in terms of a syndrome of aggressive and bizarre behavior; aggression towards other people, towards the self, towards inanimate objects, running amok, uncontrollable writhing, self-anointing with, or eating, ashes, dirt, or dung.

Thus spirit possession occupies an important role in Digo folk psychology but it is only one type of spirit possession, specified in terms of a behavior pattern which everybody knows, that becomes the subject of therapy.

The main therapeutic apparatus consists of public exorcism ceremonies conducted by *aganga* (doctors) who are experts in divination, counterwitchcraft, herbal and magical medicine as well as exorcism and whose powers are themselves held to be based on an association with a familiar spirit.[3] While different *aganga* claim to specialize in the exorcism of different spirits, the *mganga* contracted to exorcise usually just happens to be the right expert for the job. This is in itself explained by the *mganga's* power to "call" those spirits over whom he has some influence.

Possession is usually cross-sexual; male spirits possessing women, female spirits possessing men: the spasms, writhings, and moanings associated with possession are interpreted as an indication of sexual intercourse taking place between host and spirit. Exorcism is a costly business.[4] Nearly all cases of possession leading to exorcism involve possessed women. Exorcism ceremonies are nearly always provided for women by men; by husbands for wives, by fathers, brothers, and mother's brothers for unmarried women.

Etiology

The sort of spirit possession which leads to exorcism is an overwhelmingly female affliction.[5] While women of all ages may be afflicted, first attacks seem to occur especially in the earlier years of marriage, and to a lesser extent during betrothal. In an earlier paper I described at length the position of women in Digo society (Gomm 1972), but this needs to be summarized here briefly.

Digo women are legal minors. Theoretically they remain under the control of men throughout their lives. In practice this means that men (and senior patrilateral kinswomen) make rules for their behavior which they are constantly breaking. Digo women are excluded from the important businesses of Digo life; politics, religion, and arranging major economic and kinship enterprises. Taking male life as a basis of comparison we might say that in these spheres female activities are trivialized or are problematic in the sense that they breach male rules or threaten male interests. Economically while women bear the brunt of agricultural labor for domestic consumption and for cash crop production, their own ability to make money through farming is severely limited by their obligations to provide food for children, husband, and his guests. Too much attention to gardening by women on their own account is inevitably regarded as a dereliction of marital duties. They are excluded also from major trading, being restricted to selling small quantities of garden produce, cooked foods, snuff, perfume sachets, thatch tiles, and other low profit commodities. Because they are excluded from major economic enterprises and from the organization of the kinship occasions which require large cash outlays, they are seen by men to have little serious need for money.

While women can and do inherit land and valuable tree crops, they rarely inherit a controlling interest; rather they inherit a general right to share in the income from an estate managed by a trustee. Such income as is derived from the estate is apportioned according to the importance of the needs of the various heirs for money. Trustees are males: a woman's demands for cash for consumer spending are unlikely to be taken as seriously as a male co-heir's demand for cash to pay brideprice, provide a wedding feast, repay a mortgage, or pay tax.

The best opportunity a woman has for making money is through her sexuality. Adultery causes gossip, divorces, compensation suits, and ill feeling between men. Given a political system of constant jockeying for the goodwill and support of other men, marital disruption is a threat to hard won networks of support and feeds the hostility between factions.

The kinship situation of the Digo woman is a fertile milieu for generating conflicts which lead to marital disruption (Gomm 1972:109-112) and, it can be argued, for conflicts which are sometimes translated into the symptoms of spirit possession. For instance first marriages for girls are usually arranged by fathers seeking to make or consolidate useful alliances. At least 20 percent of betrothals are ended by premarital pregnancy and/or elopement. Now while the Digo generally accept an elopement which breaks a betrothal as a *fait accompli* (by accepting marriage payments) they do not usually do so gladly. In extreme cases fathers may curse their daughters which is tantamount to denying the relationship between them and places the girl at risk of misfortune. [6] A folk picture of the typical suicide in Digo society is a girl unwillingly betrothed to a man whom she does not want to marry. Such suicides do not seem to be very frequent occurrences but this typification indicates a recognition of the tensions sometimes generated by arranged marriage.

Once married, a young girl who marries a young man may find herself as the most insignificant member of her husband's residential group, under the domination and vigilance of her husband's father's wives. She is given the most arduous and menial tasks to perform for a period before she is allowed to establish an independent kitchen and she should bear abuse and gossip without rebut. As the sole wife of her husband a woman sooner or later faces the prospect of having to accept a co-wife, and in the households of established polygynists the squabbles of envious co-wives are notorious. Husband and wife relationships offer plenty of opportunity for discord which is frequently phrased in terms of the wife's unbecoming behavior, or the husband's financial meanness towards his wife.

Digo women are not well socialized for subjection. On the one hand, contemporary Digo society has grown out of a social order in which women had considerably more freedom and autonomy (Kayamba 1932; 1947). On the other hand, young women tune into local radio stations which purvey both a pop culture stressing romantic love and propaganda supporting female equality as an ideal for a modernizing society.

Conflicts which arise in marriage are frequently resolved by marital dissolution, usually by the wife deserting her husband, rarely by the husband divorcing the wife. While affinal relationships are highly valued as a basis for support in the many moots through which political and legal matters are settled among the Digo and as a basis for favorable trading arrangements, mortgages and so on, marital discord, in so far as it involves both husband and wife lobbying the wife's kin for support, and marital breakdown bring affinal relationships into question. There is a risk of conflict between husband and his wife's father, between husband and his wife's brothers, between wife's father and her brothers and mother's brothers, between wife's father and wife's mother: conflict about what happened, about who was to blame, about how much brideprice is to be returned and in what installments and by whom (Gomm 1972:106-108). While a woman's father and especially her male matrilateral relations have a duty to look after her interests in marriage and will intervene to prevent her from being ill-used, they are rarely pleased at the prospect of a desertion or divorce. Unless serious ill treatment has occurred, or unless there is gossip about the way in which they allow their kinswoman to be treated as if she were a slave (Gomm 1972:105), her relations are likely to counsel the wife to behave herself and obey her husband. Where desertion occurs the idiom in which affines discuss the return of the brideprice (and by implication future relationships between them) invokes male notions of female psychology which characterize women as unpredictable, irresponsible, childish, and wilful. This frequently facilitates the maintenance of good relationships between male affines *despite* marital breakdown, blaming the unfortunate turn of events on the wife. Thus women who do not obey their husbands, or cause trouble by deserting them, or girls who abscond from a betrothal run the risk of falling into bad odor with their male kin. As a strategy for resolving marital problems, desertion followed by the doubtful benefits of re-marriage, or the difficulties of life as a prostitute, must be set against the ill feeling of a woman's closest kinsmen.

It can be argued then that the manifestation of spirit possession symptoms by women offers a structural alternative to marital breakdown for coping with the tensions of Digo marriage, and one which is likely to be most attractive when male kinsmen are concerned to perpetuate a marriage.

Some evidence for this interpretation comes from looking at the demands made by the possession spirit during an exorcism ceremony.

The most important stage of an exorcism ceremony is the interrogation of the possessing spirit by the exorcist through the medium of his spirit familiar. Once he has discovered the name of the spirit he seeks to negotiate a price which the spirit will accept in order to go away. This is generally a present, the cost of which is borne by the woman's husband or a remission from some obligation or responsibility. More rarely a sacrifice is requested. Certainly the most common requests are for *leso*, women's clothes. Perhaps it should be explained that *leso* are printed cottons bearing a design and a motto. New *leso* appear on the market each week and husbands are constantly pestered, and almost as constantly refuse to buy their wives the latest design. Other common requests include money for bus fares, or for buying cloth, petrol stoves, soft furnishings, kitchen utensils and transistor radios, and "sweet foods." [7] It is exactly these sorts of items that feature in quarrels between husband and wife which lead wives to characterize husbands as mean, and husbands to characterise women as extravagant. Gerlach (1961: 431) reports that in Lungalunga spirit possession cases reach epidemic proportions during the coconut harvest when men have money to spend, and in Waa where many Digo are workers commuting into Mombasa, there are regular exorcism ceremonies on paydays.

In an exorcism ceremony the sort of demands made by women in marriage and refused, are made in the voice of a male spirit and granted. Husbands are publicly bound to provide the goods which will be used by the wife in the name of the spirit after "cure" has been effected.

Other spirit demands are interesting. A betrothed girl is possessed by a spirit who will not go away unless a promise is made that she will have nothing to do with the sea. Her betrothed is a fisherman. A married woman is possessed by a spirit who frequents the place far inland where her husband has opened a new farm. She will certainly be repossessed if she goes to work there. The clerk's wife who remains behind in Tiwi cannot be cured unless she leaves Tiwi (to join her husband in Mombasa). Gerlach (1961:430, sqq.) quotes a case where a wife, threatened by the imminent second marriage of her husband, manifested spirit possession symptoms until all the money that he would have used for brideprice was spent in providing exorcism ceremonies and gifts.

To some extent then we can regard spirit possession as an alternative to desertion, and as an alternative which has some advantages. While a wife who deserts her husband risks being the center of ill feeling between kinsfolk and affines, the "patient" possessed by a spirit is the center of sympathetic concern. Such concern is shown by the way in which relatives and friends come to the exorcism ceremony, contribute to its cost, and help by dancing and drumming. It is worth noting that this is a way in which her male kin can demonstrate concern for her well-being in marital difficulties without siding with her against her husband. [8]

So far there is nothing that I have said which runs counter to Lewis's (1971:32) contention that "... possession works to help the interests of the weak and downtrodden who otherwise have few effective means to press their claims." However, so far I have dealt with spirit possession only as a problem of etiology, asking "Where do the tensions which manifest themselves as spirit possession symptoms come from?" It can also be viewed as a problem of diagnosis; "How is it that people are known to be possessed by spirits?"

Diagnosis

This is not simply a matter of presenting a patient to a diviner for a diagnosis. People have first to be seen to fall into the category of people about whose behavior something should be done. Now the "classic" syndrome of spirit possession—running amok, hitting people, and so on—is known by everyone: every Digo child can perform it. However, it does not seem that such symptoms have to be manifested before exorcism is carried out, nor do all people who behave in this way become the central actors in exorcism ceremonies.

For instance Digo men are known to be violent. They will seize a panga and rush from the house to avenge an insult. Usually they are stopped by well-wishers before they can perpetrate a seriously violent act, but their displays of violence and aggression are credited with meaning, even if they resist being restrained, make as if to strike their friends, and slash at trees and huts, it is assumed that they have some good reason for behaving as they do. Digo women on the other hand are not thought to be naturally violent, particularly towards men. Displays of anger by women risk being interpreted as evidence of possession. Consider this case:

> *Mwanasha was accused by her husband Rashidi of committing adultery. Her adulterous relationship with*

Hamisi was common gossip. However Rashidi was in the process of raising a mortgage with Mwanasha's father. Moreover Hamisi was the son of the local sub-chief and Rashidi was himself using tree-crop land belonging to the subchief for growing a crop of ground-nuts. To sue Hamisi for malo (compensation) at the level of the local moot was not likely to be successful since the subchief was at that time the most powerful voice there and the attempt was likely to jeopardize his crops. To divorce Mwanasha was also unattractive because of the mortgage he hoped to raise from her father. Yet Rashidi was in the intolerable position of being the butt of local gossip and of constant nagging by his own father to do something about his wayward wife.

The situation resolved itself when Mwanasha cheeked Rashidi's father when he rebuked her for her behavior. He raised his hand to strike her and she flew at him scratching his face and then ran off into the bush. Rashidi and his brothers caught her and delivered her to a mganga, who divined spirit possession as the cause of her behavior. The exorcism ceremony resulted in Rashidi providing his wife with several expensive gifts, but it also altered the situation in his favor. The situation was translated from one involving a husband who could not satisfy his wife sexually and was not man enough to control her behavior, into one in which a woman was possessed by a lascivious and uncontrollable spirit.

An obvious case of spirit possession, but it hardly needs saying that had the complexities of Rashidi's life been different, divorce and an adultery suit would have been the outcome rather than exorcism.

Again women are known to be naturally lascivious, while men are much more self-controlled sexually. Thus a woman who refuses to have intercourse with her husband has either just had intercourse with another man or is possessed by a spirit. Such was the case of Mamuna, whose symptoms consisted in kicking her husband out of bed.

In considering cases of spirit possession both we and the Digo have to face the problem of authenticity. Do husbands who present their wives for treatment believe them to be possessed, or are they cynically utilizing a diagnosis of possession to represent a situation in terms favorable to themselves? Or, is the woman genuinely possessed, does she believe that she is possessed, or is she feigning? Digo men are certainly very suspicious that they are being taken for a ride.

From our point of view there are obviously two dimensions to the problem of authenticity, because there are at least two parties concerned in defining a person as possessed: the person who is putatively possessed, and others. So far as the deviant is concerned her behavior might be a cynical feigning of the appropriate symptoms to gain gifts and attention; it might be what a psychiatrist would regard as a "genuine" hysterical episode brought on by a build up of "intrapsychic tension" (Freed and Freed 1967:313-317) and cast into what is a culturally given "presenting syndrome;" or it might be an acting out of an unshakeable diagnosis made by others. It might also consist of a denial of possession, interpreted during exorcism as evidence of possession by a very difficult spirit.

The behavior of others towards the deviant might consist in a public refusal to believe in the authenticity of the attack; a private belief that the attack is feigned but a public acceptance of its authenticity; a genuine belief in the reality of the possession; or a cynical use of a spirit possession label to redefine a problem of control as a problem of possession.

I have spelt these alternatives out at some length because it can be argued that the existence of these alternatives does not constitute merely a technical problem of anthropological interpretation. The problem of authenticity is rather, an invariable feature of a class of phenomena which for want of a better term I will call "mendicity" (Gomm 1974).

Mendicity

It can be argued that peripheral spirit possession belongs to a class of social phenomena in which someone can be represented as bargaining for something, not on the basis of what he or she has to offer in return, but on the basis of what he lacks, is about to lose, suffers from, or is deficient in. Within this class we can include the suicide on the parapet, the invalid, the beggar, the victim of witchcraft attack, and certain types of behavior bracketed as "mental illness" in advanced societies. Similar are pleas of mitigation at law and in everyday life when someone makes a shortcoming an excuse for otherwise unacceptable behavior. Recently Wyllie (1973) has drawn attention to close parallels between witchcraft characterized by voluntary and unsolicited confessions and peripheral spirit possession. I have used the term mendicity to draw attention to the fact that these phenomena all involve a particular type of asymmetrical transaction.

Mutatis mutandi they have in common all or most of the following characteristics.

1. That someone who occupies such a mendicant role "properly" is one who is not deemed fully responsible for his own condition, and that

2. He is deemed incapable of behaving in any other way (McHugh 1970:152-179).

3. Occupancy of the role entails special privileges which would not be granted to someone of his latent/previous status . . .

4. But usually entails putting at risk and sometimes losing other values, such as autonomy, credibility, esteem, personal integrity, position, friendship, and so on. [9]

5. That because these are situations in which someone is seen to be getting something for nothing, they are usually situations which involve doubt about whether the someone "deserves what he gets." Thus it is characteristic of mendicant situations that there are either strict procedures for ascertaining culpability and authenticity (1 and 2 above) and/or that doubt prevails about the moral probity of the mendicant.

Gouldner (1960) in his article on the norm of reciprocity has cogently argued the importance of reciprocity as facilitating stable patterns of interaction.

> *Status duties shape behaviour because the status occu-*
> *pant believes them binding in their own right, they*
> *possess a kind of prima facie legitimacy for properly*
> *socialized group members. The general norm of reci-*
> *procity is however a second order defence of stability; it*
> *provides a further source of motivation and an addi-*
> *tional moral sanction for conforming with specific status*
> *obligations [Gouldner 1960:175-176].*

It is Gouldner's contention, and one which I believe is widely accepted, that the norm of reciprocity is an important social stabilizer in all societies (although not upon all occasions):

> *The norm is a kind of plastic filler capable of being*
> *poured into the shifting crevices of the social structure,*
> *and serving as a kind of all purpose moral cement*
> *[Gouldner 1960:175].*

Gouldner directs special attention to relationships where little or no reciprocity seems to occur — relationships such as those characteristic of a mendicant situation.

He suggests that:

> *If empirical analysis fails to detect the existence of*
> *functional reciprocity, or that it has been disrupted, it*
> *becomes necessary to search out and analyse the*
> *compensatory arrangements that might provide means*
> *of controlling the resultant tensions, thereby enabling*
> *the problematic pattern to remain stable [Gouldner*
> *1960:164].*

Rewarded mendicant behavior is behavior which is problematic in this sense. How is it that people can be persuaded to lay out sometimes large sums of money, to grant privileges, to overlook or suffer insult, abuse, and insubordination without hope of reciprocation from the recipient of such largess?

At one level the answer to this question lies within the field of Digo political organization. Men work hard to ensure the goodwill of other

131

men. The redefinition of a problem of marital relationships as a problem of spirit possession (however the translation is made) places the husband in such a position that he risks alienating his affines and public opinion if he refuses to provide exorcism ceremonies or to accede to spirit demands—in a way that refusing to buy his wife a new dress does not. Spirit possession behavior ("genuine" or "faked") thus levers the husband into a publicly visible situation where the correct behavior for the good husband is clearly defined. Alternatively, since a competent man is one who knows how to handle women, be they wives, sisters, or daughters, the redefinition of a problem of discipline as a problem of possession (whether genuinely believed in or not) enables men to maintain a stance of competence in the face of conflicting evidence—although at a financial cost. Further, while in cases of marital discord a woman's kin face problems of deciding whom to side with, the translation of the problem into one of possession enables all parties to co-operate in effecting a "cure." Thus spirit possession can be represented as a set of strategies for redefining situations which is available to all; it can be used by husbands to manipulate their wives, and fathers to manipulate their daughters, as well as by wives to manipulate their husbands.

Gouldner, however, asks the question not at the level of motivation, but at the level of "functional reciprocity." Applied to the Digo his question would be, "How does spirit possession stand in relation to the *status quo* in Digo society?" This is to address the problem of "supposing everybody did it, what then?" For in so far as the occupancy of a mendicant status sets aside normal obligations, we must consider what mechanisms exist for limiting recruitment to such roles.

As stated above, in situations in which someone is allowed to get something for nothing, there are usually strict procedures for ascertaining whether they deserve what they get. Crucially this means authenticating the affliction as genuine, and as being no fault of the afflicted. Unless these two conditions are seen to be met, then rights to the privileges of a mendicant status will not be granted readily.

The authentication of spirit possession as genuine may be the task of a female diviner consulted before a *mganga* is contracted, but female credibility is low and patients may be delivered direct to the male *mganga*. The *mganga* both in divination and in the practice of exorcism authenticates the reality of possession. From this point of view exorcism ceremonies can be seen as an apparatus for confirming a spirit possession diagnosis as well as for attempting a cure. The exorcism ceremony is so structured that the possessed is rewarded for confirming the diagnosis by speaking with the voice of a possessing spirit. Indeed even this is not necessary, for failing the co-operation of the patient the *mganga* may use ventriloquism or claim that the spirit speaks silently in a way that only his familiar can hear. The authentication of the spirit possession attack as genuine is relatively unproblematic once exorcism is involved. Note that it is not necessary to convince everyone that the attack is genuine, but merely to bring opinion to the state where it is publicly said to be. The Digo are not unaware of the interested nature of the *mganga's* involvement, but private doubts on this basis do not hinder co-operation in exorcism.

The personal culpability of the host is another matter. Relationships with spirits are not necessarily seen as involuntary. People are said sometimes to court spirits for the favors they give. For instance, it is well known that spirits lead people to buried treasure or cause fish to swim into nets, and of course the *mganga* and the diviner base their powers on the control of familiars. Sometimes such relationships with spirits run out of control.

For spirit possession to be regarded as an affliction worthy of sympathy and attention, demanding of people to spend money on exorcism, it must be seen as involuntary. Husbands are unlikely to provide exorcism ceremonies for their wives if they imagine their wives to be actively colluding in their own possession, and this is exactly what is imagined to be happening if women become possessed recurrently. The more frequently a woman has been possessed before, the less likely it is that her husband will bear the cost of a further exorcism. While it may be the case that refusal to provide exorcism outrages the woman's kin and they may provide a ceremony themselves, it also happens that husband and affines agree that this is a hopeless case, unlikely to be dealt with successfully. An acceptable formula to both parties is an agreement that while possession is genuine and involuntary, nonetheless the spirit involved is so strong that it is unlikely to be driven out by exorcism. The end state of a woman who is recurrently possessed is one in which no one takes upon himself the responsibility for bearing the cost of exorcism ceremonies. Such women tend to hand around the compounds of exorcists, receiving small sums of money for helping them with their work, and for providing gossip essential for their counter-witchcraft activities. They supplement their income with earnings from prostitution.[10] Some operate as diviners. When they manifest the symptoms of spirit possession they are allowed to run through the bush, attack trees, tear their hair, and eat ashes and dirt without hindrance. It can be seen, I think, that as a technique for obtaining favors from men, spirit possession has a time limited utility.

Islam among the Digo gives to women an inferior ritual status. Their ritual activities are regarded by men as dirty and as against the *sharia*. Pertinently here, this includes the traditional propitiation of nature spirits; once it would seem, an important aspect of Digo religion (Prins 1952:88) involving both men and women, but now almost solely a female concern. Such minor cults do involve mediumship (controlled possession) by women which can be used for divination and for communication with the spirits. However such activities as these, performed by women, are not usually taken seriously by men. Involvement in such a cult and possession by such spirits do not grant women any favors from their kinsfolk—how could it, when favors are granted on the basis that possession is an involuntary affliction?

An important difference between the Digo and many other well documented examples of peripheral possession is that the exorcist does not achieve his status through a transition from spirit victim to spirit controller. *Aganga* reach their status through a system of apprenticeship whereby young men are bound for a fee to senior kinsmen. Involuntary possession is thus not a step on an upward career ladder as has been claimed for the *zar* cult in Ethiopia (Messing 1958), the Ba Venda in Southern Africa (Stayt 1931:301, sqq.), the Pokomo of Mafia Island (Lewis 1971:108), or voodoo adherents in the West Indies (Lewis 1971:107). While in none of these cases is it clear as to what constraints operate to prevent everyone from becoming an exorcist or medium, it *is* clear that opportunities for improving social status are restricted to those who become "therapists" and are not available to the majority of their "patients."[11] As Lewis has pointed out, the status of the therapist is controlled by suspicions and accusations of witchcraft against those who show the ability to *control* spirits. This is true also among the Digo but here, from start to finish, therapy is controlled by the male establishment.

Among the Digo, involuntary possession may proceed from acute states to chronic ones and the recidivist experiences what might be termed downward mobility in terms of moral standing, although gaining a measure of individual freedom not shared by other women. Some women may be seen to gain control over a spirit and to be able to charge a small fee for divination, scarcely an impressive upward movement. Moreover a woman who claims to control a spirit loses any capacity to bargain for privileges on the basis of being involuntarily afflicted.

An important feature of any social control system is the conceptual apparatus used to explain deviance. If what passes for normal behavior is regarded (as it usually is) as "natural" behavior, then what are counted as serious deviations have to be explained, and explained in such a way that they do not count as evidence against the taken-for-granted notions of natural behavior. Most folk-theorizing on deviance can be represented as saving a prevailing theory of conformity.

In coastal Digo spirit possession, men regard themselves as the natural superiors of women, with the right and the competence to make rules for their behavior and to enforce them. From the point of view of the anthropologist, it can be argued that the difficulties of maintaining the goodwill between men prevents them from enforcing such rules as they make. Women are constantly "getting away with it." Moreover the tensions which are manifested in the form of spirit possession attacks are themselves generated by this control system. The concepts of spirit possession mystify the sources of discontent and the failure of control by separating cause from effect and attributing problems of control to causes outside the social and moral order: to the meaningless actions of adventitious and capricious spirits. The reality of possession is authenticated by a male practitioner in the practice of exorcism. Those who suffer from possession are set in a system of rewards and punishment which enables them to be manipulated to confirm a theory. The privileges permitted and the gifts granted to possessed women are part of this matrix.

It can be argued with some truth that spirit possession attacks may redress the disadvantages of a lowly and deprived status, but at the same time the way in which this amelioration is obtained ensures that deviants confirm a mystifying theory which is an essential element in the control system which maintains them as lowly and deprived persons.

The privileges of spirit possession are seen by the Digo as a benign response to affliction, which may be abused by some people. Faced with frequent possession, or controlled possession they invoke the culpability clause. Women who can be seen as courting possession are denied the rights accorded to those who are seen to suffer through no fault of their own.

There are two ways in which younger women can evade male controls.[12] One is through full time prostitution, in which role women service the sexual desires of Digo men awaiting marriage or deserted by their wives. The other is through chronic spirit possession. Both are conditions of low esteem in which the evasion of male control poses little in the way of a threat to the theory of male dominance. One group is by definition a group of bad women, the other if you like, a group of "mad" women, in the sense of being seen incapable of sustained rational action. Moreover, the badness of one group is frequently explained with reference to their probable possession by spirits, while the madness of the other is frequently attributed to their bad behavior in courting spirits for personal gain.

CONCLUSION

If we turn from Digo spirit possession to other types of mendicant situation we can see that the problem of sorting the deserving from the undeserving is one which is addressed in all cases. They include distinguishing the sick from the malingerers (Daniels 1970:182-205; Szasz 1961:37-64; Field 1953; Bagley 1971), the insane murderer from the rational murderer,[13] the genuine suicide from the cry-for-help suicide (Sudnoe 1967), the woman raped from the seductress who changed her mind, the educationally deprived from the lazy, and the unfortunate from the careless. Distinguishing between the deserving and the undeserving poor has dominated income-maintenance policy in England and America throughout recent history.[14] The set of typifications of occupants of mendicant roles always includes a typification of someone who occupies the status illegitimately, the person who is abusing the system.

This is not surprising, since mendicity is a setting aside of the normal

136

rules of behavior to accommodate those deemed incapable of conforming. It constitutes a loophole which must be closely guarded.

In dealing with mendicity then we are dealing with bodies of ideas which are used to legitimate the setting aside of normal criteria for behavior, whether these be status obligations or more generally reciprocal ones. It can be seen that where a group of mendicants is drawn from those of low status, then the body of ideas used to sanction the granting of privileges is usually one which mystifies the causes of their condition.

Thus the poor may be succored on the grounds of their personal incompetence and depravity (Graham 1965; Matza 1953; Ryan 1971), mystifying the processes which actually distribute income and wealth; the working class child may be given "compensatory education" on the grounds of his "cultural deprivation" (Friedman 1967; Bernstein 1970; Keddie 1973; Labov 1973), mystifying the control which elite groups exert on the class-specific criteria for educational success. And Digo women are granted privileges on the grounds that their behavior derives not from a male dominated culture, but from adventitious spirits. Part of the mystifying apparatus is the low credibility accorded to the mendicant. The poor lack "insight" or "intelligence," the educationally deprived are "inarticulate," the mad are mad and the possessed are after all possessed. Their behavior is exhausted of the meanings they might attribute to it and given other meanings (Cohen 1971:19).

Cherished and convenient ideologies are preserved. Many examples of mendicity involve manipulating the deviant to confirm the control theory, or perceiving only those features of his/her behavior which do (Young 1971; Rosenhan 1973; Gomm 1974; Braginski *et al.* 1969; Schatzman 1969), as here exorcism confirms spirit possession.

To re-address Gouldner's question about the relationship between asymmetrical transactions and the *status quo;* where recipients of apparently unreciprocated largess are the poor and the oppressed, the privileges they receive may frequently be regarded as rewards for colluding in their own oppression.

NOTES

Acknowledgments. This is an amended version of a paper first read at a staff seminar at Swansea University in May, 1974. The author would like to thank participants for their comments and Dr. Margaret Kenna for making the seminar possible. He would also like to thank Professor Ioan Lewis for his encouragement to publish this paper. The contents however remain the views of the author. The fieldwork on which this paper is based was carried out in 1967-68 with the aid of a James A. Swan Fellowship from the Pitt Rivers Museum, Oxford and an Emslie Horniman Scholarship from the Royal Anthropological Institute.

[1] This paper refers principally to the Digo, who are the largest tribe on the South Kenya coast. However, much of what is said here applies also to minority Bantu groups such as the Rabai and Segeju and to the many families who are the descendants of slaves brought from Tanzania by the Arabs in the 19th century.

[2] See, for instance, Caplan (1969), Harris (1957), Lewis (1966), Messing (1958), Onwuejeogwu (1969), Parkin (1972), Shack (1966), and Wilson (1967).

[3] An alternative to the procedure described here is a regime of dieting, purging, and steam bathing under the direction of a female Arab doctor, during which period the afflicted person lives in the household of the doctor. This therapy is far less frequently used by the Digo than public exorcism.

[4] In 1967 the cost of an exorcism ceremony at Tiwi carried out on two successive nights was about K300/—, the bulk of which was paid by the husband (and his father and brothers), the remainder in small contributions by other attenders. Most of the money is kept by the

mganga, who makes small payments to people who assist in various ways (some of whom will themselves have contributed to the cost).

5 It is difficult to give a numerical value to the ratio between male and female hosts undergoing exorcism. Concentrating on one *mganga* only, the number of exorcisms carried out in three months was twenty-five, involving eighteen patients, only one of whom was male.

6 "Cursing" involves the withdrawal of a blessing which is deemed operative until withdrawn.

7 It is worth drawing attention to the modesty of spirit demands; women ask for bus fares, not buses.

8 I say little in this paper about group psychotherapeutic aspects of exorcism ceremonies. It has sometimes been rather glibly assumed that gathering around the patient a supportive group of kin and friends is "therapeutic" in the sense of "curing" an affliction. Certainly Digo exorcism ceremonies show nothing in the nature of bringing into the open underlying conflicts and tensions which might be the cause of the problematic behavior, as convincingly described by Turner (1964). Rather, underlying conflicts and tensions are obfuscated by the ceremony (see above). Throughout this paper the term "therapy" is used without a value load after the manner of Berger and Luckman (1971).

9 Readers will recognize that this is essentially a reformulation of Parsons' description of the sick role in western societies (Parsons 1951: 428-479). See also Bagley (1971).

10 It should not be thought that these women are entirely destitute. They continue to garden on their own account. It is usually the case, however, that their children born in marriage are removed by their husbands.

11 So far as cult members gaining in social status is concerned, this is not well demonstrated in the literature. Lewis (1971: 107) points to favorable treatment in trading and jobs being given to cult members of voodoo groups, but this is set in a situation in which voodoo groups compete for membership. Upward social mobility claimed by Messing (1958) for *zar* cult members seems to consist in being able to rub shoulders with members of higher status groups during *zar* ceremonies. If anything his data suggest that the *zar* cult has become declassé as it has become more and more associated with those of depressed status. One example, however, stands out clearly as an exception: the case of "therapeutic Islam" among the Giriama. Here where Islam is a peripheral religion, possession by Islamic spirits who

demand adherence to Islamic ways enables upwardly mobile entrepreneurs to evade the financial drag of kinship obligations towards their pagan kin (Parkin 1972: 42-46).

12 Women with married sons are granted considerably more freedom in Digo society.

13 For a discussion of the MacNaghten Rule see Mechanic (1968: 82-83) and references cited therein.

14 From the problem of "sturdy beggars" in Tudor times to "scroungers on the dole" today: " 'There is nothing legally wrong. It would not be fair to call it scrounging if the person is genuinely seeking work. But some people are taking advantage of their rights as citizens in an awkward way' " — Richard Crossman as Secretary of State for Social Services (*Sunday Times*, August 1969).

REFERENCES CITED

Bagley, C.
    1971   The Sick Role, Deviance and Medical Care. Journal of Social and Economic Administration 5(3): 42-57.
Berger, Peter L., and Thomas Luckmann
    1971   The Social Construction of Reality: A Treatise in the Sociology of Knowledge. Harmondsworth, England: Penguin.
Bernstein, Basil
    1970   Education Cannot Compensate for Society. New Society 15: 344-347.
Braginsky, Benjamin M., Dorothea D. Braginsky, and Kenneth Ring
    1969   Method of Madness: The Mental Hospital as a Last Resort. New York: Holt, Rinehart and Winston.
Caplan, Ann Patricia
    1969   Non-Unilineal Kinship on Mafia Island, Tanzania. Ph.D. dissertation, Anthropology Department, University of London.
Cohen, Stanley, ed.
    1971   Images of Deviance. Harmondsworth, England: Penguin.
Daniels, Arlene K.
    1970   The Social Construction of Military Psychiatric Disorders. *In* Recent Sociology: Patterns of Communicative Behavior. Vol. 2. Hans Peter Dreitzel, ed. Pp. 182-205. New York: Macmillan.

Field, Mark G.
1953 Structured Strain in the Role of the Soviet Physician. American Journal of Sociology 58: 493-502.

Freed, Stanley A., and Ruth S. Freed
1967 Spirit Possession as Illness in a North Indian Village. *In* Magic, Witchcraft, and Curing. John Middleton, ed. Pp. 295-320. New York: Natural History Press, for the American Museum of National History.

Friedman, Norman L.
1967 Cultural Deprivation: A Commentary in the Sociology of Knowledge. Journal of Educational Thought 1(2): 88-99.

Gerlach, L.P.
1961 The Social Organisation of the Digo of Kenya. Ph.D. dissertation, Anthropology Department, University of London.

Gomm, Roger
1972 Harlots and Bachelors: Marital Instability among the Coastal Digo. Man (n.s.) 7: 95-113.
1974 The Claimant as Mendicant: Four Approaches to Welfare Benefits. Social Work Today 5(12): 369-372.

Gouldner, Alvin W.
1960 The Norm of Reciprocity: A Preliminary Statement. American Sociological Review 25: 161-178.

Graham, Elinor
1965 The Politics of Poverty. *In* Poverty as a Public Issue. Ben B. Seligman, ed. Pp. 231-250. New York: Free Press.

Harris, Grace
1957 Possession "Hysteria" in a Kenya Tribe. American Anthropologist 59: 1046-1066.

Kayamba, H.M.T.
1932 The Modern Life of the East African Native. Africa 5: 50-60.
1947 Notes on the Wadigo. Tanganyika Notes and Records, No. 23 (June): 80-96.

Keddie, Nell, ed.
1973 Tinker, Tailor: The Myth of Cultural Deprivation. Harmondsworth, England: Penguin.

Kennedy, John G.
1967 Nubian *Zar* Ceremonies as Psychotherapy. Human Organization 26: 185-194.

Labov, William
1973   The Logic of Nonstandard English. *In* Tinker, Tailor: The Myth of Cultural Deprivation. Nell Keddie, ed. Pp. 21-66. Harmondsworth, England: Penguin.

Lewis, I.M.
1966   Spirit Possession and Deprivation Cults. Man (n.s.) 1: 307-329.
1971   Ecstatic Religion: An Anthropological Study of Spirit Possession and Shamanism. Harmondsworth, England: Penguin.

McHugh, Peter
1970   A Common-Sense Perception of Deviance. *In* Recent Sociology: Patterns of Communicative Behavior. Vol. 2. Hans Peter Dreitzel, ed. Pp. 152-180. New York: Macmillan.

Matza, David
1953   The Disreputable Poor. *In* Class, Status, and Power: Social Stratification in Comparative Perspective. Reinhard Bendix and Seymour Martin Lipset, eds. Pp. 289-302. New York: Free Press. (Second ed., 1966.)

Mechanic, David
1968   Medical Sociology: A Selective View. New York: Free Press.

Messing, Simon D.
1958   Group Therapy and Social Status in the *Zar* Cult of Ethiopia. American Anthropologist 60: 1120-1126.

Onwuejeogwu, Michael
1969   The Cult of the *Bori* Spirits Among the Hausa. *In* Man in Africa. Mary Douglas and Phyllis M. Kaberry, eds. Pp. 279-305. London: Tavistock.

Parkin, David J.
1972   Palms, Wine, and Witnesses: Public Spirit and Private Gain in an African Farming Community. San Francisco: Chandler.

Parsons, Talcott
1951   The Social System. Glencoe, Illinois: Free Press.

Prins, Adriaan H.J.
1952   The Coastal Tribes of the North-Eastern Bantu (Pokomo, Nyika, Teita). Ethnographic Survey of Africa: East Central Africa, Vol. 3, Part 1. London: International African Institute.

Rosenhan, D.L.
 1973   Sane in Insane Places. Science 179: 250-258.
Ryan, William
 1971   Blaming the Victim. 1st ed. New York: Pantheon Books.
Schatzman, Morton
 1969   Madness and Morals. *In* Counter Culture. Joseph Berke,
 ed. Pp. 288-313. London: Peter Owen.
Shack, William A.
 1966   The Gurage: A People of the Ensete Culture. London:
 Oxford University Press, for the International African Institute.
Stayt, Hush A.
 1968   The Bavenda. London: Cass. (Originally published,
 1931.)
Sudnow, David
 1967   Passing On: The Social Organization of Dying. Englewood Cliffs, New Jersey: Prentice-Hall.
Szasz, Thomas S.
 1961   The Myth of Mental Illness: Foundations of a Theory of
 Personal Conduct. New York: Hoeber-Harper.
Turner, Victor W.
 1964   An Ndembu Doctor in Practice. *In* Magic, Faith, and
 Healing: Studies in Primitive Psychiatry Today. Ari Kiev, ed.
 Pp. 230-263. New York: Free Press of Glencoe.
Wilson, Peter
 1967   Status Ambiguity and Spirit Possession. Man (n.s.) 2:
 366-378.
Wyllie, R.W.
 1973   Introspective Witchcraft among the Effutu of Southern
 Ghana. Man (n.s.) 8: 74-79.
Young, Jock
 1971   The Role of the Police as Amplifiers of Deviancy, Nego-
 tiators of Reality and Translators of Fantasy: Some Consequences of Our Present System of Drug Control as Seen in
 Notting Hill. *In* Images of Deviance. Stanley Cohen, ed. Pp.
 27-61. Harmondsworth, England: Penguin.

SUGGESTIONS FOR FURTHER READING

Collier, Jane
   1974   Women in Politics. *In* Woman, Culture, and Society. Michelle Zimbalist Rosaldo and Louise Lamphere, eds. Pp. 89-96. Stanford: Stanford University Press.
   A brief but provocative essay criticizing views of women as passive recipients of men's decisions. Argues that women are important political actors and strategists whose goals and decisions influence male options and behaviors in a variety of social contexts.
Friedl, Ernestine
   1967   The Position of Women: Appearance and Reality. Anthropological Quarterly 40: 97-108.
   Discusses how the "myth" of formal male dominance can obscure the realities of female power in a Greek peasant community.
Lewis, I.M.
   1971   Ecstatic Religion: An Anthropological Study of Spirit Possession and Shamanism. Harmondsworth, England: Penguin.
   The author's major thesis is that spirit possession may serve ". . . as an oblique aggressive strategy" for politically and economically dependent segments of a population (1971: 32). Examines women's possession cults as political protest groups.

JURAL RELATIONS BETWEEN THE SEXES AMONG
THE BARABAIG

George Klima

Many accounts of African tribal societies lack information concerning the role of women in social control and political organization. Social control is seen largely as the prerogative of males, even in societies where matriliny serves as a basis for establishing rules of succession to positions of authority. Of course, there are exceptional cases where authority and political leadership has been vested in women, e.g., the Lobedu of the Transvaal, but generally speaking, the establishment and maintenance of law and order by legitimate authority, within a specific territory, has been considered by many anthropologists to be almost exclusively the preoccupation and franchise of the male members of a society.

In a specific area of a political territory, such as a village, neighborhood, ward, or district, different sets of rights and obligations may co-exist for different purposes but their totality constitutes the political system within the geographic area. Co-existent principles of social grouping, based on kinship, age, residence, or locality, may entail different sets of rights and obligations, the violation of rights and the nonperformance or lack of observance of obligations, giving rise to a

Reprinted by permission of the author and the International African Institute from *Africa* 34(1):9-20, 1964. Portions of this paper were reprinted in *The Barabaig: East African Cattle-Herders*, by George J. Klima, copyright 1970 by Holt, Rinehart and Winston. Reprinted by permission of the author and publishers.

145

social sanction of some kind emanating from persons or groups operating within a particular territorial base.

Among the Barabaig of [Tanzania, formerly British] Tanganyika, a fourth principle of social grouping, based on sex dichotomy, constitutes an important principle in grouping people socially and politically in every neighborhood and ward in Barabaig territory. Although the neighborhood group of women is not structurally or functionally equal to the men's group in the exercise of authority within the jurisdiction of the neighborhood, they are, nevertheless, a constituent element in the political organization of Barabaig society.

Before proceeding to a discussion of jural relations between men and women in Barabaig society, it is necessary to furnish a brief summary of some aspects of Barabaig social, economic, and political organization so that the character of social control, on a local level, may become more apparent.

The Barabaig of [Tanzania] are the largest of several subtribes comprising a widely dispersed ethnic group who call themselves *Datog*. According to Joseph Greenberg (1957, personal communication), the Barabaig language can be tentatively classified as belonging to the same eastern Sudanic language group as the Nandi and Suk.

The Barabaig are predominantly semi-nomadic pastoralists who follow a transhumant pattern of residence in response to climatic and vegetational changes. The size of the cattle herd and the carrying capacity of the land are factors which contribute to individual variations in the location of homesteads and in the frequency of moving. For example, two owners of large cattle herds would not care to build their homesteads in the same neighborhood because of the competition for grazing which would ensue. There are no rights to grazing land either individually or collectively. Anyone may graze his cattle, or cultivate (if he is so inclined), wherever he wishes and build his homestead in the vicinity of any clan or lineage member, or affine, with whom he wishes to establish closer social relations. Therefore the social composition of a neighborhood changes periodically as neighbors move to other areas and are subsequently replaced by new families.

Cattle are the most valued property among the Barabaig and belong to both sexes. Although descent, succession to political office, and inheritance of cattle are determined patrilineally, the existence of dowry for married daughters confers a high economic status on women which may, or may not, be linked with their relatively high jural status. A payment of bridewealth, a small barrel of honey, and a heifer, called *ded gadyeld,* is given to the father of the bride by the parents of the bridegroom. In return, the bride's family will give her from two to forty head of cattle, depending on the economic status of her family. These dowry cattle, called *dug badaid,* "cattle of the back," will be kept in trust and later redistributed to her sons as marriage and inheritance cattle and as dowry for her daughters. [1]

Segmentation of Barabaig society into clans and lineages is not accompanied by any stable territorial localization of descent groups. All sixty-odd clans are dispersed throughout Barabaig territory. Thus, the social composition of neighborhoods is not determined by membership in a particular social grouping, although the larger clans may have a larger representation of members in some neighborhoods, and, indeed, may have at least one representative in every neighborhood. Barabaig clans are part of a larger dual division which separates the tribe according to magico-religious functions. The two divisions are the *Daremgadyeg,* the priestly or ritual clans, and the *Homat'k,* which are laical or secular clans. These divisions are nonexogamous in character and membership is determined by patrilineal descent.

Although the political system of the Barabaig is segmentary in character, with positions of ritual and jural authority within clans and lineages determined patrilineally, there also exists a central authority in the person of the chief, *nutamid,* who inherits his title patrilineally and whose authority is backed by supernatural powers since he is the possessor of the *gadyak't,* a magic fire used as war magic in the days prior to the advent of European colonial rule. Following the pacification of tribes in the interior of Tanganyika, traditional chiefship among the Barabaig has operated *sub rosa* and the paramount chiefship created by colonial government functions within a different sphere of rights and obligations from the indigenous paramountcy. Traditional chiefship today is limited to the authorization of circumcision and funeral ceremonies and to the application of excommunicative sanctions against tribal members who have been insubordinate to the chief, have violated tribal obligations and promises, or who have killed a fellow Barabaig. [2]

The Barabaig political community is composed of territorial segments —the tribal territory, the ward, and the neighborhood. Within each spatial unit, and between units, political relations are structured according to different principles, based on kinship, age, locality, and sex. It is on the neighborhood level that the latter two principles, locality and sex-division, can best be observed; whereas, kinship and age-associational principles are more diffuse and extend beyond a particular locality. For the present discussion, I choose to trace some of the ways in which social behavior is regulated and controlled in the milieu of the neighborhood.

The extent of a neighborhood cannot be delimited solely in terms of physical boundaries, although a certain area can be identified by name. The difficulty in delimitation of a neighborhood stems from the fact that it is not the periphery which is identifiable but the "center" around which at varying distances a number of homesteads are distributed at random. Therefore, the reference name of the neighborhood derives from some physical landmark, such as a lake, hill, ravine, rock outcrop, or the name of some elder who had received a stone cairn burial.

Variation in the physical area of different neighborhoods is the result of the number and distribution of homesteads which comprise the various neighborhoods. In other words, there is no fixed radius or periphery. Nor are neighborhoods necessarily contiguous but may be separated by unoccupied land, especially in the dry season when land otherwise suitable for settlement is too far away from a permanent water supply. The periphery of a neighborhood may be extended or contracted, depending on the arrival or departure of families who have identified and interacted socially with those families whose homesteads are closer to the identifying landmark. Since anyone may build his homestead wherever he chooses, those homesteads nearer the "center" do not assume any special social or political importance as a nucleus for the formation of a neighborhood group. The temporary character of residence applies equally to homesteads near the "center" of the neighborhood as well as to those on the periphery.

Social interaction of people sharing the same geographic area, such as a neighborhood, may be more intense than relations on either the ward, district, or tribal level. Public affairs in the neighborhood, linked with conditions of drought, famine, disease, witchcraft, death, or non-

148

co-operative behavior of a fellow neighbor, are generally managed by concentrated action of the male elders. A neighborhood council, called *girwaged gischeud*, may be convened by any local elder, who is then referred to as *ghamata girgwaged*, "mother of the council," for it is he who "gave birth" to the assemblage. Only male elders and young men may attend the meetings. Neighborhood councils are empowered to deliberate and judge only those matters which are of public concern for the neighborhood at large.

The transient nature of residence in a neighborhood linked with the cyclical growth and depletion of grazing areas does not permit the establishment of permanent membership and leadership in any territorial group. In addition, the absence of any localized kin groups precludes the possibility of a clan or lineage forming the nucleus for a formal political structure with permanent authority. Although each Barabaig family and homestead is pursuing economic self-interest and advantage, in terms of the welfare and increase of their own cattle upon which they are vitally dependent, they are still reliant on group co-operation and effort in areas of noneconomic activity as well as in situations requiring common defence against disease, predatory animals, and cattle raids.

Transient leadership is a characteristic feature of a Barabaig neighborhood political system. Some elders are more skilled in oratory, better informed about judicial procedure and precedents, and will, therefore, be informally recognized as spokesmen, since positions of leadership are not formally identified by name on the neighborhood level. These spokesmen may eventually move away from the neighborhood and be replaced by other spokesmen. Thus, leadership in a neighborhood is in the same state of flux as the social composition of the neighborhood, with the assumption of leadership by specific individuals contingent upon the character and ability of potential candidates. In other words, status as a spokesman in a neighborhood is achieved by personal accomplishment rather than derived or ascribed on the basis of hereditary succession. Since neighborhood groups are not permanent with respect to permanent membership, they assume a somewhat voluntary character in recruitment of members. But once new members are settled in the neighborhood, participation in social activities such as ritual becomes obligatory.

149

Within any neighborhood, there are different spheres of authority and jurisdiction, depending on the nature of the social situation which leads to jural action, i.e., the nature of the delict determines the character of authority which will be activated and directed toward the resolution of the breach in social relations. Disputes over inheritance of cattle, violations of the rule of exogamy in marriage, and fighting are considered to be under the jurisdiction of clan councils convened *ad hoc*. The sphere of clan authority extends across neighborhood boundaries and the clan council replaces the neighborhood council in assuming responsibility for the administration of justice and the restoration of peace in situations where clan rights and obligations are involved.

So far, I have discussed briefly some aspects of social control exercised by males as individuals and groups in Barabaig political organization. When attention is focused on the exercise of social control within the neighborhood, it becomes apparent that there exists another constituent element, namely, the group of neighborhood women, who must be included in any discussion of the Barabaig political system.

Regulation of social relations between the sexes appears to be largely the prerogative of women. Women, collectively and individually, hold certain rights, which I would designate as *jus feminarum*, the infringement of which leads to a spontaneous reaction from the women of the neighborhood in which the delict occurred. The legal status of Barabaig women is reflected in the jural institution of *girgwaged gademg*, "council of women," a moot composed of neighborhood women who collectively act and deliberate as a judicial body, adjudicate, and enforce their own decisions. The ability of Barabaig women to hold *ad hoc* moots, to pass judgement on men who have violated certain of their rights, and to impose legal sanctions against men, is validated by myth and actualized by communal opinion and action of the women. Mythical validation of *ghordyod gademg*, "fine of the women," relates to the promiscuous state of men and women before the institution of marriage was created by Udameselgwa, a female deity held in high reverence by Barabaig women. The limited scope of this paper doe not allow explication of the myth.

The general status of Barabaig women is high, even though the society is strongly patriarchal. An investigation of possible status determinants indicates that there is no single factor responsible for the relatively high social and jural status held by women.

The ritual status of women may be linked with their high social status. Certain magico-religious rituals are carried out exclusively by Barabaig women. It would be difficult to assign a dominant or subordinate role to women in the ritual activities of the society, since a large part of their rituals is complementary to rituals being performed at the same time by the men's groups. However, in their singing of religious "hymns" to solicit aid from God, Aset, and the spirits of deceased "priests" from the ritual clans who are intermediaries, the women display a ritual competence acknowledged by the men as essential for the general welfare of the society in times of disease, epidemic, and drought. Therefore, the role of women in religious activity is subordinate to the men's role only in their lack of religious specialists or priests. Their knowledge and performance of hymns to God and spirit intermediaries are considered an integral and vital part of the Barabaig religious ritual system.

The jural status of women does not seem to derive from the jural aspects of marriage. The first installment of the bridewealth, a barrel of honey, called *Maled Anog,* "honey of the breast milk," is usually sufficient to give the future husband the right to remove his intended bride from her family homestead before marriage. During the betrothal period, while residing in her fiancé's homestead, the girl has a subordinate role and is treated as a novice who must learn the customary behavior of her future affines. Therefore, the early removal of the intended bride away from her parents and her subordination in her future father-in-law's homestead might be interpreted as a reflection of the future husband's jural status, rather than an index of rights held by the girl or her father.

The payment of bridewealth also conveys rights to the husband over the procreative ability of his wife. The husband's right to children of the marriage is unequivocal, as is the right of filiation by which the children are assigned membership of their father's clan and lineage. However, the transfer of bridewealth does not give the husband any economic rights over the woman except those rights pertaining to domestic labor, such as cooking and herding cattle. Economic rights in a woman, such as ownership of her dowry cattle, belong to her father, or, more often, to her eldest full brother. Dowry cattle and their progeny are returnable to a woman's father or brother, in the event of a son not being born of her marriage which has terminated in divorce or death. The birth of a son prevents the possibility of any future return of bridewealth or dowry cattle between two families when affinal ties are no longer operant.

In many households, the total number of dowry cattle controlled by the wives may far exceed the number of cattle owned by the husband. Although he has nominal control over all the cattle in his homestead, he must customarily ask permission from his wife before he can sell any of her dowry cattle. A woman's dowry cattle will eventually be distributed among her sons and daughters on the occasion of their marriage, but until this happens, the dowry will be a source of dissension and conflict between the husband and wife.

The existence of dowry gives a woman economic leverage in her relations *vis-à-vis* the husband, which diminishes somewhat with the birth of a son but increases again when the son reaches an age where he and his mother could separate from the father's homestead and set up a separate homestead in a different neighborhood. Therefore, I submit that the economic status of Barabaig women appears to reinforce the mythological validation of women's right to jural action against the men, although its actual contribution to the jural status held by women is difficult to assess.

When a Barabaig woman believes that one or more men in the neighborhood have committed an offence against her by violating certain rights of women, she complains to other women of the neighborhood who decide informally whether or not to convene a moot. No distinction is made between a private and a public delict. An offence committed against one woman is seen as an offence committed against all women, thus inciting the female members of the community in which the delict occurred to seek redress by jural retaliation.

The emergence of leadership among neighborhood women follows along lines similar to the assumption of leadership by neighborhood men. Knowledgeable women, skilled in oratory, emerge as spokesmen during the judicial proceedings, and may continue to be recognized as "leaders" during their residence in the neighborhood. Since residence during betrothal and marriage is virilocal, a neighborhood group of women will consist of women belonging to many different patriclans. Therefore virilocal marriage residence does not allow the formation of a kin-based group of women. Transient residence of households comprising a neighborhood also militates against the establishment of permanent territorial groupings. Hence the absence of localized kin groups; ecological imbalance, with its concomitant changes in the personnel comprising a neighborhood, prevents the emergence of permanent, formalized, political leadership among the men's and women's neighborhood groups.

The group of neighborhood women are not acting in the Durkheimian (1933) sense as the "authorized interpreters of collective sentiments." They are representative only of the "collective conscience" of the female half of the neighborhood population. The delict arouses a different collective sentiment and conscience in the male members of the community who object to the impending jural action of the women which may, by the imposition of a fine, deprive a man of cattle, the property most valued in Barabaig society. Between the sexes there will be feelings of antagonism, but for different reasons; the sentiments of the women being offended because their rights have been violated by a man, and the sentiments of the men aroused because the women will deprive a man of property. The disgruntled state of the men is manifested in the oft-repeated phrase, "They [the women] are going to 'eat' [consume] cattle needlessly." Therefore, it appears that the delict affects the neighborhood group differentially, depending on the common sentiments specific to each sex grouping.

Much of the women's juridical procedure is strikingly similar to the pattern of behavior exhibited by the men during their councils. The council place is usually under a shade tree previously selected by some of the council members. Every day, during the course of the trial, which may last from three to six days, the women leave their homesteads and gather at the designated place of council. The deliberations begin in the late morning and last until late afternoon, at which time the women disperse and return to their homesteads to cook the evening meal. It is obligatory for all married women of the neighborhood to attend the meetings. Exemptions are made in cases of sickness, childcare, and herding duties.

The male offender may be present to explain and defend his actions, but sometimes a man chooses to avoid risking further antagonism and does not attend. In any event, the opportunity to challenge the allega-

153

tions of women is available to those who would choose to debate the issue. Sometimes the moot is prolonged by internal dissension. Wives, female members of the defendant's clan, and friends may try to defend the transgressor, even when they realize that an unfavorable verdict is inevitable. Precedents and parallels between the present delict and delicts punished in the past will be cited by knowledgeable older women in the group. However, certain precedents may not be known or remembered by the women who comprise a particular moot and therefore deliberation may be more difficult. Still, there is a body of common knowledge which refers to some of the delicts which have, in the past, evoked the sanction called *ghordyod gademg,* "fine of the women."

An investigation of the delicts subject to a cattle fine indicates that there are certain basic concepts embodied in abstract rules, such as the sanctity of the female body, domestic harmony during the critical period of childbirth, which, when challenged or threatened, may incite legal action on the part of the neighborhood women. Some delicts which are liable to prosecution are the following:

If a husband kicks his wife's cooking-stones, his action implies a wish for her death.

If a husband beats his wife after she has just returned from a *ghadowed,* a women's pilgrimage to the homestead of an influential *daremgadyand,* a magico-religious specialist possessing curative powers.

If the husband beats his wife during her one-month convalescence after childbirth, the period called *ghereg.*

If the husband beats his wife after she returns from a *werwerik,* a neighborhood mission of condolence for a woman who has just given birth.

If the midwife hears the husband beating another wife during the time when his pregnant wife is about to give birth.

If the husband swears at the midwife while she is still performing her duty, or if he wishes to send her away before her customary attendance period has lapsed.

If a husband hits his wife over the head with his stick.

If the husband takes away his wife's clothes and sends her away from the homestead in a naked condition.

If any man, including a husband, witnesses a childbirth.

If a goat, sheep, or bullock is solicited from a male neighbor, in order to provide food for a convalescent mother in the neighborhood, and the man refuses to contribute the animal.

If a man rapes a prepubescent girl.

If a man ill-treats a wanton by physical abuse.

Each day of the council, the neighborhood women assemble under the designated shade tree and display their oratory. Formal procedure is at a minimum, but some rules are obviously operative. Only married women are permitted to attend the moot. One female elder stands before the group and addresses her remarks to a "receiver," called *giripshochand*, a woman selected by the speaker to reinforce her verbal delivery from time to time by assenting and repeating key words of the oration, thus lending emphasis to the speaker's pleading.

The gesturing and oratory of the women closely resembles the pattern of behavior in evidence during the councils of Barabaig men. Such actions as striking the ground with a stick in order to emphasize certain points in an argument, swinging the stick and exhorting the audience (who respond with a chorused shout of approval), modulating the voice from a barely audible level until it rises gradually to emotional shouting, grimacing, expressions of anger and disgust, are some of the oratorical devices used for effect. However, for the most part, the jural proceedings are conducted with a modicum of emotion.

The women's council, numbering about fifty women, is an "open" meeting in the sense that any married woman may have the opportunity to speak before the group and, unlike male councils which exclude women, the women permit men to attend the moot. A few men, usually less than ten in number, sit apart from the women's group but within hearing distance of the proceedings. Neighborhood men may try to defend their accused neighbor by pitting their oratorical skills against female protagonists, but rarely are moot decisions reversed because of the intervention of neighborhood men. Some men take the opportunity of expression to chide and rebuke the women about "unjust" decisions in the past. The obstructive tactics of the men appear to be aimed at defending the accused man and disparaging and discrediting the jural institution of the *girgwaged gademg*. I have observed men complaining bitterly about the existence of *girgwaged gademg* and have heard them voice the wish for its abolition, but the small attendance of the men at women's councils may be an indication that dissension has not yet generated organized opposition on a large scale.

During the council proceedings, numerous deviations from the objective of the moot occur frequently and appear to be beyond the control of women informally recognized as "spokesmen." The occasion of the moot provides an opportunity to air a wide variety of grievances concerning such things as a husband's sale of part of his wife's dowry cattle, child welfare, and the iniquities of men in general, as well as the one on trial.

Discussion of hearsay evidence of precedents and parallels is weighed against firsthand accounts of previous delicts and their disposition. There is an apparent effort to arrive at some degree of accuracy in recounting former delicts, defendants, and councils associated with different neighborhoods.

When the oratory is exhausted, usually three to six days after the moot has been convened, the women apparently reach a consensus concerning the guilt of the accused and the sanction to be imposed. I have never seen a women's council end in an acquittal for the defendant, although there have been instances when the women's decision pertaining to the sanction has been modified because of certain circumstances surrounding the defendant. These circumstances will be discussed in a later section.

The customary sanction levied against the man is a cattle fine. He is ordered to send one black bullock to the women's group, where an attempt will be made to beat it to death with sticks. Whether or not this action is symbolic of what the women would like to do to the man who violated their rights but instead inflict physical punishment and death on his surrogate cannot be ascertained at this time. Therefore, to say that the cattle fine may serve concurrently as retribution and restitution would be conjectural.

Until the moment when the cattle fine is paid, neighborhood men will actively try to dissuade the women from carrying out their decision. The men place themselves between the advancing group of women and the bullock being led to the women's group by the defendant or his assistant. They try to obstruct the passage of the women, but the women drive them away by threatening to hit them with their sticks. The action and pleading of the men does not usually alter the course of legal action of the women.

Not all the women present in the council are permitted to hit the bullock with their sticks. Custom dictates that only those women who are married to a man belonging to the same generation-set, called *saiged*, as the male offender are considered eligible to beat the bullock. Also, no woman who is a member of the same clan as the offender would consider killing an animal belonging to her clan.

Informal structural continuity for a neighborhood group of women is made possible by the generation-set principle, which appears to be a facilitating condition for group action. Propinquity alone does not serve to define the enforcement agency which emerges to implement the decision of the moot. Since the generation-set membership of the male offender and, affinitively, his wives' memberships provide the eligibility criterion for selecting members to comprise the sanction-enforcement group, the constitution of the enforcement agency is situational. Therefore, the jural institution of *girgwaged gademg* operates within a framework provided by the generation-set principle.

After the eligible women hit the bullock, but usually without killing it, some neighborhood men assist the women in killing the bullock by tossing it to the ground and suffocating it in the prescribed manner employed during animal sacrifice. The legs are bound with leather thongs and a leather thong is tied around the bullock's face, holding the jaws shut. Hands are placed over the bullock's nostrils and, in a matter of minutes, the animal is suffocated. It is mandatory in any ritual killing of an animal, whether a bull or a sheep, that no bones be broken or blood drawn. After the bullock is dead, each woman in the council is permitted to touch the carcass with her stick. The women sing a song of approval and dance around the carcass and later the meat of the dead animal will be divided among the women, first choice of portions going to the women who comprised the eligible group which first administered the beating.

157

In cases where the guilty man is a member of a priestly or ritual clan, i.e., a *daremgadyand,* the women are not permitted to beat the bullock with their sticks. Instead, the customary alternative is for the women to sing their religious songs while a group of neighborhood men, in the ritual manner of animal sacrifice, suffocate the bullock inside the *kraal* [cattle enclosure] of the offender. Thus the killing of the bullock takes place in a context of propitiation, even though the initial intent of the women was to impose a legal sanction.

In almost all the cases of *ghordyod gademg* which I have either witnessed or heard of, the convicted men have recognized the jural authority of the women to hold moots and pass judgement on males and have paid their fines, although rather grudgingly. Not all fines have been cattle fines. If a man with a small herd of cattle is not able to pay the cattle fine, the women may consider a fine of several gallons of raw honey as indemnification. The honey is then consumed on the spot by the women. If a man had a ritually unclean condition called *gak,* "bones," because he, or his father or grandfather, had killed a tribal member, the cattle fine would be waived and a fine of honey substituted in its stead. The rationale for this action may be seen in the sacred nature of honey and the profane character of the man's cattle. Whereas the women would abhor eating any of the meat of an animal belonging to a man who had *gak* for fear of becoming contaminated, the eating of honey would be permissible, since honey is considered sacred and is not capable of being contaminated by a man who is ritually unclean.

One case is illustrative of a rare situation in which a Barabaig man refused to comply with the decision of the women's council and challenged their authority to impose a fine. In 1955 Ghutadyonda, son of Mwal, was away from his homestead when a bullock was taken from his herd and killed to provide food for a convalescent mother in the neighborhood. Ghutadyonda encountered the women skinning his bull and became so angry that he threw a spear at them to chase them away. The women convened a moot and fined Ghutadyonda, who refused to pay the cattle fine. His refusal brought into action the women's sanction of *gibuhand,* a devastating fine and curse. The women tore down his *kraal* fence and returned his wives to their fathers. They went into the huts of the wives and threw the ashes from the hearth on to the bed and scattered the remainder around the room, all the while making mourning cries to symbolize that a death had occurred in the homestead — Ghutadyonda's death.

For one year, Ghutadyonda's relatives continued to plead with the neighborhood women to reconsider their action. A moot was convened and it was decided that before Ghutadyonda's wives could be returned to him, and the curse of death removed, Ghutadyonda would have to pay a fine of two black bullocks and would have to brew honey beer to take away the curse which they had imposed on him. This time, he recognized the jural authority of the women and complied with their decree. Social relations were again restored between Ghutadyonda and the women of the neighborhood.

Although the women's council is convened presumably to help restore harmony in social relations between the sexes in the neighborhood, some women discussants manifest strong feelings of antagonism toward men in general. Expressions of ridicule and contempt comprise a part of the tangential and inappropriate discussions that emerge during the judicial proceedings.

There are other social contexts in which women display antagonism toward Barabaig men. During a wedding, *nyangid,* neighborhood women engage in a special song and dance called *dumd dumod,* "dance of the penis," in which a singing rivalry emerges between women who boast of their sexual prowess in vanquishing the males of their husbands' clans. The presence of ritual obscenity and ridicule during a wedding reception is only one indication of sexual antagonism manifested by women towards men. Another part of the wedding ritual consists of a mime play in which one woman, acting the role of "husband," is deceived and made to look ridiculous by a second woman playing the part of the "new wife" cooking her first meal for her husband. The female spectators howl with delight over the antics of the two performers, but none of the men present in the *kraal* cares to see either the play or the lewd dancing and singing of the *dumd dumod.*

Another occasion when antagonism between the sexes is manifested in ritual behavior occurs during a séance. Although the audience at a séance is mixed, women spectators considerably outnumber the men.

The medium, who is always a woman, elicits the spirit of a man named Gidamagir, who proceeds to vilify and harass the women attending the séance. According to myth, Gidamagir's hostility towards women originates from the time women refused to pull out an arrow from his body when he returned from battle with a tribal enemy. He finally located a small boy who succeeded in extracting the arrow, but Gidamagir died shortly after. It is believed that, to this day, his spirit continues to rebuke and deprecate women for their refusal of aid which would have saved his life. Shortly after Gidamagir's bitter and violent denunciation, the spirit of Udameselgwa, the female deity, intercedes on behalf of the women and is heard quarrelling with Gidamagir until both spirit voices fade away.

The rest of the séance is devoted to the elicitation of spirits of deceased priests, *mang,* who answer questions concerning personal problems put to them by the audience.

The women's council, *girgwaged gademg,* operates as part of the legal machinery which goes into action to mend the breach in neighborhood relations caused by an offence committed against a female member of the community, and its potential threat covertly regulates the day-to-day relations between the sexes occupying the same communal territory. The *girgwaged gademg* also functions to preserve the relatively high social and legal status of Barabaig women, as is evident in the fact that the women's council is convened only when a delict has been committed by a man against a woman. It is not convened to pass judgement on women, nor is there any traditional jural body which is empowered to impose a cattle fine on women, even though women possess cattle universally, and in sufficient numbers to warrant their inclusion in a system of sanctions.

The redressive mechanism of the *girgwaged gademg* appears to be a possibly unique social phenomenon which, so far as this investigator is aware, does not exist among any of the related eastern Sudanic groups to which the Barabaig belong, nor does mention of women's councils empowered to impose punitive sanctions against men appear in literature dealing with other African societies. Although the function of the jural institution may be understood in its present operation, its origin and conception cannot be explained in terms of any specific historical preconditions. The *girgwaged gademg* continues to be an effective instrument in maintaining social cohesion within a given Barabaig neighborhood, the smallest but not the least important political segment in Barabaig society.

NOTES

Acknowledgments. This paper was presented at the April 1963 meetings of the Southwestern Anthropological Association held at the University of California, Riverside, California.

Data for this paper derive from field research carried out in 1955-56 and 1958-59. I should like to thank Professor Michael G. Smith, [formerly of the] University of California, Los Angeles, for reading an earlier version of the paper and offering valuable criticisms and suggestions. However, I alone bear full responsibility for the contents of this paper.

[1] The exchange of cattle between the two families is more complex than is here presented, and the limited scope of this paper does not allow a more detailed description of the transfer network between donors and recipients.

[2] I have described aspects of traditional chiefship as they existed during the periods 1955-56 and 1958-59. I have no information regarding chiefship among the Barabaig under the newly independent government of [Tanzania].

REFERENCE CITED

Durkheim, Émile
    1933   The Division of Labor in Society. George Simpson, trans. New York: Free Press.

SUGGESTIONS FOR FURTHER READING

Dwyer, Daisy Hilse
  1977 Bridging the Gap between the Sexes in Moroccan Legal Practice. *In* Sexual Stratification: A Cross-Cultural View. Alice Schlegel, ed. Pp. 41-66. New York: Columbia University Press. Examines the politico-jural roles of the female *'arifa*, an institutionalized intermediary, between the male-dominated legal system and women in a sexually segregated society.

Eastwood, Mary
  1979 Feminism and the Law. *In* Women: A Feminist Perspective. Jo Freeman, ed. Pp. 385-403. 2nd ed. Palo Alto, California: Mayfield.
  A brief assessment of cases and legislation in the United States concerning equal treatment for women under the law and protection from sex discrimination.

Juviler, Peter H.
  1977 Women and Sex in Soviet Law. *In* Women in Russia. Dorothy Atkinson, Alexander Dallin, and Gail Warshofsky Lapidus, eds. Pp. 243-265. Stanford: Stanford University Press. Surveys changes in women's legal status as sexual partners, childbearers, and spouses from the Bolshevik Revolution to the Russian Republic Code of Marriage and the Family of 1970.

Mohsen, Safia K.
  1967 The Legal Status of Women among Awlad 'Ali. Anthropological Quarterly 40: 153-166. (Reprinted in Peoples and Cultures of the Middle East. Vol. 1: Cultural Depth and Diversity. Louise E. Sweet, ed. Pp. 220-233. Garden City, New York: Natural History Press, for the American Museum of Natural History, 1970.)
  Describes women's legal rights and disabilities in a seminomadic herding society in the Western Desert of Egypt. By forfeiting their inheritance in return for protection by their male kin, married women acquire a significant measure of legal independence from their husbands.

"SITTING ON A MAN:" COLONIALISM AND THE LOST POLITICAL INSTITUTIONS OF IGBO WOMEN

Judith Van Allen

In the conventinal wisdom, western influer.ce has "emancipated" African women — through the weakening of kinship bonds and the provision of "free choice" in Christian monogamous marriage, the suppression of "barbarous" practices, the opening of schools, the introduction of modern medicine and hygiene, and, sometimes, of female suffrage.

But westernization is not an unmixed blessing. The experience of Igbo women under British colonialism shows that western influence can sometimes weaken or destroy women's traditional autonomy and power without providing modern forms of autonomy or power in exchange. Igbo women had a significant role in traditional political life. As individuals, they participated in village meetings with men. But their real political power was based on the solidarity of women, as expressed in their own political institutions - their meetings (*mikiri* or *mitiri*), their market networks, their kinship groups, and their right to use strikes, boycotts, and force to effect their decisions.

British colonial officers and missionaries, both men and women, generally failed to see the political roles and the political power of Igbo women. The actions of administrators weakened. and in some cases destroyed women's bases of strength. Since they did not appreciate

Reprinted by permission of the author and publisher from *Canadian Journal of African Studies* 6(2):165-181, 1972.

women's political institutions, they made no efforts to ensure women's participation in the modern institutions they were trying to foster.

Igbo women haven't taken leadership roles in modern local government, nationalist movements, and national government, and what roles they *have* played have not been investigated by scholars. The purpose in describing their traditional political institutions and source of power is to raise the question of why these women have been "invisible" historically, even though they forced the colonial authorities to pay attention to them briefly. We suggest that the dominant view among British colonial officers and missionaries was that politics was a man's concern. Socialized in Victorian England, they had internalized a set of values and attitudes about what they considered to be the natural and proper role of women that supported this belief. We suggest further that this assumption about men and politics has had a great deal to do with the fact that no one has even asked, "Whatever happened to Igbo women's organizations?" even though all the evidence needed to justify the question has been available for thirty years.

IGBO TRADITIONAL POLITICAL INSTITUTIONS

Political power in Igbo society was diffuse.[1] There were no specialized bodies or offices in which legitimate power was vested, and no person, regardless of his status or ritual position, had the authority to issue commands which others had an obligation to obey. In line with this diffusion of authority, the right to enforce decisions was also diffuse: there was no "state" that held a monopoly of legitimate force, and the use of force to protect one's interests or to see that a group decision was carried out was considered legitimate for individuals and groups. In the simplest terms, the British tried to create specialized political institutions which commanded authority and monopolized force. In doing so they took into account, eventually, Igbo political institutions dominated by men but ignored those of the women. Thus, women were shut out from political power.

The Igbo lived traditionally in semi-autonomous villages, which consisted of the scattered compounds of seventy-five or so patrikin; related villages formed "village-groups" which came together for limited ritual and jural purposes. Villages commonly contained several hundred people; but size varied, and in the more densely populated areas there were village-groups with more than 5,000 members (Forde and Jones 1950: 39; Harris 1940: 141). Disputes at all the levels above the compound were settled by group discussion until mutual agreement was reached (Uchendu 1965: 41-44).

The main Igbo political institution seems to have been the village assembly, a gathering of all adults in the village who chose to attend. Any adult who had something to say on the matter under discussion was entitled to speak—as long as he *or she* said something the others considered worth listening to; as the Igbo says, ''a case forbids no one'' (Green [1947] 1964: 78-79; Uchendu 1965: 41).

Matters dealt with in the village assembly were those of concern to all—either common problems for which collective action was appropriate (''How can we make our market 'bigger' than the other villages' markets?'') or conflicts which threatened the unity of the village (Harris 1940: 142-143; Uchendu 1965: 34, 42-43).

Decisions agreed on by the village assembly did not have the force of law in our terms, however. Even after decisions had been reached, social pressure based on consensus and the ability of individuals and groups to enforce decisions in their favor played a major part in giving the force of law to decisions. As Green ([1947] 1964: 137) put it:

> [O]ne had the impression . . . that laws only establish themselves by degrees and then only in so far as they gain general acceptance. A law does not either exist or not exist: rather it goes through a process of establishing itself by common consent or of being shelved by a series of quiet evasions.

Persuasion about the rightness of a particular course of action in terms of tradition was of primary importance in assuring its acceptance, and the leaders were people who had the ability to persuade.

The mode of political discourse was that of proverb, parable, and metaphor drawn from the body of Igbo tradition.[2] The needed political knowledge was accessible to the average man or woman, since all Igbo were reared with these proverbs and parables. Influential speech was the creative and skillful use of tradition to assure others that a certain course of action was both a wise and right thing to do. The accessibility of this knowledge is indicated by an Igbo proverb: "If you tell a proverb to a fool, he will ask you its meaning."

The leaders of Igbo society were men and women who combined wealth and generosity with "mouth," the ability to speak well. Age combined with wisdom brought respect, but age alone carried little influence. The senior elders who were ritual heads of their lineages were very likely to have considerable influence, but they would not have achieved these positions in the first place if they had not been considered to have good sense and good character (Uchendu 1965: 41). Wealth in itself was no guarantee of influence: a "big man" or "big woman" was not necessarily a wealthy person, but one who had shown skill and generosity in helping other individuals and, especially, the community (Meek [1937] 1950 : 111; Uchendu 1965: 34).

Men owned the most profitable crops such as palm oil, received the bulk of the money from bridewealth, and, if compound heads, presents from the members. Through the patrilineage, they controlled the land, which they could lease to nonkinsmen or to women for a good profit. Men also did most of the long distance trading which gave higher profit than local and regional trading, which was almost entirely in women's hands (Green [1947] 1964: 32-42).

Women were entitled to sell the surplus of their own crops and the palm kernels which were their share of the palm produce. They might also sell prepared foods or the products of special skills, for instance, processed salt, pots, and baskets. They pocketed the entire profit, but their relatively lower profit levels kept them disadvantaged relative to the men in acquiring titles and prestige (Leith-Ross 1939: 90-92, 138-139, 143).

For women as well as for men, status was largely achieved, not ascribed. A woman's status was determined more *by her own achievements* than by the achievements of her husband. The resources available to men were greater, however; so that while a woman might rank higher among women than her husband did among men, very few women could acquire the highest titles, a major source of prestige (Meek ([1937] 1950): 203; Uchendu 1965: 86).

At village assemblies men were more likely to speak than were women; women more often spoke only on matters of direct concern to them (Green [1947] 1964: 169). Title holders took leading parts in discussion and were more likely to take part in consultation. After a case had been thoroughly discussed, a few men retired in order to come to a decision. A spokesman then announced the decision, which could be accepted or rejected by the assembly (Uchendu 1965: 41).

Apparently no rule forbade women to participate in consultations, but they were invited to do so only rarely. The invited women were older women, for while younger men might have the wealth to acquire the higher titles and thus make up in talent what they lacked in age, younger women could not acquire the needed wealth quickly enough to be eligible (Meek ([1937] 1950): 203).

Women, therefore, came second to men in power and influence. While status and the political influence it could bring were achieved and there were no formal limits to women's political power, men through their ascriptive status (members of the patrilineage) acquired wealth which gave them a head start and a life-long advantage over women. The Igbo say that "a child who washes his hands clean deserves to eat with his elders" (Uchendu 1965: 19). But at birth some children were given water and some were not.

WOMEN'S POLITICAL INSTITUTIONS

Since political authority was diffuse, the settling of disputes, discussions about how to improve the village or its market, or any other problems of general concern were brought up at various gatherings such as funerals, meetings of kinsmen to discuss burial rituals, and the marketplace, gatherings whose ostensible purpose was not political discussion (Green [1947] 1964: 132-138; Meek ([1937] 1950): 125).

The women's base of political power lay in their own gatherings. Since Igbo society was patrilocal and villages were exogamous, adult women resident in a village would almost all be wives, and others were divorced or widowed "daughters of the village" who had returned home to live. Women generally attended age-set gatherings (*ogbo*) in their natal villages, performed various ritual functions, and helped to

167

settle disputes among their "brothers" (Green [1947] 1964: 217-232). But the gatherings which performed the major role in self-rule among women and which articulated women's interests *as opposed to* those of men were the village-wide gatherings of all adult women resident in a village which under colonialism came to be called *mikiri* or *mitiri* (from "meeting") (Leith-Ross 1939: 106-108).

Mikiri were held whenever there was a need (Green [1947] 1964: 178-216). In *mikiri* the same processes of discussion and consultation were used as in the village assembly. There were no official leaders, as in the village, women of wealth and generosity who could speak well took leading roles. Decisions appear often to have been announced informally by wives telling their husbands. If the need arose, spokeswomen—to contact the men, or women in other villages—were chosen through general discussion. If the announcement of decisions and persuasion were not sufficient for their implementation, women could take direct action to enforce their decisions and protect their interests (Green [1947] 1964:180; Leith-Ross 1939:106-107).

Mikiri provided women with a forum in which to develop their political talents among a more egalitarian group than the village assembly. In *mikiri*, women could discuss their particular interests as traders, farmers, wives, and mothers. These interests often were opposed to those of the men, and where individually women couldn't compete with men, collectively they could often hold their own.

One of the *mikiri's* most important functions was that of a market association to promote and regulate the major activity of women: trading. At these discussions prices were set, rules established about market attendance, and fines fixed for those who violated the rules or who didn't contribute to market rituals. Rules were also made which applied to men. For instance, rowdy behavior on the part of young men was forbidden. Husbands and elders were asked to control the young men. If their requests were ignored, the women would handle the matter by a boycott or a strike to force the men to police themselves or they might decide to "sit on" the individual offender (Harris 1940: 146-147).

"Sitting on a man" or a woman, boycotts, and strikes were the women's main weapons. To "sit on" or "make war on" a man involved

168

gathering at his compound, sometimes late at night, dancing, singing scurrilous songs which detailed the women's grievances against him and often called his manhood into question, banging on his hut with the pestles women used for pounding yams, and perhaps demolishing his hut or plastering it with mud and roughing him up a bit. A man might be sanctioned in this way for mistreating his wife, for violating the women's market rules, or for letting his cows eat the women's crops. The women would stay at his hut throughout the day, and late into the night, if necessary, until he repented and promised to mend his ways (Green [1947] 1964:196-197; Harris 1940:146-148; Leith-Ross 1939: 109). Although this could hardly have been a pleasant experience for the offending man, it was considered legitimate and no man would consider intervening.

In tackling men as a group, women used boycotts and strikes. Harris (1940: 146-147) describes a case in which, after repeated requests by the women for the paths to the market to be cleared (a male responsibility), all the women refused to cook for their husbands until the request was carried out. For this boycott to be effective, *all* women had to co-operate so that men could not go and eat with their brothers. Another time the men of a village decided that the women should stop trading at the more distant markets from which they did not return until late at night because the men feared that the women were having sexual relations with men in those towns. The women, however, refused to comply since opportunity to buy in one market and sell in another was basic to profit making. Threats of collective retaliation were enough to make the men capitulate.

As farmers, women's interests conflicted with those of the men as owners of much of the larger livestock—cows, pigs, goats, and sheep. The men's crop, yams, had a short season and was then dug up and stored, after which the men tended to be careless about keeping their livestock out of the women's crops. Green ([1947] 1964: 210-211) reports a case in which the women of a village swore an oath that if any woman killed a cow or other domestic animal on her farm the others would stand by her.

A woman could also bring complaints about her husband to the *mikiri*. If most of the women agreed that the husband was at fault, they would collectively support her. They might send spokeswomen to tell the husband to apologize and to give her a present, and if he was recalcitrant they might "sit on" him. They might also act to protect a right of wives. Harris (1940: 146-147) describes a case of women's solidarity to maintain sexual freedom:

> *The men . . . were very angry because their wives were openly having relations with their lovers. The men . . . met and passed a law to the effect that every woman . . . should renounce her lover and present a goat to her husband as a token of repentance . . . . The women held . . . secret meetings and, a few mornings later, they went to a neighboring [village], leaving all but suckling children behind them . . . . [The men] endured it for a day and a half and then they went to the women and begged their return . . . . [T he men gave [the women] one goat and apologized informally and formally.*

Thus through *mikiri* women acted to force a resolution of their individual and collective grievances.

COLONIAL PENETRATION

Into this system of diffuse authority, fluid and informal leadership, shared rights of enforcement, and a more or less stable balance of male and female power, the British tried to introduce ideas of native administration derived from colonial experience with chiefs and emirs in northern Nigeria. Southern Nigeria was declared a protectorate in 1900, but it was ten years before the conquest was effective. As colonial power was established in what the British perceived as a situation of "ordered anarchy," Igboland was divided into Native Court Areas which violated the autonomy of villages by lumping many unrelated villages into each Court Area. British District Officers were to preside over the courts, but were not always present as there were more courts than officers. The Igbo membership was formed by choosing from each village a "representative" who was given a warrant of office. These Warrant Chiefs were also constituted the Native Authority. They were required to see that the orders of the District Officers were executed in their own villages and were the only link between the colonial power and the people (Forde n.d.: 9-13).

It was a violation of Igbo concept to have one man represent the village in the first place and more of a violation that he should give orders to everyone else. The people obeyed the Warrant Chief when they had to, since British power backed him up. In some places Warrant Chiefs were lineage heads or wealthy men who were already leaders in the village. But in many places they were simply ambitious, opportunistic young men who put themselves forward as friends of the conquerors. Even the relatively less corrupt Warrant Chief was still, more than anything else, an agent of the British (Anene 1966: 259; Forde n.d.: 9-13; Meek ([1937] 1950): 328-330).

The people avoided using Native Courts when they could do so. But Warrant Chiefs could force cases into the Native Courts and could fine people for infractions of rules. By having the ear of the British, the Warrant Chief could himself violate traditions and even British rules, and get away with it since his version would be believed (Forde n.d.: 12).

Women suffered particularly under the arbitrary rule of Warrant Chiefs, who were reported as having taken women to marry without conforming to the customary process, which included the woman's right to refuse a particular suitor. They also helped themselves to the women's agricultural produce and to their domestic animals (Onwuteaka 1965: 274).

Recommendations for reform of the system were made almost from its inception by junior officers in the field and by senior officers sent out from headquarters to investigate. But no real improvements were made (Gailey 1970: 66-74; Meek ([1937] 1950): 329-330).

ABA AND THE WOMEN'S WAR

The Native Administration in the years before 1929 took little account of either men's or women's political institutions. In 1929, women in southern Igboland became convinced that they were to be taxed by the British. This fear on top of their resentment of the Warrant Chiefs led to what the British called the Aba Riots, and the Igbo, the Women's War. The rebellion provides perhaps the most striking example of British blindness to the political institutions of Igbo women. The women, "invisible" to the British as they laid their plans for Native Administration, suddenly became highly visible for a few months, but as soon as they quieted down, they were once again ignored, and the reforms made in Native Administration took no account of them politically. [3]

In 1925 Igbo men paid taxes, although during the census count on which the tax was based the British had denied that there was to be any taxation. Taxes were collected without too much trouble. By 1929, the prices for palm products had fallen, however, and the taxes, set at 1925 levels, were an increasingly resented burden (Gailey 1970: 94-95; Meek ([1937] 1950): 330-331). In the midst of this resentment, an overzealous Assistant District Officer in Owerri Province decided to update the census registers by recounting households and household property, which belonged to women. Understandably, the women did not believe his assurances that new taxes were not to be invoked. They sent messages through the market and kinship networks to other villages and called a *mikiri* to decide what to do.

In the Oloko Native Court area of Owerri Province, the women decided that as long as only men were approached in a compound and asked for information, the women would do nothing. They wanted clear evidence that they were to be taxed before they acted (Gailey 1970: 107-108). If any woman was approached, she was to raise the alarm and they would meet to discuss retaliation.

On November 23, the agent of the Oloko Warrant Chief, Okugo, entered a compound and told a married woman, Nwanyeruwa, to count her goats and sheep. She retorted angrily, "Was your mother counted?" Thereupon "they closed, seizing each other by the throat" (Perham 1937: 207). Nwanyeruwa's report to the Oloko women convinced them that they were to be taxed. Messengers were sent to neighboring areas. Women streamed into Oloko from all over Owerri Province. They massed in protest at the district office and after several days of protest meetings succeeded in obtaining written assurances that they were not to be taxed, and in getting Okugo arrested. Subsequently he was tried and convicted of physically assaulting women and of spreading news likely to cause alarm. He was sentenced to two years' imprisonment (Gailey 1970: 108-113).

News of this victory spread rapidly through the market *mikiri* network, and women in sixteen Native Court areas attempted to get rid of their Warrant Chiefs, as well as the Native Administration itself. Tens of thousands of women became involved, generally using the same traditional tactics, though not with the same results as in Oloko. In each Native Court area, the women marched on Native Administration centers and demanded the Warrant Chiefs' caps of office and assurances that they would not be taxed. In some areas the District Officers assured the women to their satisfaction that they were not to be taxed and the women dispersed without further incident. But the British in general stood behind the Warrant Chiefs; at that point they interpreted the women's rebellion as motivated solely by fear of taxation, and Oloko was the only area in which a Warrant Chief had directly provoked the women's fears of taxation by counting their property.

Women in most areas did not get full satisfaction from the British, and, further, some British District Officers simply panicked when faced by masses of angry women and acted in ways which made negotiation impossible.

In most of the Native Court areas affected, women took matters into their own hands—they "sat on" Warrant Chiefs and burned Native Court buildings, and, in some cases, released prisoners from jail. Among the buildings burned were those at Aba, a major administrative center from which the British name for the rebellion is derived. Large numbers of police and soldiers, and on one occasion Boy Scouts, were called in to quell the "disturbances." On two occasions, clashes between the women and the troops left more than fifty women dead and fifty wounded from gunfire. The lives taken were those of women only —no men, Igbo or British, were even seriously injured. The cost of property damage—estimated at more than £60,000, was paid for by the Igbo, who were heavily taxed to pay for rebuilding the Native Administration centers (Esike 1965; Harris 1940: 143; Perham 1937: 209-212).

The rebellion lasted about a month. By late December, "order" was somewhat restored but sporadic disturbances and occupation by government troops continued into 1930. In all, the rebellion extended over an area of six thousand square miles, all of Owerri and Calabar Provinces, containing about two million people (Gailey 1970: 137; Perham 1937: 209-212).

The British generally saw the rebellion as "irrational" and called it a series of "riots." They discovered that the market network had been used to spread the rumor of taxation, but they did not inquire further into the concerted action of the women, the grassroots leadership, the agreement on demands, or even into the fact that thousands of women showed up at Native Administration centers dressed in the same unusual way: wearing short loincloths, their faces smeared with charcoal or ashes, their heads bound with young ferns, and in their hands carrying sticks wreathed with young palms (Harris 1940: 147-148; Meek ([1937] 1950): ix; Perham 1937: 207 ff.).

In exonerating the soldiers who fired on the women, a Commission of Enquiry spoke of the "savage passions" of the "mobs," and one military officer told the Commission that "he had never seen crowds in such a state of frenzy." Yet these "frenzied mobs" injured no one seriously, which the British found "surprising" (Perham 1937: 212-219).

It is not surprising if the Women's War is seen as the traditional practice of "sitting on a man," only on a larger scale. Decisions were made in *mikiri* to respond to a situation in which women were acutely wronged by the Warrant Chiefs' corruption and by the taxes they believed to be forthcoming. Spokeswomen were chosen to present their demands for the removal of the Warrant Chiefs and women followed their leadership, on several occasions sitting down to wait for negotiations or agreeing to disperse or to turn in Warrant Chiefs' caps (Perham 1937: 212 ff.). Traditional dress, rituals, and "weapons" for "sitting on" were used: the head wreathed with young ferns symbolized war, and sticks, bound with ferns or young palms, were used to invoke the powers of the female ancestors. 4 The women's behavior also followed traditional patterns: much noise, stamping, preposterous threats, and a general raucous atmosphere were all part of the institution of "sitting on a man." Destroying an offender's hut—in this case the Native Court buildings—was clearly within the bounds of this sanctioning process.

The Women's War was coordinated throughout the two provinces by information sent through the market *mikiri* network. Delegates travelled from one area to another and the costs were paid by donations from the women's market profits (Gailey 1970: 112). Traditional rules were followed in that the participants were women—only a few men were involved in the demonstrations—and leadership was clearly in the hands of women.

The absence of men from the riots does not indicate lack of support. Men generally approved, and only a few older men criticized the women for not being more respectful toward the government. It is reported that both men and women shared the mistaken belief that the women, having observed certain rituals, would not be fired upon. The men had no illusions of immunity for themselves, having vivid memories of the slaughter of Igbo men during the conquest (Anene 1966: 207-224; Esike 1965: 11; Meek ([1937] 1950): x; Perham 1937: 212 ff.). Finally, the name given the rebellion by the Igbo—the Women's War— indicates that the women saw themselves following their traditional sanctioning methods of "sitting on" or "making war on" a man.

Since the British failed to recognize the Women's War as a collective response to the abrogation of rights, they did not inquire into the kinds of structures the women had that prepared them for such action. They failed to ask, "How do the women make group decisions? How do they choose their leaders?" Since they saw only a "riot," they explained the fact that the women injured no one seriously as "luck," never even contemplating that perhaps the women's actions had traditional limits.

Because the women—and the men—regarded the inquiries as attempts to discover whom to punish, they did not volunteer any information about the women's organizations. But there is at least some question as to whether the British would have understood them if they had. The market network was discovered, but suggested no further lines of inquiry to the British. The majority of District Officers thought that the men organized the women's actions and were secretly directing them. The Bende District Officer and the Secretary of the Southern Province believed that there was a secret "Ogbo Society" which exercised control over women and was responsible for fomenting the rebellion (Gailey 1970: 130 ff.). And the women's demands that they did not want the Native Court to hear cases any longer and that all white men should go to their own country, or, at least, that women should serve on the Native Courts and one be appointed District Officer—demands in line with the power of women in traditional society—were ignored (Leith-Ross 1939: 165; Perham 1937: 165 ff.).

All these responses fall into a coherent pattern: *not* of purposeful discrimination against women with the intent of keeping them from playing their traditional political roles, but of a prevailing blindness to the possibility that women had *had* a significant role in traditional politics and should participate in the new system of local government. A few political officers were ". . . of the opinion that, if the balance of society is to be kept, the women's organizations should be encouraged alongside those of the men" (Perham 1937: 246). Some commissioners even recognized ". . . the remarkable character of organization and leadership which some of the women displayed" and recommended that ". . . more attention be paid to the political influence of women" (Afigbo 1967: 187). But these men were the exception; their views did not prevail. Even in the late 1930s when the investigations of Leith-Ross (1939) and Green ([1947] 1964) revealed the decreasing vitality of women's organizations under colonialism, the British still did not include women in the reformed Native Administration. When political officers warned that *young men* were being excluded, however, steps were taken to return their traditional political status (Meek ([1937] 1950): 336).

"REFORMS" AND WOMEN'S LOSS OF POWER

In 1933 reforms were enacted to redress many Igbo grievances against the Native Administration. The number of Native Court Areas was greatly increased and their boundaries arranged to conform roughly to traditional divisions. Warrant Chiefs were replaced by "massed benches" —allowing large numbers of judges to sit at one time. In most cases it was left up to the villages to decide whom and how many to send (Perham 1937: 365 ff.). This benefitted the women by eliminating the corruption of the Warrant Chiefs, and it made their persons and property more secure. But it provided no outlet for collective action, their real base of power.

As in the village assembly, the women could not compete with the men for leadership in the reformed Native Administration because as individuals they lacked the resources of the men (Meek ([1937] 1950): 203). In the various studies done on the Igbo in the 1930s, there is only one report of a woman being sent to the Native Court and her patrilineage had put up the money for her to take her titles. [5]

176

Since the reformed Native Administration actually took over many functions of the village assemblies, women's political participation was seriously affected. Discussions on policy no longer included any adult who wished to take part but only members of the Native Courts. Men who were not members were also excluded, but men's interests and point of view were represented, and, at one time or another, many men had some chance to become members; very few women ever did (Leith-Ross 1939: 171-172; Lord Hailey [1950/53] 1951: 160-165).

The political participation and power of women had depended on the diffuseness of political power and authority within Igbo society. In attempting to create specialized political institutions on the western model with participation on the basis of individual achievement, the British created a system in which there was no place for group solidarity, no place for what thereby became extralegal or simply illegal forms of group coercion, and thus very little place for women.

The British reforms undermined and weakened the power of the women by removing many political functions from *mikiri* and from village assemblies. In 1901 the British had declared all jural institutions except the Native Courts illegitimate, but it was only in the years following the 1933 reforms that Native Administration local government became effective enough to make that declaration meaningful. When this happened, the *mikiri* lost vitality, although what has happened to them since has not been reported in detail (Leith-Ross 1939: 110, 163, 214). The reports that do exist mention the functioning of market women's organizations but only as pressure groups for narrow economic interest and women's participation in Igbo unions as very low in two towns (Bretton 1966: 61; Smock 1971: 65, 137).

The British also weakened women's power by outlawing self-help—the use of force by individuals or groups to protect their own interests by punishing wrongdoers. This action—in accord with the idea that only the state may legitimately use force—made "sitting on" anyone illegal, thereby depriving women of one of their best weapons to protect wives from husbands, markets from rowdies, or coco yams from cows (Leith-Ross 1939: 109).

The British didn't know, of course, that they were banning "sitting on a man;" they were simply banning the "illegitimate" use of force. In

177

theory, this didn't hurt the women, as wife-beaters, rowdies, and owners of marauding cows could be taken to court. But courts were expensive, and the men who sat in them were likely to have different views from the women's on wife-beating, market "fun," and men's cows. By interfering with the traditional balance of power, the British effectively eliminated the women's ability to protect their own interests and made them dependent upon men for protection against men.

Since the British did not understand this, they did nothing to help women develop new ways of protecting their interests within the political system. (What the women *did* do to try to protect their interests in this situation should be a fruitful subject for study.) What women did *not* do was to participate to any significant extent in local government or, much later, in national government, and a large part of the responsibility must rest on the British, who removed legitimacy from women's traditional political institutions and did nothing to help women move into modern political institutions.

MISSIONARY INFLUENCE

The effect of the colonial administration was reinforced by the missionaries and mission schools. Christian missions were established in Igboland in the late 19th century. They had few converts at first, but their influence by the 1930s was considered significant, generally among the young. [6] A majority of Igbo eventually "became Christians"—they had to profess Christianity in order to attend mission schools, and education was highly valued. But regardless of how nominal their membership was, they had to obey the rules to remain in good standing, and one rule was to avoid "pagan" rituals. Women were discouraged from attending *mikiri* where traditional rituals were performed or money collected for the rituals, which in effect meant all *mikiri* (Ajayi 1965: 108-109; Leith-Ross 1939: 110).

Probably more significant, since *mikiri* were in the process of losing some of their political functions anyway, was mission education. English and western education came to be seen as increasingly necessary for political leadership—needed to deal with the British and their law—and women had less access to this new knowledge than men. Boys were more often sent to school, for a variety of reasons generally related to their favored position in the patrilineage (Leith-Ross 1939: 133, 196-197, 316). But even when girls did go, they tended not to receive the same type of education. In mission schools, and increasingly in special "training homes" which dispensed with most academic courses, the girls were taught European domestic skills and the Bible, often in the vernacular. The missionaries' avowed purpose in educating girls was to train them to be Christian wives and mothers, not for jobs or for citizenship.[7] Missionaries were not necessarily against women's participation in politics—clergy in England, as in America, could be found supporting women's suffrage. But in Africa their concern was the church, and for the church they needed Christian families. Therefore, Christian wives and mothers, not female political leaders, was the missions' aim. As Mary Slessor, the influential Calabar missionary, said: "God-like motherhood is the finest sphere for women, and the way to the redemption of the world" (Livingstone 1916: 328).

VICTORIANISM AND WOMEN'S INVISIBILITY

The missionaries' beliefs about woman's natural and proper role being that of a Christian helpmate, and the administration's refusal to take the Igbo women seriously when they demanded political participation, are understandable in light of the colonialists having been socialized in a society dominated by Victorian values. It was during Queen Victoria's reign that the woman's-place-is-in-the-home ideology hardened into its most recent highly rigid form (Smith 1970: 58-76; Stenton 1957: 312-344). Although attacked by feminists, it remained the dominant mode of thought through that part of the colonial period discussed here; and it is, in fact, far from dead today, when a woman's primary identity is most often seen as that of wife and mother even when she works forty hours a week outside the home (Figes 1970; Hartley 1959).

We are concerned here primarily with the Victorian view of women and politics which produced the expectation that men would be active in politics, but women would not. The ideal of Victorian womanhood— attainable, of course, by only the middle class, but widely believed in throughout society—was of a sensitive, morally superior being who was the hearthside guardian of Christian virtues and sentiments absent in the outside world. Her mind was not strong enough for the appropriately masculine subjects: science, business, and politics.[8] A woman

179

who showed talent in these areas did not challenge any ideas about typical women: the exceptional woman simply "had the brain of a man," as Sir George Goldie said of Mary Kingsley. [9]

A thorough investigation of the diaries, journals, reports, and letters of colonial officers and missionaries would be needed to prove that most of them held these Victorian values. But preliminary reading of biographies, autobiographies, journals and "reminiscences," and the evidence of their own statements about Igbo women at the time of the Women's War, strongly suggest the plausibility of the hypothesis that they were deflected from any attempt to discover and protect Igbo women's political role by their assumption that politics isn't a proper, normal place for women. [10]

When Igbo women with their Women's War forced the colonial administrators to recognize their presence, their brief "visibility" was insufficient to shake those assumptions. Their behavior was simply seen as aberrant. When they returned to "normal," they were once again invisible. Although there was a feminist movement in England during that time, it had not successfully challenged basic ideas about women nor made the absence of women from public life seem to be a problem which required remedy. The movement had not succeeded in creating a feminist consciousness in any but a few "deviants," and such a consciousness is far from widespread today; for to have a feminist consciousness means that one *notices* the "invisibility" of women. One *wonders* where the women are—in life and in print.

Understanding the assumptions about women's roles prevalent in Victorian society—and still common today—helps to explain how the introduction of supposedly modern political structures and values could reduce rather than expand the political lives of Igbo women. As long as politics is presumed to be a male realm, no one wonders where the women went. The loss of Igbo women's political institutions—in life and in print—shows the need for more western scholars to develop enough of a feminist consciousness to start wondering.

NOTES

Acknowledgments. An earlier version of this paper was presented at the Annual Meeting of The African Studies Association, Denver, Colorado, November, 1971.

[1] The Igbo-speaking peoples are heterogeneous and can only be termed a "tribe" on the basis of a common language and a contiguous territory. They were the dominant group in southeastern Nigeria during the colonial period numbering more than three million, according to the 1931 census. The Igbo in Owerri and Calabar, the two southernmost provinces, were relatively homogeneous politically, and it is their political institutions which are discussed here. Studies in depth were done of the Igbo only in the 1930s, but traditional political institutions survived "underneath" the native administration, although weakened more in some areas than in others. There were also many informants who remembered life in the precolonial days. The picture of Igbo society drawn here is based on reports by two Englishwomen, Leith-Ross (1939) and Green ([1947] 1964), who had a particular interest in Igbo women; the work of a government anthropological officer, C.K. Meek ([1937] 1950); a brief report by Harris (1940); and the work of educated Igbo describing their own society (Onwuteaka 1965; Uchendu 1965).

[2] The sources for this description are Uchendu (1965) and personal conversations with an Igbo born in Umu-Domi village of Onicha clan in Afikpo division who, however, went to mission schools from the age of seven and speaks Union Igbo rather than his village dialect.

[3] Information on the Women's War is derived mainly from Gailey (1970) and Perham (1937, 1956, 1960), who based their descriptions on

the reports of the two Commissions of Enquiry, issued as Sessional Papers of the Nigerian Legislative Council, Number 12 and 28 of 1930, and the Minutes of Evidence issued with the latter. Gailey (1970) also used the early 1930s Intelligence Reports of political officers. Meek ([1937] 1950) and Afigbo (1967) also provide quotations from the reports, which were not, unfortunately, available to me in full.

4 Harris (1940: 143-145) reports a curse sworn by the women on the pestles: "It is I who gave birth to you. It is I who cook for you to eat. This is the pestle I use to pound yams and coco yams for you to eat. May you soon die!"

5 She was divorced and had to remain unmarried as a condition of her family's paying for her title, as they wanted to be sure to get their investment back when future initiates paid their fees to the established members. If she remarried, her husband's family, and not her own, would inherit her property (Meek [1937] 1950: 158-159).

6 See Leith-Ross (1939: 109-118) and Meek ([1937] 1950: xv). Maxwell (1927: 150-152) states that by 1925 there were twenty-six mission stations and sixty-three missionaries (twelve of them missionary wives) in Igboland. The earliest station was established in 1857, but all but three were founded after 1900. Fifteen mission stations and thirty missionaries were among Igbo in Owerri and Calabar Provinces.

7 According to Leith-Ross (1939: 189-190), in the ". . . girls' training homes . . . the scholastic education given was limited, in some of the smaller homes opened at a later date almost negligible, but the domestic training and the general civilizing effect were good." Evidence of these views among missionaries can be found in Ajayi (1965: 142-144), Basden (1927: 13, 16, 33, 55, 77, 86), Bulifant (1950: 163 and pass.), Livingstone (1916: iii-vi), and Maxwell (1927: 55, 118).

8 See Houghton (1957: 349-353). Numerous studies of Victorian and post-Victorian ideas about women and politics describe these patterns. In addition to Houghton (1957), Smith (1970), and Stenton (1957), see, for example, Amundsen (1971), Bernard (1971), Mill and Mill (1970), Vicinus (1972), and Woodham-Smith (1951). It was not until 1929 that all English women could vote; women over thirty who met restrictive property qualifications received the vote in 1918.

9 See Stephen Gwynn, *The Life of Mary Kingsley* (1932: 252). Mary Kingsley along with other elite female "exceptions" like Flora Shaw Lugard and Margery Perham, all of whom influenced African colonial policy, held the same values as men, at least in regard to

women's roles. They did not expect ordinary women to have political power any more than the men did, and they showed no particular concern for African women.

10 See, for nonmissionary examples, Anene (1966: 222-234), Crocker (1936), Kingsley (1897, 1899), Meek ([1937] 1950), Perham (1937), and Wood (1960).

REFERENCES CITED

Afigbo, A.E.
   1967   *Review of* Igbo Village Affairs. By Margaret M. Green. Journal of the Historical Society of Nigeria 4(1): 186-190.
Ajayi, J.F. Ade
   1965   Christian Missions in Nigeria, 1841-1891: The Making of a New Elite. Evanston, Illinois: Northwestern University Press.
Amundsen, Kirsten
   1971   The Silenced Majority: Women and American Democracy. Englewood Cliffs, New Jersey: Prentice-Hall.
Anene, Joseph C.
   1966   Southern Nigeria in Transition, 1885-1906: Theory and Practice in a Colonial Protectorate. Cambridge: Cambridge University Press.
Basden, George T.
   1927   Edith Warner of the Niger, the Story of Thirty-three Years of Zealous and Courageous Work amongst Ibo Girls and Women. London: Seeley, Service.
Bernard, Jessie S.
   1971   Women and the Public Interest: An Essay on Policy and Protest. Chicago: Aldine-Atherton.
Bretton, Henry L.
   1966   Political Influence in Southern Nigeria. *In* Africa: The Primacy of Politics. Herbert J. Spiro, ed. Pp. 49-84. New York: Random House.
Bulifant, Josephine C.
   1950   Forty Years in the African Bush. Grand Rapids, Michigan: Zondervan Publishing House.

Crocker, Walter R.
   1936   Nigeria: A Critique of British Colonial Administration. London: Allen and Unwin.
Esike, S.O.
   1965   The Aba Riots of 1929. African Historian 1(3): 7-13.
Figes, Eva
   1970   Patriarchal Attitudes. New York: Stein and Day.
Forde, C. Daryll
   n.d.   Justice and Judgment among the Southern Ibo under Colonial Rule. Unpublished manuscript prepared for Interdisciplinary Colloquium in African Studies, University of California, Los Angeles.
Forde, C. Daryll, and G.I. Jones
   1950   The Ibo-and-Ibibio-Speaking Peoples of South-Eastern Nigeria. London: Oxford University Press, for the International African Institute.
Gailey, Harry A.
   1970   The Road to Aba: A Study of British Administrative Policy in Eastern Nigeria. New York: New York University Press.
Green, Margaret M.
   1947   Igbo Village Affairs, Chiefly with Reference to the Village of Umueke Agbaja. London: Sidgwick and Jackson. (Reprinted New York: Frederick A. Praeger, 1964.)
Gwynn, Stephen L.
   1932   The Life of Mary Kingsley. London: Macmillan.
Hailey, Baron William Malcolm
   1950/53   Native Administration in the British African Territories. Part 3, 1951, West Africa: Nigeria, Gold Coast, Sierra Leone, Gambia. London: Her Majesty's Stationary Office.
Harris, Jack
   1940   The Position of Women in a Nigerian Society. Transactions of the New York Academy of Sciences, Series II, Vol. 2., No. 5. Pp. 141-148. New York: New York Academy of Sciences.
Hartley, Ruth E.
   1959   Children's Concepts of Male and Female Roles. Merrill-Palmer Quarterly 6(2): 83-91.
Houghton, Walter E.
   1957   The Victorian Frame of Mind, 1830-1870. New Haven: Yale University Press, for Wellesley College.

Kingsley, Mary H.
1897 Travels in West Africa, Congo Francais, Corisco and Cameroons. London: Macmillan.
1899 West African Studies. London: Macmillan.
Leith-Ross, Sylvia
1939 African Women: A Study of the Ibo of Nigeria. London: Faber and Faber.
Livingstone, William P.
1916 Mary Slessor of Calabar, Pioneer Missionary. London: Hodder and Stoughton.
Maxwell, John L.
1927 Nigeria: The Land, the People and the Christian Progress. London: World Dominion Press.
Meek, Charles K.
1937 Law and Authority in a Nigerian Tribe: A Study in Indirect Rule. London: Oxford University Press. (Reprinted London: Oxford University Press, 1950.)
Mill, John Stuart, and Harriett Taylor Mill
1970 Essays on Sex Equality. Alice S. Rossi, ed. Chicago: University of Chicago Press.
Onwuteaka, V.C.
1965 The Aba Riot of 1929 and its Relation to the System of Indirect Rule. The Nigerian Journal of Economic and Social Studies 7(3): 273-282.
Perham, Margery F.
1937 Native Administration in Nigeria. London: Oxford University Press.
1956 Lugard: The Years of Adventure, 1858-1898. Part 1. London: Collins.
1960 Lugard: The Years of Authority, 1898-1945. Part 2. London: Collins.
Smith, Page
1970 Daughters of the Promised Land: Women in American History. Boston: Little, Brown.
Smock, Audrey C.
1971 Ibo Politics: The Role of Ethnic Unions in Eastern Nigeria. Cambridge: Harvard University Press.
Spiro, Herbert J., ed.
1966 Africa: The Primacy of Politics. New York: Random House.

Stenton, Doris M.
1957 The English Woman in History. London: Allen and Unwin.
Uchendu, Victor C.
1965 The Igbo of Southeast Nigeria. New York: Holt, Rinehart and Winston.
Vicinus, Martha, ed.
1972 Suffer and Be Still: Women in the Victorian Age. Bloomington: Indiana University Press.
Wood, A.H. St. John
1960 Nigeria: Fifty Years of Political Development among the Ibos. *In* From Tribal Rule to Modern Government. Raymond Apthorpe, ed. Pp. 121-136. Lusaka, Northern Rhodesia: Rhodes-Livingstone Institute for Social Research.
Woodham-Smith, Cecil B.
1951 Florence Nightingale, 1820-1910. New York: McGraw Hill.

SUGGESTIONS FOR FURTHER READING

Hoffer, Carol P.
1972 Mende and Sherbro Women in High Office. Canadian Journal of African Studies 6(2): 151-164.
Describes the structure of chiefships in Sierra Leone, Africa that encouraged the rise of women to high office. In these societies femininity is an important asset for women leaders, contrary to western notions of the political liabilities of womanhood.
Lebeuf, Annie M.D.
1963 The Role of Women in the Political Organization of African Societies. *In* Women of Tropical Africa. Denise Paulme, ed. H.M. Wright, trans. Pp. 93-119. London: Routledge and Kegan Paul.
Reviews the wide range of women's participation in traditional political institutions of centralized and tribal societies in Central and South Africa.

Lynn, Naomi B.
   1979   American Women and the Political Process. *In* Women:
   A Feminist Perspective. Jo Freeman, ed. Pp. 404-429. 2nd ed.
   Palo Alto, California: Mayfield.
   A general historical overview of American women's voting
   patterns, political participation, office holding, and administrative positions in government.
Nelson, Cynthia
   1974   Public and Private Politics: Women in the Middle Eastern
   World. American Ethnologist 1: 551-563.
   Examines the problem of conceptualizing politics as the socially
   important public domain of men. Criticizes anthropological
   studies of women and power in Middle Eastern societies.
Rogers, Susan Carol
   1975   Female Forms of Power and the Myth of Male Dominance: A Model of Female/Male Interaction in Peasant Society.
   American Ethnologist 2: 727-756.
   Argues that androcentric perspectives have biased anthropological studies of politics by emphasizing the formal aspects of
   political roles, which are often held by men. The author cites
   evidence from the literature and her research in rural France to
   show that peasant women are important political actors within
   their own homes and in the community at large.

GOING HOME TO MOTHER: TRADITIONAL MARRIAGE AMONG THE IRIGWE OF BENUE-PLATEAU STATE, NIGERIA

Walter H. Sangree

The Irigwe live about twenty miles west of the town of Jos and Bukuru in euphorbia-enclosed, extended-family compounds that are clustered closely together to form a belt of almost continuous settlement running north and south for about four miles just above the western escarpment of the Jos Plateau. Numbering around 17,000, they speak a distinctive Niger-Congo language, one not understood by any other group to my knowledge but clearly closely related to those of several nonadjacent peoples to the west. The Irigwe gain their subsistance primarily from a traditional system of hoe agriculture. Each extended family compound has its own proximate seedling beds and garden patches, but most of the farming is done on scattered outlying fields as much as six or seven miles away from the settled area.

Since forceful British intervention in 1905, the Irigwe have refrained from hunting the heads of enemies and have come to accept the imposition of a centralized tribal administration. Hunting and the preservation of the skulls of certain categories of big game, however, remain passionately pursued, dry-season activities of great social and religious significance.

By 1965 about three percent of the Irigwe had forsaken their traditional religious practices for Christianity. Perhaps an equal number, mostly

Reprinted by permission of the author and the American Anthropological Association from *American Anthropologist* 71(6):1046-1057, 1969.

Christians, had received some formal schooling of British type, but not more than two or three dozen had by 1965 gone on to complete their secondary school education. It had become common practice throughout Irigwe, however, for most of the women and girls to walk to Jos or Bukuru several times a year to sell and buy at the markets there. Many younger men seek occasional employment as laborers in these towns or in the nearby mine fields for several weeks after the farming season is over to earn money to pay the annual poll tax and to buy clothing, kerosine lamps, and the like. In spite of this regular contact with modern urban centers, traditional patterns of lineage and family activities still largely prevail in the ritual, economic, and, to a lesser extent, political spheres among probably 95 percent of the population. I shall limit myself in this paper to discussing the traditionalist illiterate majority as I found them in 1963-65.

The Irigwe repeatedly utilize the idiom of generation and sex (i.e., parent-child and male-female) to characterize and classify aspects of their world, both social and geographical. There are twenty-four agnatically based Irigwe subdivisions or "sections," as the Irigwe call them, each with its own shrine house, rather womb-like in shape, called a *branyi*. Each Irigwe section regards its *branyi* as sacred and as its center of strength and regeneration, and skulls and other relics of warfare and hunting are preserved therein. Each *branyi* is presided over by a senior man of the section's seniormost lineage. The twenty-four sections are grouped into two geographically discrete divisions. Rigwe (Kwon District), the "parent" division, which lies south of the River Ngell, has ten sections, which together control a major portion of the important tribal ritual. Nyango (Miango District), the "child" division, with fourteen sections, is north of the Ngell. In addition sections are regarded as either "male" or "female." There are seven male and two female sections in the parent division, plus one section that is probably regarded as male (but I remain uncertain about this section). Then there are nine male and four female sections in the child division, plus one section that cannot be clearly classified as either. Each section has its ritual specialization of significance to the entire tribe. Female sections share the responsibility for most of the ritual concerning wet-season planting and crop growth, whereas male sections direct the ritual regulating hunting and most other dry-season activities. Sections in the parent division are felt, with one exception, to have ritual status superior to that of sections in the child division. This one exception is the section called *Rae* ("Red Earth"), which is the most senior female section and is situated in the child division.

Most sections in the parent division are regarded as having diverse agnatic origins. The male sections in the parent division are ritually ranked and specialized according to their putative order of arrival in Irigwe. The most senior male section presides over the most important dry-season and planting rituals for the entire tribe. The more junior sections in the parent division have their own relatively minor ritual specializations, which are for the most part concerned with dry-season activity. The three female sections in the parent division are all of essentially equal ritual status; one carries out planting ritual for one of the important grain crops; a second has ritual to control the lightning; the specialty of the third remains unclear to me.

Rae ("Red Earth"), the most senior female section as noted above, is situated in the child division. The Red Earth section presides over the principal farming and first-fruits ritual for all of Irigwe. Elders of *Rae* recount the following Irigwe origin myth:

> *Long ago, Weze, the original Red Earth ancestor, descended from the sun to a spot in the child division (Nyango). A descendant of his first brought forth fire from a hole in the rock by the river that separates the parent and child divisions. A later descendent moved south of the river to what is now the parent division area (Rigwe) and met a man named Audu wandering by. He bore the name Audu, which is an Irigwe nick- name for Jarawa, because he had come for the Jarawa tribal group situated east of Irigwe. The Red Earth people invited Audu to live with them, and he married and became the original ancestor of the most senior Irigwe male section. Audu came bringing as a gift the fruit of the Inhwiae tree [I was unable to identify this tree botanically], and the Irigwe section he founded is known as Nuhwie in remembrance of this gift. At that time Audu had no crops, his people eating only game, fruits, and berries. The Red Earth people gave Audu crops and asked him to distribute them among his people. They agreed to respect each other as mother*

190

and son and as man and woman (which also means husband and wife in the Irigwe language). Then, combining their hunting and gathering and farming skills, they together founded the Irigwe tribe.

With the passing of time the tribe grew to have quite a few sections, some arising from the incorporation of immigrant groups and others being formed by the splitting off of patrilineages from already established Irigwe sections. Then a great migration took place. A man from a junior male section led members of his own lineage, together with offshoots of other male and female sections, to the north side of the river where they formed a new "son" section not far from where the original Red Earth ancestor had descended from the sun. Very soon afterwards the entire Red Earth section followed this new son section to the new settlement. Several other lineages from male and female sections came later. The descendants of all these migrants now comprise Nyango, the child division of Irigwe.

With the exception of the Red Earth section and two offshoot sections from it, each section of the child division recognizes its origin from a "parent" section in the parent division and serves as its ritual subordinate. Thus a section in the child division is regarded as "female" if it is derived from a female parent section and as "male" if it is derived from a male parent section. It is noteworthy that the elders of Nuhwie, the most senior male section, do not accept the Red Earth origin myth given above and dispute the seniority of the Red Earth section. They assert that Nuhwie was the first Irigwe section and insist that the Red Earth section is merely their daughter (a rather ungrateful daughter at that) on whom they have bestowed female ritual leadership through the magnanimity of their paternal affection.

Most Irigwe sections are subdivided into several exogamous lineages (*énūcíe*). Although extended family compounds of any particular lineage and section tend to be spatially clustered, there are many cases of compounds that adjoin or are surrounded by compounds of other lineages or even other sections. Thus it is not possible to identify either a compound's lineage or section affiliation solely by its location. Sections vary greatly in size; the largest comprises ninety-nine separate extended family compounds, and the smallest has only two. A compound usually has about 35 members, but they too vary greatly in size from as few as 3 people to over 150.

Irigwe hunt all during the dry season, principally in groups organized on a section basis. The highlight of the hunting season is a three day tribal hunt and celebration (*Zaraci*) at the end of the dry season presided over by Nuhwie, the most senior male section. It is in the organization and ceremonial arrangements of this big hunt that one sees the parent and child divisions most explicitly counterposed. The Irigwe's passion for hunting finds its principal ceremonial expression, however, after this great hunt, early in the rains when planting is just beginning. At this time each section in turn holds a three-day ceremonial to purify and praise its hunters who during the preceeding season have brought heads of big game (and formerly human enemies) to their *branyi*. Only heads of certain dangerous game are preserved as relics, thereby qualifying their takers as *šüa* (''heroes'') to be thus honored. In recent decades big game has grown very scarce, and in several instances some of the small sections, tired of waiting many years for a member to bag the requisite game before holding a *šüa* ceremonial have paired off with other sections to hold the ceremonial jointly, thus making bigger and more frequent ceremonies possible for each.

After the climax of the *šüa* ceremonial when the heroes are annointed and ritually cleansed while seated before the *branyi*, senior representatives of every section of the tribe sit down to a feast, and girls of the host section dance and sing songs of praise, honoring past and present heroes. Although the food and beer are supplied by the host section, representatives from guest female sections help make the final feast preparations, and elders from guest male sections actually distribute the food and drink. Then, as they eat and drink, a spokesman from each section in turn comments on the skulls and their takers. As the speeches drag on and the beer flows, verbal skirmishes and sometimes fisticuffs arise over slights or departures from protocol. Finally peace and reconciliation is sought and usually achieved with shouted admonitions that all the sections are one family and that man and wife and parents and children should help and support each other. Anyhow, by that time the elders are too full of beer to care very much, and the younger men and women, girls and youths, are dancing around the big drum (*bi*), or are off trysting. Thus we come at last to the principal focus of this paper, the Irigwe marriage system. During the dry season men bend their sporting energy to chasing down game; but the beginning of the planting season, when the rains are just starting, is the time above all times for making off with other men's wives.

The published material on the Irigwe (Gunn 1953:100), and also the mimeographed administrative reports, reiterate three aspects of Irigwe social life, namely, the "looseness" of the marriage system, the high incidence of spirit possession among the women, and the large number of Irigwe female "native doctors." My own field research in Irigwe, carried out between September 1963 and June 1965, generally confirms these observations. I am led, however, to characterize the rather unusual Irigwe marriage system as mobile rather than loose. Also I have reason to believe that this mobility of marriage and the high incidence of both women's possession and woman "native doctors" are closely interrelated phenomena.

There are two basic types of Irigwe marriage. One type, arranged by the parents of the couple prior to their adolescence, is known by the men as *fo'wena*, "taking a girl," and by the women as *nynira*, "a from-to." The other type, initiated usually by the couple themselves, is called *fo mbru*, "taking a woman or wife" by the men and *vwevwe*, "sing-sing" by the women. I shall simply call the former type "primary marriage" since it usually starts a couple's conjugal career, and the latter "secondary marriage" (Smith 1953:323).

Arrangements for primary marriage are initiated by the boy's family, usually when he is still very young or even an infant. The father of the young son may approach a friend who has a daughter about the same age and ask if he and the girl's mother are willing for the girl to become engaged to his son (*à kwē wéna*, "they become engaged"). If they both give their assent the boy's father sends the girl's family a white hen for her mother and an iron bracelet (*angrá*) for the girl. Occasionally a new calabash is presented instead of the white hen, and in recent years the substitution of a small cash payment has been coming into favor. Sometimes a boy's mother or grandmother may initiate the marriage plans. I know one case where the boy's paternal grandmother arranged for his engagement to the granddaughter of one of her co-wives (a granddaughter by one of the co-wife's other husbands, it should be noted). A

193

boy's family may contract more than one primary marriage for him, but usually only one such arrangement is made for each son. Although a girl is never engaged for primary marriage to more than one boy, it is common (and held to her credit) for a popular girl as she reaches puberty to become engaged for secondary marriages to several other men even prior to the consummation of her primary marriage.

When the boy is old and strong enough to do a good day's hoeing in the fields, and when the girl's breasts are beginning to grow, the boy's father visits the girl's father and is shown fields for his son to prepare for planting. Early the next planting season the boy with the help of perhaps a dozen of his lineage brothers does about twenty-four mandays of work on the fields assigned by his father-in-law-elect. A great deal of the annual preplanting field preparation is carried out by these work bees of youths and young men of the same lineage helping with the bride service of their younger members.

Usually after three or four years of farm service, but never before the girl is well into puberty, the marriage is consummated by her taking up residence with her espoused in his father's compound. Sometimes the marriage is consummated before the boy has reached puberty; I am well acquainted with two such cases. After this no further work is due the father-in-law. Since primary marriages are characteristically arranged between families that are distant agnates or between families linked by friendship (*ne uri*) it is important to the girl's patrikin that the marriage be consummated without mishap. An Irigwe girl after she reaches puberty may feel inclined to defy parental authority and go to live with one of her secondary marriage suitors even before she has consummated her primary marriage (secondary suitors have inevitably attained puberty); thus, a prudent father hesitates to postpone his daughter's primary marriage much after she reaches puberty even though additional years of farm labor are at stake. A girl's mother, on the other hand, free from many of her husband's pressures of family or friendship, may counsel her to drag her feet a bit and postpone leaving home at least until her primary fiancé has grown up a bit. A mother's control over her children, both male and female, is reinforced by the Irigwe belief that the matrikin, that is the mother and her patrilineage (*ne tekwe*), are the best source of aid in case of illness or any other mishap, and a child learns early to heed the counsel of his mother and her agnates. Thus although the mother lacks formalized rights of control in the matter, it is often she who decides when the daughter should take up residence with her primary husband; indeed, a substantial gift in cash or kind from the boy's family to the mother usually shortly precedes a girl's consummating her primary marriage. It should be noted that in those cases where a girl take matters into her own hands and goes to a secondary suitor first, she inevitably feels obligated minimally to fulfill her parents' primary marriage commitments for her by later taking up residence with her primary husband for at least several weeks.

The initiative in arranging a secondary marriage, in contrast to primary marriage, is taken by the suitor himself. He generally uses a male friend as a go-between when first sounding out a girl (or woman), and she may either refuse or encourage his overtures. If encouraged the suitor must seek out her father (or marriage guardian) to ask for his consent. The father usually agrees after checking with his daughter unless he finds the union would be prohibited by custom, that is unless it would violate an Irigwe rule of incest or exogamy.

Primary and secondary marriages are prohibited between lineage-mates, between cognates with a common great-grandparent, and between persons born in the same compound regardless of kinship. Marriages into one's mother's compound and marriages by a man (and by another man from his compound) with more than one daughter of a compound are also prohibited; also men from the same section may never marry the same woman so long as both men are alive; nor may a man marry a widow of his own lineage until she has first gone to marry a new husband of another lineage. The section is not an exogamous unit, and primary marriages in particular are often contracted between distant agnates as well as between other distant consanguines.

Secondary marriage suitors cannot be members of her living hubands' or husband-elect's sections. As Irigwe men put it, "You can take a girl (*'wena*) but never a wife (*mbru*) from your own section." In addition a man cannot take a wife from his mother's section or his mother's mother's natal compound, that is he cannot contract a secondary marriage with a woman who is already married to these categories of his kinsmen.

Secondary marriage arrangements are, by Irigwe custom, formally conducted and become binding when the suitor makes a marriage payment to the father or marriage guardian; the amount of the payment is generally thirty to forty shillings cash. After that the girl is committed to leave her prior husband and spend a night with her new secondary husband at his compound. Usually she does this within several months' time. Unless, however, the girl's mother also favors the union and, as with primary marriage, has been given a gift of perhaps ten shillings, the girl can be expected to postpone going to the secondary husband indefinitely. After an Irigwe father has granted permission and received marriage payment for two or three of his daughter's secondary marriages, it is usual for him to select one of his lineage brothers to be her marriage guardian (*bae bi nva*) and oversee and receive payment for her future secondary marriages.

When a woman goes to a secondary husband she leaves behind everything except the clothes and jewelry she is wearing. (Occasionally an older woman will take one or more of her younger children with her.) Generally her prior husband fetches her back the morning after she has forsaken him for a secondary husband. On a subsequent visit, however, the woman may choose to stay and take up residence with her new husband. The husband receiving her must be prepared to supply her with a hut and everything she needs for housekeeping if he expects her to stay more than a night. If a woman stays with a husband from planting time on through the harvest season he can be counted on to give her grain for her dry season cooking needs and her own small granary to store it in. Young girls who have just consummated their primary marriages go off to their secondary husbands any season, although they favor the hunting and early planting seasons when drumming and dancing are allowed. But once a woman has stayed with a man long enough for him to have given her a granary and grain she seldom leaves him for a secondary husband before the beginning of another farming season when she has already used up the grain.

At dawn after a man has received a new secondary wife the women of his compound announce the fact by shrill ululation. Before long, the prior husband, or one of his brothers, shows up to call her back. She then promptly returns to her prior husband's compound, accompanied by a stream of ululating girls if she herself is still a young girl. The prior husband tarries at the wife-taker's compound to drink his fill of the beer that custom demands must be offered him. It is considered bad manners for a prior spouse to sulk or give direct expression to his annoyance at this time, but he never misses a chance to criticize the quality of their beer, while at the same time encouraging lots of people from his own compound to follow him there to drink up as much as possible. Later in the day the girls from the wife-taker's compound, if the wife has come to him for the first time, announce his success by begging pennies at the compounds of his friends and from others of his section.

A woman is not obliged to sleep with a secondary spouse for more than one night, and she must return to her prior husband when he comes for her. But her reputation will suffer and she may incur the wrath of her father or marriage guardian if she isn't willing to go to the secondary husband two or three times. She probably won't go to him a fourth time, however, unless she has decided to shift her residence from her prior husband to his; at that juncture the prior husband usually doesn't bother to call her home to him any more. In any case the prior husband isn't served beer by the secondary husband except the first time he calls her back. The traditional Irigwe marriage system has no divorce. A woman's prior marriages are never formally terminated by her switching residence to another spouse; she may return to any of her spouses at any time and usually finds herself welcomed back and given a hut and everything else she needs for housekeeping.

In order to be a real success at the secondary marriage game a man needs to have two or three reliable friends outside his own section who, being able to move freely and partake of festivities in compounds where he would be suspect, can sound out possible secondary marriage alliances, carry messages for him, and the like. The *quid pro quo* of such friendships is to give reciprocal aid in courtship and never to take wives from each other's compounds. Friends may, however, marry daughters from each other's compounds. Women, for their part, depend heavily upon their co-wives, including their husbands' siblings' wives, when planning and carrying out secondary alliances. Indeed the Irigwe word *urī* means just two things: "a man's friend," as described above, and "co-wife." Two people calling each other *urī* (both two men who are friends and co-wives) often in later life further consolidate their relationship by arranging for a primary marriage between each other's children or grandchildren. Exogamy rules, however, strictly circumscribe the opportunities for arranging such a primary marriage.

Irigwe men have much to gain and relatively little to lose by contracting many marriages. The initial expenses of procuring a wife are offset probably within a year by her domestic and agricultural labor if she can be induced to stay that long. It will be seen later, however, that keeping a wife resident for a number of years is generally quite expensive for the husband. A man receives a lot of kudos from others in his compound and section and from his friends for taking many wives, especially if he can also keep a number of wives resident at the same time. When a wife leaves him for another husband both the example and counsel of his section peers exhort him to cool his anger, be civil towards her other husband so as not to annoy her, promptly call her back, and seek further to regain face by endeavoring to marry someone else's wife. From the husband's point of view every new marriage means minimally another woman who will cohabit with him, always at his own compound, for at least two or three nights, and who may settle with him more or less permanently and bear him children.

An Irigwe woman, as mentioned earlier, always has the right to refuse any secondary marriage proposal prior to the marriage payment from the suitor to her father or marriage guardian. She is never able, however, to contract a marriage without her father's or marriage guardian's consent; few Irigwe women will risk the epithet of *mbrúnjē* (promiscuous woman) and the accompanying loss of further desirability as a wife that sexual relations without this paternal permission quickly brings. A woman always has someone in her lineage who has the inalienable right to bestow her as a legitimate sexual partner; if her father and the marriage guardian he chose for her both die, her lineage selects another marriage guardian for her. A father or marriage guardian, of course, never grants exclusive sexual access to his marriage ward; since there is no divorce a husband competes with his wife's other husbands, both present and future, for her sexual favors.

A husband also, in effect, competes with a wife's other husbands for the paternity of the children she bears. In contrast to the rights of bestowal of sexual access, which remain always with the woman's father, his appointee, or his lineage heirs, the father surrenders all control over rights *in genetricem* (Bohannan 1949:287) early in a woman's marriage career, at a ceremony called *sa tese* (literally, "putting outside") usually held about the sixth month of her first pregnancy. Thenceforth the question of paternity is settled and legally confirmed by the actions of the woman and her spouses. It may be adjudicated by the Irigwe elders, and sometimes today by the District Court, but this is seldom necessary. A child's paternity is usually bestowed without contention upon whichever husband the mother was residing with when she was pregnant and when she bore the child. A woman seldom shifts to another husband while she is pregnant. If it turns out a wife went to another husband about the time she conceived, the prior husband's paternal rights to the child are not disputed provided he called the wife back to him promptly, and provided he took responsibility for the baby's infancy rites. The infant's permanent section affiliation is the same as the pater's, that is, it is reckoned agnatically.

When a wife makes it clear that she is shifting her residence to another husband, the husband she is leaving generally asserts his right to keep all the children she bore him except for those under three or four years of age whose return he may later demand, and then he puts out the welcome mat for her return. Wives come and wives go, but a man lives on in the familiar surroundings of his ancestral home with the company of his sons and unmarried daughters. In his old age he is supported by his sons and cooked for by their wives if he has no resident wives of his own, while he turns his energies to ritual and judidical affairs that include looking after the marriages of his daughters and/or marriage wards.

All older Irigwe women have had a plurality of husbands. In a complete census I took of 5 compounds, totalling over 250 people, every girl pubescent or older had had a primary marriage arranged for her; all women past their teens had at least one secondary spouse, and most had had two or more; fully half of the women middle aged or over had borne children for two or more husbands. A girl's primary marriage is merely her marital debut whence she usually leaps into a round of secondary alliances, gaining thereby not only the excitement and pleasures these afford, but also the admiration of both peers and parents. Fathers are pleased and proud to have a daughter who has four or more secondary marriages to her credit, and co-wives admire such a woman. Some young women, however, soon become very attached to one or another secondary—or even their primary—spouse and go on to take other husbands only to avoid annoying their father or marriage guardian; for it is believed that a father's annoyance, even unexpressed, may lead to his daughter's barrenness, illness, or even to the illness of her children.

It is usual for a woman to settle down for a relatively protracted period with a husband for whom she has borne a child or two. Sooner or later, however, she almost inevitably moves either back to an old or on to a new husband. Often she is prompted to do so by a diviner's diagnosis that her own health or that of one of her children needs the change. The Irigwe consider it a prime duty of both parents to go visit any of their children who have fallen seriously ill and then to stay on until the child's health improves or until the funeral. In this society about half of the infants healthy at birth die from illness before their sixth birthday. Thus sometimes her own health, but more frequently the health of her children, becomes a prime factor sometimes in abetting and other times in inhibiting a mother's marriage mobility. "Spoiled stomach" (*owie 'dzio*) is the Irigwe idiom generally used to denote grief, including homesickness and bereavement. On several occasions I saw just that literally occur to a child upon the departure of the mother for another husband, and once I saw the child get sick enough so that the mother postponed her planned shift of residence.

The Irigwe have a belief they use as the basis of a sort of litmus paper test as to whether or not a man should consider taking any particular woman as his secondary wife. The belief is that if a man who is ill or injured is visited or aided by a man with whom he has shared a woman's favors (if, for example, he is visited by a co-husband) he will take a sudden turn for the worse and probably die. This belief enjoins men to be particularly sure they know all a woman's husbands before taking her in secondary marriage, so they can avoid inadvertently becoming the co-husband of anyone such as a friend or section-brother with whom casual and friendly relations are desired or ritually pre-scribed. It also leads a prudent man to choose his hunting partners with care; and whenever he is hunting with people from other sections he feels it wise to seek out a "friend" or close uterine kinsman to stay nearby and lend him assistance if he should accidentally be injured. It will be recalled that it is both rude and poor strategy to express hostility openly towards a man who married your wife. Thus it is not surprising to have had the belief arise that co-husbands are dangerous to have around in times of illness.

Open accusations of witchcraft or sorcery in Irigwe, although they occur, are rare, and I have no cases of their arising between rivals for a woman. On the other hand, fights between hunters over division of

200

game, especially between men of different sections and rivals for the same woman, are very common, and resultant bodily injury occurs all too frequently. I never, however, was able to uncover an example of intratribal homicide in Irigwe, and elders claim that there was no traditional compensation, retribution, or punishment for murder or homicide within the tribe. There are strong sanctions, mostly ritual in nature, militating against a section's bifurcating. Elders, however, can recall several instances of this happening within the last sixty or seventy years. Sometimes a dispute over the division of game was cited as the cause of the split, and in other instances a man's taking a wife of a member of another lineage of his own section was put forth as the start of the division; all agreed, however, that the taking of wives of section members of other lineages confirmed the splits even where they did not initiate them.

Irigwe is a segmentary society that brings its own refinement to the use of marriage as a social mechanism for establishing ties between segments. In many segmentary societies in Africa cross-cutting ties are forged by "marrying your enemies," i.e., by marrying the daughters of outsider clans. The Irigwe system, however, serves directly to reenforce intrasegment solidarity while also forging intersegment links. The Irigwe marry their friends and distant kinsmen in primary marriage, and then they marry their enemy's wives in secondary marriage, with most of the secondary marriages being between partners from different sections.

Often in her old age a woman returns to live her last days in a compound where she has a grown son. If she is without surviving sons, she may choose to spend her declining years either with one of her surviving spouses, to contract a new marriage with an elderly man, or to return to her paternal compound "to retire." An Irigwe woman takes an active, but not central, role in the mortuary rites of her husband if she is resident with him when he dies, and vice versa, but within a month she moves from her deceased husband's compound back to her paternal home whence she later may be married to a new husband of another section. Irigwe spouses are never buried in the same grave; indeed they even fear going near the graves of their deceased spouses.

Irigwe old men are prone to wax both sentimental and possessive about the daughters of their section; I remember overhearing an audible revery of some old men basking on a rock in the evening sun, about "those wonderful daughters of our section, all of them belonging to us, all of them!" An Irigwe section may lose daughters' children to other sections, but they always retain the right to bestow each of their daughters in marriage again and again. And when a woman dies, the husband or son she was resident with may choose to bury her in a crypt of his lineage, but her lineage of birth can always intervene and demand the body back if they feel the burial arrangements are in any way unsatisfactory. It would seem that Irigwe men draw an intense satisfaction from holding veto power over the whereabouts of their daughters, a veto that contrasts so to a man's limited power to keep a wife with him and a child's inability to hold onto his mother (except by getting sick).

As my fieldwork in Irigwe progressed I grew more and more troubled about Irigwe marriage because I couldn't see how women, not to mention the children, could stand a life that was such an interminable succession of separation experiences. Irigwe men, of course, must also endure frequent separations, first as children from one or another parent and extended family group and then as adults from a succession of wives, sometimes parting temporarily, sometimes permanently. As adults, however, Irigwe men may derive whatever solace can be drawn from remaining resident in their paternal compound, from regular participation in their compound's and their section's yearly cycle of ceremonies, and from leading their daily lives always with the same core of male patrikinsmen. Irigwe women, in contrast, must not only endure frequent separation from one or another of their husbands and children but must also experience concomitant changes of residence and of women with whom to pass their work-a-day lives. From my earliest weeks in Irigwe I frequently attended women's possession dances and saw women cry, speak in tongues, and flail about after the frenetic drumming, dancing, singing, and rattling leg irons had induced a dissociated state in them. From my census I found that over 95 percent of the women past their middle twenties felt themselves to be afflicted with troublesome spirits they call *rije,* which if not brought out and assuaged from time to time cause illness. In contrast less than 2 percent of the men were so afflicted. It wasn't until over a year of field-work had passed, however, and I saw a woman whom I had come to know well in the agony of a sudden and protracted state of dissociation, "struck," as they say, by her *rije*, that I made the connection between the Irigwe marriage-go-round and women's possession.

Two aspects of this woman's seizure led to my new insight. First, her behavior was in such striking contrast to her usual gay and confident manner. Normally she was the most self-possessed and affable of three young resident wives of a widely liked young man who was generally viewed as a model husband. She had borne him one child then about three years old. Her co-wives had noticed that she had been moody since she had had a miscarriage about a month before, and then suddenly she had been overcome while making beer. Possession specialists, both male and female, were immediately called in, and by the time I arrived on the scene they and perhaps a dozen members of the compound were trying to humor and calm her as she lay sobbing and groveling on the floor of her hut. It was fully two hours before she calmed down, quite exhausted by then, and was able even to recognize her own child. The second aspect was the nature of the seizure itself. Her flailing about while possessed, her barely coherent demands for this and that emitted between heart-rending wails, reminded me all too forcefully of two- and three-year-old children I had seen in my own culture reacting to one or another major frustration. In contrast, silence, listlessness, and quite often "spoiled stomach" are Irigwe toddlers' characteristic responses to a severe frustration or trauma such as the departure of the mother. Irigwe children learn very early to suppress, indeed to repress the felt need for violent emotional outbursts. They find that tantrums usually bring tongue-lashings and abrupt shooings from their elders, whereas in contrast the silent and wan or the clearly ill child is endlessly snuggled and whispered words of affection and reassurance. Thus it appears that only under the cultural guise of being possessed by *rije* may Irigwe usually give vent without castigation to their repressed feelings of anguish arising from their repeated separations from loved ones, separations first occurring in infancy and childhood, and later a major aspect of married life, especially the married life of women.

Subsequent systematic inquiries revealed that instances such as the one just described are very common. When a woman is first struck down by her *rije* the people on hand call in an expert diagnostician who quickly establishes which of several varieties of *rije* have afflicted her. The diagnostician then blames the presence of the *rije* for some recent disaster in the patient's life such as a miscarriage or illness. After the woman has recovered from this initial attack she must seek treatment at a compound "owning her *rije*," that is, owning the medicine and ritual to control them. There she is inevitably advised that if she ever wants to escape the ill effects, and in time perhaps gain control, of the *rije* that have come to reside in her she should as soon as possible have a major ceremonial held for her called *nyi rije* ("making *rije*"). The *nyi rije* ceremonial is very expensive. All the patient's paternal and maternal kin, and all of the kinsmen of the husband with whom she resides must be invited and served beer. Also a hundred shillings or more worth of grain must be supplied as payment to female ritual practitioners of the compound owning the *rije*, and additional grain must be given to elder women of other compounds also possessed by that type of *rije* who come to help preside. The services of perhaps a dozen possession drummers and singers (always men) must be paid for. Finally, and most costly of all, the practitioners, interpreting the babblings of the possessed women, inevitably assert that the *rije* possessing the patient demands cloth, lots of expensive cloth, some of which must be given to the patient prior to the ceremony, and some afterwards, to assure its effectiveness. Usually it takes an Irigwe husband a number of months, or even a year or more, to raise the capital and finish arrangements for one of these ceremonials. And that's generally not the end of it. Most women need repeat ceremonials every several years to keep their *rije* under control. Happily *rije* can be "placed" (*sa rije*), that is, pacified temporarily, by holding relatively simple and inexpensive all night possession dances requiring only the services of one or two drummer-singers whom the women can find money to reimburse themselves. In the case of the big *nyi rije* ceremonials, however, most women are dependent on the larger resources available only to the menfolk. A wife will, if necessary, keep leaving one husband for another until she finds one willing and able to hold a *nyi rije* ceremonial for her. A husband soon develops a reputation among womenfolk as stingy or generous in such matters, a reputation that strongly affects his subsequent success in marrying wives and holding them resident.

A woman in middle age may develop skill in calling forth her *rije* (*hurae rije*) and becoming possessed by them at will. She will then be sought after to help preside at *nyi rije* ceremonials and novices afflicted with her kind of *rije*, and she will receive payment for her services. Some older women learn to call and utilize their *rije* as a source of divinatory and curing power; a few build up a large clientele of patients and even become independently wealthy through fees received for their services. Thus it would seem that many years later and in a displaced and disguised form a woman may receive substantial compensation for the psychic stresses she has suffered from workings of the Irigwe marriage-go-round.

The Irigwe language is replete with ambiguities, and puns are a favorite form of Irigwe humor. The expression *nje na ridae* means "I am going courting," i.e., looking for a secondary wife. But it also means "I am going home to mother." Never sure whether I'd miss a subtle phonemic distinction or a crucial toneme, I asked again and again about this ambiguity, and usually for an answer I got a laugh followed either by a shrug, or a terse retort, "It's the same thing." Thus in closing may I suggest that it is a meaningful metaphor to speak of an Irigwe man's life and loves in large measure as a continuing quest for his wandering mother? Bearing in mind the part of the Red Earth origin myth where the Red Earth section followed a son section to its present locale in Nyango, and also that a son's compound is indeed the favorite place for a woman's "retirement" in old age, is it not fair also to say that an Irigwe woman's life can be viewed as an ongoing quest for her son?

NOTES

Acknowledgments. This essay is a composite of two papers on aspects of Irigwe marriage read at the 1966 and 1968 American Anthropological meetings. The field research on which it is based was funded by the National Science Foundation. I am indebted to Lucinda Sangree for her most helpful suggestions and editorial comments.

REFERENCES CITED

Bohannan, Laura
    1949   Dahomean Marriage: A Revaluation. Africa 19: 237-287.
Gunn, Harold D.
    1953   Peoples of the Plateau Area of Northern Nigeria. *In* Ethnographic Survey of Africa: Western Africa, Part 7. London: International African Institute.
Smith, M.G.
    1953   Secondary Marriage in Northern Nigeria. Africa 23: 298-323.

Gillespie, Dair L.
    1975   Who Has the Power? The Marital Struggle. *In* Women: A Feminist Perspective. Jo Freeman, ed. Pp. 64-87. 1st ed. (Originally published in Journal of Marriage and the Family 33: 445-458, 1971.)
    Criticizes sociological interpretations of American marriage as a free contract among equals. Examines sources of power in marriage and concludes that husbands exercise greater control over the decision-making process than wives.

Gomm, Roger
    1972   Harlots and Bachelors: Marital Instability among the Coastal Digo of Kenya. Man (n.s.) 7: 95-113.
    Digo marriage, like that described by Sangree (this volume) for the Irigwe, is characterized by frequent divorce and the circulation of wives among several spouses (see also Gomm, this volume). The author attributes Digo marital conflict to ". . . separate male and female view-points and aspirations" (1972: 101).

Gregor, Thomas A.
    1974   Publicity, Privacy, and Mehinacu Marriage. Ethnology 12: 333-349.
    Discusses the public and private dimensions of marital relations among the Mehinacu Indians of central Brazil.

McC. Netting, Robert
    1969   Women's Weapons: The Politics of Domesticity among the Kofyar. American Anthropologist 71: 1037-1046.
    Interesting discussion of marital relations in a patrilineal society of northern Nigeria. Women exercise considerable economic power, accept lovers in their husbands' homesteads, and terminate their marriages at will.

WOMAN-MARRIAGE, WITH SPECIAL REFERENCE TO THE LOVEDU—ITS SIGNIFICANCE FOR THE DEFINITION OF MARRIAGE

Eileen Jensen Krige

The marriage of a woman to a woman, found in many African societies, has not been given the attention it warrants and is still imperfectly understood. Herskovits (1938 I:319-320) imputed to it sexual overtones that are foreign to the institution when, after stating quite definitely that such marriage did not imply a homosexual relationship, went on to add, "... although it is not to be doubted that occasionally homosexual women who have inherited wealth ... utilize this relationship to the women they marry to satisfy themselves." He made no attempt to substantiate his statement. And Lucy Mair (1971:60, my italics), for all the clarity and grasp displayed in her excellent book on marriage, seems to have failed to appreciate the nature of the institution when she says, "According to Evans-Pritchard's account of the Nuer it is usually barren women who make such marriages, *and indeed it is hard to imagine a woman who had her own children doing so.*" In actual fact it is usually married women with children of their own who contract such marriages, except, it would appear, among the Nuer. By woman-marriage we mean the institution by which it is possible for a woman to give bridewealth for, and marry, a woman, over whom and whose offspring she has full control, delegating to a male genitor the duties of procreation.

Reprinted by permission of the author and the International African Institute from *Africa* 44(1):11-37, 1974. Diagrams 1 and 2, Figure 3, Appendix 1, and portions of this paper are omitted.

Misconceptions such as those of Herskovits are rooted in the central place accorded to the husband-wife relationship in current concepts and definitions of marriage. In the article on marriage in the *Encyclopedia of the Social Sciences,* Robert F. Winch (1968:2) says, "Marriage may be defined as a culturally approved relationship of one man and one woman (monogamy), of one man and two or more women (polygyny), or of one woman and two or more men (polyandry), in which there is cultural endorsement of sexual intercourse between the marital partners of opposite sex and, generally, the expectation that children will be born of the relationship . . . ." Leach (1961:105) criticizes the definition of marriage given in *Notes and Queries on Anthropology* (1951), viz., "A union between a man and a woman such that children born to the woman are recognized, legitimate offspring of both partners." He considers it too limited, particularly in failing to cover cases of adelphic polyandry. He says, "Marriage is (to borrow Maine's phrase) 'a bundle of rights;' hence all universal definitions of marriage are vain;" but he then goes on to enumerate ten classes of rights with which marriage is concerned, and *all* except one of these centers on the husband-wife relationship (Leach 1961:107-108). P.G. Rivière (1971:63) in his essay, "Marriage: A Reassessment" goes as far as to say, "The constituent units of marriage are men and women and this seems to be marriage's single, universal feature. The study of marriage must in the first place concentrate on the categories male and female and the relationship between them." He is aware that this definition ". . . does not take account of such famous unions as the Nuer woman-marriage," but he dismisses this by citing Evans-Pritchard's (1951:108-109) statements that such a woman is playing the part of a man, and suggests that the problem can be overcome by describing the marital union as being a union between ". . . the conceptual roles of male and female" instead of as between "man and woman" (Rivière 1971:68-69). Whether this meets the problem had best be considered later. We need merely note here Rivière's emphasis on the husband-wife relationship as the single universal feature of marriage.

I propose in this paper to discuss in some detail woman-marriage as practiced today among the Lovedu, with whom I have been associated over a long period. For greater clarity and perspective I give also some comparable material from other African peoples for whom information is available and, finally, consider the relevance of this material for the definition of marriage. We begin with a brief examination of the Nuer case.

BARRENNESS AND OWNERSHIP OF WEALTH AS FACTORS IN WOMAN-MARRIAGE

A Barren Nuer Woman Considered as a Man

Evans-Pritchard, who has coined the term "woman-marriage," has shown that among the Nuer woman-marriage is but one of a variety of other forms of union, besides what he terms simple legal marriage; these range from simple concubinage to widow concubinage, woman-marriage, and ghost-marriage. Simple concubinage is found in almost every village. Here the woman is unmarried and the children belong to the mother's lineage (unless legitimized by the payment by the genitor of a substantial fee for each child). Ghost-marriage (marrying a wife to the name of a kinsman who died without male children to sacrifice to him) is almost as common as simple legal marriage. In simple legal marriage the man in whose name cattle were handed over as bridewealth is always the sociological father of the children, whether he is genitor or not, and the children belong to his lineage. But until the first child is born a married woman lives in her own home village, and only when a child is born is the union reckoned complete and the wife considered as belonging to the husband's lineage (Evans-Pritchard (1945:5).

A barren woman has very special rights in her own lineage. She is considered to be in some respects like a man, may inherit cattle and receive from her family a share of the bridewealth coming in from the marriage of girls in the family, as if she were one of the men. She is regarded as a man even to the extent that if after her death her ghost causes sickness to draw attention to her unhappy plight, her brother or her brother's son may marry a woman who will bear children to her name (Evans-Pritchard 1945:12). The children are called after the female ghost as though she were a man, while the brother counts as their paternal uncle, "for his sister has become his brother." He must not cohabit with this woman himself but must arrange for a stranger (perhaps a Dinka) to cohabit with her in the hut he has built for her in his homestead (Evans-Pritchard 1945:112). It is possible also, failing male kin, for a barren woman to marry a woman to the name of a complaining dead kinsman, usually her uterine brother. Or she may marry a wife in her own name and instruct a son of this woman to marry a wife to the name of her brother when he grows up (Evans-Pritchard 1951:111). A barren Nuer woman may become wealthy, especially if she practices as

210

a diviner, and can in this way acquire several wives. She is their legal husband and can demand damages if they have relations with men without her consent.

Family Arrangements in Nuer Woman-Marriage

Evans-Pritchard (1945:31) gives as an example of woman-marriage in operation the case of one Nyaluthni who had three wives. She chose as genitor a kinsman in the case of one wife and in others a stranger. These men did not live in her homestead but visited or stayed the night. "They hoe her gardens, are given meals when they are present and on the marriage of the daughters they have begotten the genitors receive a cow from the bridewealth of each" (Evans-Pritchard 1945:31). The female husband administers her home and herd as a man would do, being treated by her wives and children with the deference they would show to a male husband and father. Her children address her as "father," and she speaks of their mothers as "my wives." Such marriages are by no means uncommon in Nuerland and they must be regarded as a form of simple legal marriage, says Evans-Pritchard (1951:108), for the female husband marries her wife in exactly the same way as a man marries a woman and with the same marriage rites. He nowhere states clearly, however, whether all barren women remain unmarried to men and continue living where their parents are. He tells us that a woman who marries a woman is "generally barren," but he does not say whether a woman who was not barren or who was herself married to a man could in any circumstances contract such a marriage. If such marriages are "by no means uncommon" they could hardly be confined to barren women. Further, if married women sometimes contract such marriages it would be interesting to know whether the children in that case are considered to belong to the husband's lineage (as among the Lovedu).

The Seligmans (1965:221) reported a type of woman-marriage for the Nuer which Evans-Pritchard does not specifically mention. They say an elderly, childless widow whose husband has left property may raise up seed to her husband among the Nuer, as also among the Dinka (presumably such a woman has lost her children by death). It is important to note that the children in this case belonged to the lineage from which the property had come, viz., that of the deceased husband.

211

A barren Nuer woman, then, may marry a woman to raise up seed in ghost-marriage to a dead kinsman (Evans-Pritchard 1951) or a childless widow to a deceased husband (Seligman and Seligman 1965). A barren woman may also, using her own property, marry a woman in her own name, the children calling her "father" and being counted as members of her paternal lineage.

Woman-Marriage and Property in West Africa

In contrast to the Nuer, where only a barren woman can acquire wealth, there is a number of societies in West Africa, with its advanced arts and crafts and well developed system of trade and markets run largely by women, in which any woman can, by her personal earnings or by inheritance, acquire property in the form of farms, money, palm groves, etc. This gives women a good deal of independence. In these circumstances a barren wife in Dahomey, for example, is able to overcome the disadvantages of her position by using her own property to acquire a woman whom she will give to her husband. Any children born to a wife so acquired will be known as her own children (Herskovits 1938 I:342). Talbot (1926:111, 431, 439, 441) reports a similar arrangement for the Ibo and Ijo of southern Nigeria. Such a wife will never have her own, independent house, as does a wife in the case of ordinary marriage or of woman-marriage. It is not a separate marriage. The wife merely forms part of the establishment of the older woman. For this reason, and in the absence of more detailed information on the West African examples, one hesitates to consider these cases as falling under the term woman-marriage even though the bridewealth has been supplied by the woman. It is common among the Ibo for a married woman to pay bridewealth for a wife for her son or husband. The children belong to the lineage of the man to whom she is married (G.I. Jones n.d., personal communication). Here, though the property used belongs to the woman and she is said to have a "moral right" over the wife so acquired, her rights are not legal rights (such a case, it is stated, would never come to court), and the nature of her control is not clear. It is doubtful here too whether such an arrangement should be called woman-marriage. If, however, an Ibo woman, X, obtained a divorce by repaying her husband the bridewealth he gave for her and then married a woman, Y, the situation would be different. X would then be defined as the "husband" of Y; her role would have changed to a male role; her

212

wife Y's children would then take her name and in course of time become one of the segments of her father's lineage (G.I. Jones n.d., personal communication). Legally such repayment had to be made by the person who originally received it or his heirs and it was open to the husband to refuse the refund. In the latter case the children of Y would belong to the home of the husband of X. Before an Ibo woman was able to refund bridewealth and marry a wife of her own ". . . she was already in an anomalous position: i.e., she was wealthier than most men and barren or without a son. If she had children there would be no need for a change as she already had a 'house' and the woman for whom she paid bridewealth could be married to her son or grandson" (G.I. Jones n.d., personal communication).

According to Herskovits (1938 I), any woman of means in Dahomey can marry a wife; she supports all payments and gifts decreed for full marriage as if she were a man, she builds a house for her "wife" near her own home and chooses a genitor from among her husband's relatives or her male acquaintances. He visits the woman but cannot take her to his own home, and chooses a genitor from among her husband's relatives or her male acquaintances. He visits the woman but cannot take her to his own home. The genitor makes no payment, is under no obligation of 1938 I:320). The genitor gets nothing at all for his sexual services. The advantage to him in such an arrangement appears to be that he has an extra woman with whom he may seek satisfaction, and she is available to him without any expenditure or responsibility on his part. The wife of the woman has considerable freedom, and the man to whom she has been given may at any time find other men in her house. If no child is conceived she may simply reject him; but if there are children this would not be so easy, as both her own family and the woman she has married might bring pressure to bear on her to retain him as genitor (Herskovits 1938 I:346).

By marrying a "wife" a woman in Dahomey establishes a "house" which may become a new compound. Herskovits does not mention whether she must first divorce her husband. Since the owner of a farm and palm groves requires labor, a woman of wealth (single or married, but usually married), will find it in her interest to employ her resources to marry as many women as she can afford in order to build up a compound and obtain control over many children, who will carry on its affairs and provide for its perpetuation (Herskovits 1937:358).

213

In woman-marriage the female husband has contracted full marriage with transfer of rights over the children to herself as sociological father. It is relevant here to mention that a form of marriage without transfer of rights to the children appears to be common in many parts of West Africa as an alternative to full marriage. The Ijo recognize two forms of marriage called respectively *eya* and *egwa*. The marriage rituals are the same in both forms but in *eya* a considerable sum of money is paid as bridewealth while in *egwa* marriage only a little is given and rights to the children are not transferred. The woman and her children belong to her natal group. This corresponds to the *vidotohwe*, child-stays-at-the wife's father's home form of marriage in Dahomey (Herskovits 1938 I: 422-424) in which the husband may not take his wife home but builds her a house in her father's compound where he visits her from time to time. "He must provide for his children and . . . his mother-in-law must approve of the manner in which he keeps up the household" (Herskovits (1938 I:846). "He has no legal right to the children but receives a share of them as a moral right" (Herskovits 1938 I:323). [1]

WOMAN-MARRIAGE AMONG THE LOVEDU

Characteristic Features

We have seen that the right of women to acquire and dispose of wealth is important for woman-marriage. Among the Lovedu women also have the right to acquire and control property. But woman-marriage here, far from being the privilege of those who have acquired wealth by their own efforts, is within the reach of any woman in certain fortuitous circumstances. It is bound up with the right, enforceable at law, of every woman to a daughter-in-law (to render services to her and marry her son) from the "house" of any woman who has been acquired by means of her own bridewealth, for, failing a son, the woman may marry the girl herself. Woman-marriage of this kind is closely associated with cross-cousin marriage between children of uterine brother and sister, since it is generally the uterine brother who uses his sister's cattle. The most arresting aspect of Lovedu woman-marriage is, however, the fact that the custom of giving daughters as wives to the queen for rain or for personal or political favors and their reallocation by the queen to relatives or clients has made this institution a basic integrating factor in the political system.

The Setting of the Institution

The setting in which Lovedu woman-marriage is found is that of an economy based on subsistence agriculture and with cattle in such short supply that most of them are involved in ritual exchanges connected with marriage. There is little or no trade, there are no markets, and arts and crafts have not reached anywhere near the standard of skill found in West Africa. [2]

Wealth is, in the eyes of traditionalists even today, not something to be sought after for its own sake. Influence and prestige lie not in the accumulation of wealth but in its consumption in the entertainment of kin and neighbors. The correct use of property in the form of cattle or money is to invest it in marriage, in building up human resources by establishing a "house" which will produce chidren and a following and secure the support of affines. Hence the army pensions of many Lovedu soldiers in the Second World War went into marrying wives, and a successful doctor or diviner reckons to have many wives. The value of girls (as potential wives and mothers) for acquiring human resources is clearly perceived by the Lovedu, and girls figure in a number of transactions that to westerners appear purely economic. Thus, a girl may be handed over in lieu of a large debt which a man is unable to pay. (We saw these arrangements made in a court even in 1966 in a dispute about return of brideprice.) The most usual way of "borrowing" the wherewithal to acquire a wife was to take a small girl to a man who had cattle and promise her in marriage (or even to promise an as yet unborn daughter) against an advance of cattle for bridewealth. This may be done even today, in spite of opportunities for earning money in the European labor market. Compensation for unintentional homicide in the first decades of the century took the form of a girl sent to the family of the deceased to bear them a child, an arrangement which in the only case I knew personally ended up in the girl staying on permanently as wife of the brother of the boy who had met his death.

Yet the position of women is high among the Lovedu. The ruler is a queen. Political office as heads of districts is open to women. Women have full control over wealth they have earned after marriage. Such wealth vests in the "house" of the woman, must be used for the benefit of her house, and is inherited by her son. A woman who is on bad terms with her husband has been known to use the cattle received from the marriage of her daughter in acquiring a wife for an absent son or herself without the knowledge of her husband. Important in the setting of woman-marriage is the complementarity of uterine brother and sister. Both are of life-long importance for the development of the "house" in which they were born. The eldest brother in the chief house succeeds his father as family head, responsible for law and order and the settlement of disputes. The eldest sister even though married becomes ritual head, responsible for officiating in all major sacrifices and for the health and welfare of her brothers' children. She it is who, acting in consultation with any brothers of the father that are still alive, divides out the inheritance on the death of her father and allocates her father's wives to seed-raisers. Not only do she and her sisters usually receive some small portion of the inheritance but she, as the eldest, may, where there is no brother to succeed, become headman in her own right. She rules until her death. The son of another house rarely succeeds. A sister whose marriage-cattle have been used by a brother to marry a wife has considerable control in the "house" thus established. It is to this "house" that she looks for a daughter-in-law.[3] All these institutional arrangements are important for understanding woman-marriage among the Lovedu.

Circumstances in which Woman-Marriage Occurs

1. Right of a woman to a girl from a "house" established by her brideprice whether she has a son or not.

There are several different forms of woman-marriage among the Lovedu. One of these arises from the right of a woman, as she grows older, to have the care and services of a daughter-in-law, a bride for her son, from any "house" that has been established by means of her own bridewealth.

Thus in Figure 1, A's marriage-cattle or bridewealth were used to procure a wife for her brother, B. This is usually described as a cattle-link between them. D, the daughter of the "house" established with A's bridewealth, should marry A's son and cook for her mother-in-law, A. Should A have no son she may, using bridewealth from her daughter C's marriage, "marry" the girl D herself. (If B had no daughter, A could marry any other girl.) Two women have rights in respect of the

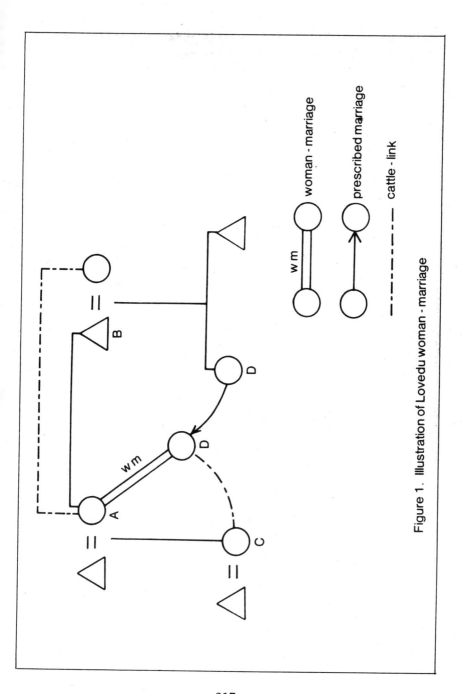

Figure 1. Illustration of Lovedu woman - marriage

217

girl D: the old mother A to her services and A's married daughter C to a daughter of D later on for her son. Technically C is the "husband" of the bride, D, and A, her mother-in-law; but C cannot take D to live with her in her *kraal* [or homestead] until after the death of her mother, A, and C has no right to D's services. (She has a right to the services of D's daughter.)

These claims of mother and daughter do not conflict because of the difference in age between them. For purposes of procreation a genitor is appointed, generally a male agnate of the female husband; alternatively the bride may be left free to have children by lovers. In certain cases the genitor is chosen from the old woman A's own lineage. The genitor, called *boho*, or "bull," should visit the girl in secret (an open secret if he resides in the same *kraal*). Unlike a levir, the genitor has no responsibilities towards the woman and her children, but he will later be given one head of cattle for his services. In practice, however, the genitor may give occasional gifts of clothing or even sometimes, nowadays, pay the school fees of the children.

The position of a woman "married" to a female husband is, on the whole, analogous to that of other young married women, especially these days when so many married men are away doing migrant labor. The services she is expected to render her mother-in-law are exactly the same and she will have her own "house" like any other married woman. When her sons marry they may move away with her to establish their own *kraal*. Where such a woman is, however, at a disadvantage today is in lacking the things that money can buy. Her mother-in-law can provide her with few clothes and, now that so large a proportion of the food consumed also has to be bought from shops, this presents a problem in the absence of a wage earner. The children of the wife of a woman are members of the family and house that has provided their mother's brideprice. They call the old woman-head of the "house" *koko*, or grandmother. Their mother calls her *matswale*, mother-in-law or *rakhadi*, father's sister, if she is a niece; and the relationships may be very cordial. The female husband i.e., the daughter of the old woman or mother-in-law, will only be called a "husband" by the woman concerned or a "father" (*papa*) by her children if she holds an important position, as in the case of the queen or of a female district head, when they live with and are controlled by her. Otherwise, if she is a cross-cousin, her "wife" will say *motsoala* (cousin). The children will

call her *rakhadi,* literally, female father. A woman in woman-marriage
has the same sense of duty towards her female husband as towards a
male husband. Thus Mamaila as "wife of her cattle" went to nurse
Bilwana, her female husband, when Bilwana was ill, even though she
was living in a different *kraal* and Bilwana's sister was available.

The most important relationship in ordinary woman-marriage in cases
where the female husband has no political position is that between the
wife and her "mother-in-law," with whom she generally lives.

Nowadays woman-marriage may take place as a result of a son's refusal
to marry the girl that has been "born for" him. He may be a Christian
and wish to have an educated Christian wife or he may be already
married in town. In this case his mother will "marry" the girl in any
case. Very often a son who has refused to marry such a girl is not averse
to "entering" her hut unofficially. Or the son in town may visit home,
find the girl attractive, and have children by her as his country wife.
There are a number of marriages arranged for sons that end up as
woman-marriage in the sense that the son remains in town or refuses to
cohabit with the girl who stays with his mother and has children by
lovers.

Once they have been to school girls today refuse to marry a woman.
They are taught by church and school that they should choose their own
husbands.

2. The need to raise an heir for a political position.

Woman-marriage by a woman headman for purposes of raising an heir
to the headmanship of a district usually differs a little from ordinary
cases of woman-marriage. In the first place the bride in this case will
generally be residing in the same *kraal* as her female husband (except
where the woman ruler is an absentee ruler). [4] When a district headman dies without a male heir in his chief house, a daughter of that
house will be chosen as ruler in preference to a son in another house.
She will be assisted by a half-brother or by a mother's brother who will
do the court work. She rules in her own right until her death, but her
son may not succeed as he does not belong to his mother's family of
orientation. She must marry a woman with cattle belonging to her

219

father's chief house to raise an heir to her deceased or nonexistent brother. This form of marriage may work out in practice to be much the same as has been described above if the female ruler's mother is still alive and the girl who has been married cooks for her and lives in her household. But it is to be distinguished in that often in this case the woman lives in the same *kraal* as her female husband; the purpose is to raise an heir, and the children call the female husband *papa* (father). A married woman has a dual responsibility: that of raising children and ensuring male descendants in the family of her husband and thus increasing the importance of the "house" established by her marriage and, in addition, that of raising a male heir to continue the house into which she was born, should this be necessary. The origin of the cattle used in woman-marriage always determines the family to which the children will belong.

3. Woman-marriage as an investment of wealth earned by women.

Women who are diviners are able to obtain wealth which puts them into a position to marry several wives. Such wives belong to the house established by the diviner's own marriage. Mathorisane, a widow who has been inherited by a levir, is a doctor of note. She has married four wives. In the case of the first, her own levir was appointed genitor. Of the others one was given to her elder son, who has since moved away with his wife, and two have been allocated to the younger son, who lives with his mother in her *kraal*.

4. Inheritance of a wife by a woman.

Just as a son may inherit the young wife of his father, more especially a girl who has not yet come to live in her husband's *kraal,* so too a daughter may inherit wives from her father. Mamolape, who, with her eldest sister divided out their deceased father's inheritance, took for herself a girl betrothed to her father. In announcing her decision the eldest sister said, *Moyana wa vomme wa tswenyeha ka ho seda. Ke mo fa motho wa ho mo sidela*—"The child of my mother is suffering by having to stamp [mealies]. I am giving her a person to stamp for her." Two of the father's five wives were given to Mamolape's uterine brother, one to the son of the deceased's elder sister, and one to a

220

brother's son. It was intended that Andrew, Mamolape's son, should enter this wife's hut as genitor, but the latter was a good deal older than he, and as he had received some school education he refused to act in this capacity. The children borne by the "wife" of Mamolape took the name of Mamolape's family of orientation, not that of her husband. Even if Andrew had "entered" the hut the children would still have belonged to his mother's family. In another case a woman, on dividing out the inheritance on the death of her brother, elected to keep for herself two of his widows. This ensured that they remained in their deceased husband's home, gave them freedom to have children by lovers, and served to give the deceased's sister a place in her parental home from which she could continue to exercise control.

A woman may also, if her parents are dead, be given the girl betrothed to, or "born for" her deceased brother if there is no other brother in that "house" to inherit her. Thus Mantika had the wife intended for her brother living as her wife in her husband's *kraal* in a hut near her own. Mantika arranged for a genitor to enter, and two boys and a girl were born (not all by the genitor). Mantika's interest in this wife was that she had been obtained with Mantika's own brideprice and so her daughter was destined for Mantika's son. But Mantika also had responsibilities as their "father;" she provided one of the boys with cattle for a wife (he in turn helped his brother with money earned from migrant labor). Their sister, Kewele, married Mantika's son. Then she absconded. There were strained relations and after a time Mantika's "wife" and her sons moved away to a European farm. Twelve years later when conditions became difficult on the farm the family returned to Mantika for asylum. They have built their own *kraal* next to Mantika's in a field that belonged to Mantika. Bonds arising from woman-marriage may be as close and strong as in ordinary marriage and the divorce rate today can hardly be said to be higher in woman-marriage than in ordinary marriage.

5. Arrangements in case of barrenness.

It is usual in the case of barrenness for the girl's family to offer the husband a younger kinswoman for his wife, e.g., a sister or brother's daughter, to raise seed to her. The husband gives brideprice again for this girl, but she is never given a hut of her own, all her children being considered as belonging to the "house" of the barren woman. Failing this kind of arrangement it is possible for the barren wife herself to use property she has acquired by her own efforts to acquire a girl whom she gives to her husband to raise seed to her. In the case of Motau there was no girl at home to be sent so she negotiated for a distant cross-cousin and married her in 1966 with her own property supplemented by some of her husband's. Her husband had access to this girl and called her "wife." There was some confusion in the kinship terminology used in this case. Motau called the girl *motsoala* (cross-cousin); the children called Motau *koko* (grandmother) as they did all the other wives of Pekela, instead of calling them "mothers," with correct age distinctions. Yet they called the adult children of these women brothers and sisters. As we have stated above, it is doubtful whether such a case of seed-raising should be called "woman-marriage" because it is not a separate marriage; it is merely a measure taken to bolster up an existing marriage by securing offspring in the "house" of a barren wife.

6. The queen's wives.

This is not the place to deal in any detail with the political importance of the institution of woman-marriage with the queen, but in a discussion of forms of woman-marriage some mention must be made of it. Just as in other Bantu societies subjects may send daughters as gifts to the chief or king, so too among the Lovedu. A girl may be given to the queen to solicit a favor, particularly some political position such as headmanship of a district; this may be done by the queen's own relatives as well as by commoners. A girl may also be required as a fine for some heinous ritual offence; or, such is the fame of Modjadji as rain-maker that foreign tribes also sent daughters for rain. There are still one or two such foreign women at court. These wives, like wives of women headmen, are, because of their importance, called *vatanoni* (not *vasadi*). They hoe the queen's fields, and those that are of royal blood or closely related to the queen are privileged to cook her food for so long as they remain virgin. Those that remain virgin for many years are given "houses" of their own and allowed to bear children to the queen, mostly by some royal relative at the capital. Usually, however, a *motanoni* is seduced after a year or two, whereupon she is sent home in disgrace to bear her child. When the child has been weaned the *motanoni* will be brought back by her father to the queen with "pardon beer." On that occasion her father must point out or name the girl who

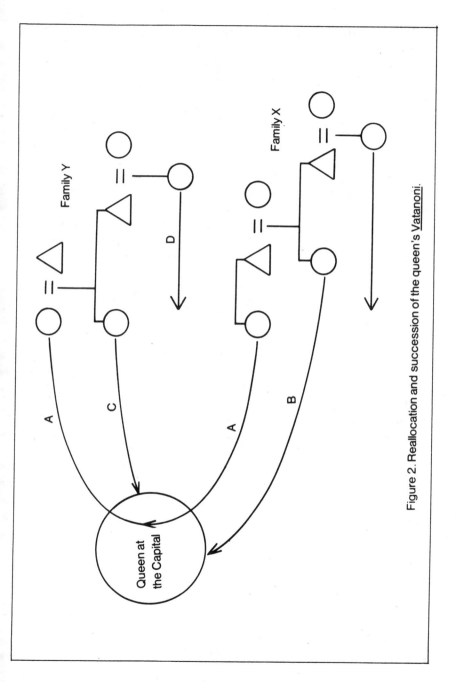

Figure 2. Reallocation and succession of the queen's <u>Vatanoni</u>.

will take her place, either a younger sister or a brother's daughter, perhaps as yet unborn, in which case the brother himself will accompany the father. If the seducer was some royal relative who is still interested in the *motanoni* she may be allowed to remain at court where her own father will build her a hut. The children she bears are the queen's and call the queen "father." The queen's own children are their brothers and sisters, as are the children of other *vatanoni* living at court. In most cases, however, the queen gives such a wife in marriage to one of her relatives or to a political client (see A in Figure 2), and the child that was born takes the name of the man to whom the mother has been given. No brideprice is paid, but later the client will have to give the queen a daughter of this woman to take the place of her mother (see C in Figure 2). When this is done the queen may give brideprice for the new *motanoni*. This will be used by her brother, who in turn will have to send a daughter to "follow" her father's sister at court (see D in Figure 2). In this way, for each wife given initially to the queen, she receives two in return, and they are followed in a long line of succession by their brother's daughters on the pattern of cross-cousin marriages.

Girls who have been to school refuse to marry women, so if in any family a girl is destined to marry the queen she is usually kept at home. Not all headmen send daughters to marry the queen but those that do tend to become important politically. Through the institution of woman-marriage the queen is linked by ties of kinship with many districts and the various districts become linked with each other by affinal ties when a daughter sent to the queen is given by her in marriage to someone else. Until the first decade of this century *vatanoni* of the queen were occasionally rewarded and honored by being given their own village in the royal district and sometimes other *vatanoni* to be their wives. A *motanoni* might also be given a district to rule, especially if she were of royal blood.

A *motanoni* closely related to the queen can, if the genitor is of royal blood, provide an heir to the throne.

Modern Developments in Woman-Marriage

Educated Christian Lovedu are not above exploiting woman-marriage when it is to their advantage to do so. Violet, a Christian woman, on becoming weak and sickly after being married for many years, paid brideprice to "marry" a distant maternal kinswoman, a girl who was mentally retarded, and allowed her to have children "in the bush" by lovers. The church was not opposed to the marriage because the husband was not cohabiting with this girl. There was also a case in which the Lovedu principal of a large school near Pretoria, too far away for his wife to cook for her mother-in-law, had offered to provide the wherewithal for his mother to "marry" a wife to help her. There were other similar cases.

Complex Family Structures Resulting from Women-Marriages

Woman-marriage may lead to complex family structures, more especially when there is in a single family a combination of several forms of woman-marriage.

The Genitor—Human and Legal Aspects of His Position

Evans-Pritchard (1945, 1951), illustrating chiefly from cases of levirate and ghost-marriage, discusses the opposition between the interests of the legal family and those of other forms of bio-domestic groups among the Nuer. This brings out clearly the problems in the life of an individual when the privileges he derives from membership of one of these groups clash with his feelings towards the people of the other to whom he is united by sentiments based on common residence and a common life. This is to some extent avoided where, as in most cases of woman-marriage and sometimes also in the levirate among the Lovedu, the genitor is not resident in the family. The Lovedu genitor in woman-marriage holds no recognized position in the life of the family and should not be known as their father by his biological children. He generally lives elsewhere and visits the woman periodically. Cases do, however, occur in which the genitor, by virtue of close relationship to the female husband and because of being resident in the same *kraal*, is able to play the part of father and to gain some control over the children. For example, a *motanoni* of the queen who had been honored by being given her own village and several of the queen's *vatanoni* to serve her as "wives," allocated one of these to her uterine brother's son. He was able to play the role of father to the children (they even

225

called him "father") and one of them used the genitor's name in his personal documents. It is because of the danger of losing control over the children that some women prefer not to appoint a genitor and leave the wife free to have children "in the bush" by lovers. [5]

Incidence of Woman-Marriage among the Lovedu

We are not given any indication of the incidence of woman-marriage in Dahomey or among the Nuer except in the most general terms. But it would appear that the incidence of woman-marriage in Africa as a whole is nowhere high in proportion to other marriages and this is what one would expect. Among the Lovedu, where one cannot remain long in the society without coming across it, I have found its highest incidence outside the royal capital itself to be only 5 percent of the total number of married women in the community. In the capital, where there were 75 married women in a population of 312, the proportion of woman-marriage was 37 percent; with a few exceptions these cases were the queen's wives. In other areas the incidence was lower, as little as 1 percent in one case. It is extremely difficult without an intimate knowledge of the people of the area enumerated to get any reliable figures on woman-marriage. When the wife is old and lives with a married son, people no longer remember that she was married to a woman and when she is young it is not always easy to tell in the case of an absent migrant whether the woman married for him is his or his mother's wife. Woman-marriage is never reflected in any official census. Its real incidence among the Lovedu is likely to be in excess of any figures one may obtain.

SUMMARY OF CONDITIONS IN WHICH WOMAN-MARRIAGE IS FOUND

Before going on to discuss the bearing of woman-marriage on the definition of marriage, let us summarize briefly the conditions in which woman-marriage is found. It is likely to be found in a concatenation of circumstances in which there is agnatic descent; where payment of brideprice is an important factor in securing a wife and obtaining legal control over her children; and where it is possible to a greater or lesser extent for women in general or certain women in particular to acquire

226

and control wealth, whether by inheritance, by their own skills, by the exercise of certain rights (as among the Lovedu), or where, as among the Zulu, a woman can, failing brothers, act in handling property for securing heirs to her father's house. In Nuer society wealth can be obtained only by barren women, who are treated as men in the inheritance of goods, who can exercise control over their own property, however acquired, and may use their property to marry wives. The children born belong to the agnatic lineage of the female husband. Among the Venda and Lovedu and also in Dahomey and eastern Nigeria a woman can acquire wealth by inheritance or by her own earnings, which she may use to marry a wife. Among the Ibo the children would belong to the lineage of the man to whom the female husband was herself married. If, however, she divorced her husband before marrying a woman the children would take the name of the female husband and belong to her father's lineage. In the case of the Lovedu or Venda, a woman, when marrying a woman with wealth she has earned herself, creates an incipient "house" within her own house (which was established by her marriage in her husband's family), as if the wife were married to a son of the house. When she marries a woman with property belonging to her father's family, the children belong to and inherit in her father's family. It is mostly only married women who contract woman-marriage, girls being married soon after puberty. In Zulu society, where there are severe limitations on the control a woman may exercise over property, it would appear that only a diviner might be in a position to marry a wife with her own earnings.

Woman-marriage may be closely bound up with rights and duties arising from the social structure. A Lovedu woman, besides being able to acquire and control property of her own, has claims and rights in relation to the house established with the bridewealth received for her and exercises control over the disposition of the bridewealth received for her daughters. She has duties in regard to the perpetuation of both her family of procreation and her family of orientation. Women here have access to wealth also through the political positions they may hold such as that of district head or queen.

Woman-marriage in Dahomey is said to be closely associated with the need for labor and the building up of an independent compound by a woman of wealth. In a rather different situation the services of a wife to her mother-in-law are important considerations, too, in Lovedu woman-marriage.

Woman-marriage as a last resort in raising a male heir to perpetuate the name and inherit the property of a man (or of a particular "house" of a polygynist) seems to be quite its most widespread form. Two other ways in which woman-marriage may occur are through inheritance, as when a woman inherits a wife from her father, and by gift, as when a Venda woman is given a wife by her mother who has contracted woman-marriage, in the same way as a son may be given such a wife.

Woman-marriage is a flexible institution that can be utilized in a number of different ways to meet a number of different situations. It is being used also in the modern situation of migrant labor, where it has the effect of cushioning disruptive influences on marriage and family life.

WOMAN-MARRIAGE AND THE DEFINITION OF MARRIAGE

Genitor or Husband?

Having reviewed some representative variations of woman-marriage, let us consider its bearing on the definition of marriage. Here the position of genitor in relation to husband is of importance. The use of a genitor is not confined to woman-marriage. It is resorted to in many parts of Africa as a substitute for an impotent husband. Among the Venda this may be done with or without the consent and knowledge of the husband by a decision of members of his agnatic family, in which case the wife is asked to choose a close agnate of her husband. The matter is always considered to be secret. Sometimes the wife is allowed to accept lovers but warned to act with discretion (Van Warmelo 1948: Part 2, number 804).

In woman-marriage the position of genitor varies, not only from one society to another but within a single society. Among the Venda and Lovedu, where the woman may be allowed complete freedom to have children by any man she likes, such a lover has no recognition whatsoever and runs the risk, in the case of the Venda, of being prosecuted for adultery if discovered. The lover of a queen's *motanoni*, too, even when given permission by the queen must not be known to the public. Where a genitor is asked to "enter," he is entitled among most of the Bantu peoples of South Africa to one head of cattle for his services after children have been born, a right enforceable at law. Among the Venda such a genitor can be called upon to render services, such as mending the fences of the woman whose hut he is entering or repairing her hut. Even though the genitor has no economic responsibilities for the woman, she is always, in practice, able to obtain a good deal of economic assistance from him for herself and the children in the form of gifts. And it would be wrong to view the position of genitor from the purely legal point of view. He operates in a situation in which human relationships are the overriding factor. We have seen how, among the Lovedu, the genitor can in certain circumstances come to be recognized by his children and by the general public as their father. Such a *de facto* situation can even be reflected in the ancestor cult. The Zulu do not allow lovers in woman-marriage, any more than they do in ordinary marriage, and they give the genitor in woman-marriage a degree of social recognition that comes close to that of a husband, though he has no rights to the children and may not remove the woman to a *kraal* of his own.

We find among the South Bantu almost every gradation in the position of genitor from the complete absence of any legal or social recognition whatever, in the case of a permitted secret lover of the Lovedu, to an honored position among the Zulu, a position not far removed from that of a husband, except that legally the children are not his own.

The position of the genitor in Dahomean woman-marriage is similar in a number of respects to that of the invited or appointed genitor among the Lovedu, in the sense that he has no responsibilities for the woman and children and renders no services other than sexual ones. But he differs in Dahomey in receiving no payment and he appears to be given social recognition as father of the children, which the Lovedu genitor is not entitled to.

Rights in *Uxorem* and *Genetricem*

Laura Bohannan (1949:286), discussing Herskovits's Dahomey material, distinguishes rights *in uxorem*, which she defines as "rights over a woman as wife, the granting of which constitutes marriage" and rights *in genetricem*, defined as "rights over a woman as to her children." She would have it that in all cases of woman-marriage and marriage without transfer of rights to the children, rights *in uxorem* have been transferred to the biological father, and all these cases therefore constitute marriage between the man and the woman. Of woman-marriage in particular she says, ''The female husband has transferred to him (the genitor) rights *in uxorem* and as the active holder of these rights he is the true husband of the woman'' (Bohannan 1949:282). But what are these rights he is holding? She does not define what she considers as rights *in uxorem* and what therefore she means by marriage. These rights are very different in the various forms of union she is considering. The genitor in woman-marriage may not reside with the woman with whom he cohabits, has no responsibilities towards her or her children other than his sexual services (which he may have to share with her lovers), and is given no recognition by the ancestors. In *vidotohwe* marriage the man, though he does not live with the woman, *has* responsibilities towards her and her children; he does not share the woman with others; he pays a portion of the brideprice and is recognized by the ancestors. In *akwenusi* or full marriage a woman lives in her husband's compound, renders him all the services of a wife, cooking and cleaning, working her own fields, and helping her husband in his (Herskovits 1938 I:350). Since these rights bear so little relation to one another and the situations are so divergent it is not clear on what grounds it is maintained that the biological father in woman-marriage and in the other cases mentioned all have rights *in uxorem*. If the concept of rights *in uxorem* is to be of any value it is surely desirable to define these rights clearly. They will not be the same in every society. Without a careful analysis of the rights and duties of different parties to a marriage the concept of rights *in uxorem* can have little meaning or value. We discuss this point more fully later.

Implications of Lovedu Woman-Marriage for the Definition of Marriage

We have seen how Rivière (1971), in seeking to define marriage, eliminates any consideration of woman-marriage on the grounds that, according to Evans-Pritchard, a Nuer woman in marrying a female is taking on the role of a man. Therefore, he argues, if instead of defining the marital union as being between a man and a woman we substitute for man and woman the words ''the conceptual roles of male and female'' we can avoid the difficulty presented by woman-marriage. He goes on to say, "It seems unnecessary to consider other examples of woman-marriage" (Rivière 1971:68). One wonders why. Does Rivière assume they are all the same as the Nuer?

There is no doubt that the "male" role of a female husband in woman-marriage has been stressed in the literature on the Nuer and on West Africa. But before it can be said that a woman is taking on the role of a man, a careful study must have been made of the roles of men and women in a particular society. It may appear, for example, that when a Lovedu woman succeeds to the headmanship of an area in the absence of a brother to succeed, and marries a wife to raise an heir to him, she is taking on the role of a man. But in a society ruled by a queen, a society in which a woman may be placed as headman of a newly formed district in her own right, to rule a district is as much a feminine as a masculine role. There are, among the Lovedu, a number of roles that can be assumed by either a male or a female. One such role is that of officiator at a beer-offering to the gods and it would seem that in Lovedu society marriage to a woman can also be undertaken by a member of either sex.

When a Lovedu woman who has no son to carry on the name of her "house" within her husband's lineage marries a girl, this can be conceived as a fictitious marriage on behalf of her nonexistent son. It may be said of such a woman that she is "marrying a wife," but mostly the Lovedu say, *O vekile noeji*—she has married a bride or daughter-in-law, (the bride is *noeji* to this woman's husband and a number of other men in the *kraal* too). A woman may also marry a woman when she *has* sons, however. If she has acquired wealth by practicing as a doctor, a woman (whom we may call A) may marry a woman, B, in order to put this wealth to use and to increase the labor resources and prestige of A's house and of A herself. Because she has used her own wealth, not the bridewealth of her daughter, the daughter in this case has no special rights over B, the bride. The female husband A may allocate B to her own husband or son for the procreation of children, but neither of them has a right to "enter" the girl B's hut and, if she wished, A could allocate B to one of her own blood kin or give her permission to have children by lovers. However, far from taking on a male role, the female doctor in marrying a woman is simply claiming her right to the labor of this girl married into her "house" and is carrying out her duty as wife and originator of this "house" of her husband's to promote its interests and increase its size. She has married the girl, not in the role of a male,

231

but in her capacity as mother-in-law, with rights to the girl's services and an interest in the growth and development of her "house." The task of genitor of the children can be delegated to others who have no rights in the marriage. An interesting case illustrating a woman's right to have a wife of her own even if she has a son is a recent one, in which the queen gave one of her royal wives to an old woman in the capital whose married son had taken his wife to live with him in an African township some ten miles distant, leaving his mother with no one to stamp and draw water for her (considered very strenuous work at her age). The old woman has allowed her son to have sexual access to the girl (which has made him a frequent visitor to his old home). But the girl is regarded as his mother's and her son may not take her away with him.

There are, then, quite clearly marriages among the Lovedu in which the main constituent units are not a man and a woman (according to Rivière [1971:63], "marriage's single universal feature"), but two or more women. Moreover, ordinary marriage among the Lovedu is not only a union between husband and wife but involves a number of different individuals (each of whom has specific rights and duties), as well as two or more groups.

Marriage, therefore, among the Lovedu is much more than the union between a man and a woman. It is a joint enterprise for securing descendants for the continuation of a "house;" it involves a number of key individuals of more than one family, each of whom has an interest in it; more than one of the key individuals in the "house" of the husband can, in certain circumstances, take the initiative and marry a girl; and, although the service of a male is necessary for the procreation of children, not one of the constituent units in a marriage needs to be a male.

The incidence of woman-marriage in Africa may be low, but the fact that it exists in the forms that have been described is of considerable significance for the light this throws on the whole institution of marriage and the relationships within it. Marriage can take widely different forms, even sometimes, within the same society, each involving different categories of rights and duties. The sexual relationship between the parties concerned in a marriage is not, as is commonly believed, central to the institution. Marriage may be entered upon by people of

232

the same sex in capacities that have no sexual connotation. Marriage in Africa is concerned largely with ensuring the continuation of groups, with the creation of new social units such as "house" or compound, with the handing down of office, the conferring of status and position. Marriage is part and parcel of the whole social structure and of the system of religious and symbolic beliefs within the society (in Africa, particularly the ancestor cult). Nor must the economic connotations of marriage, marriage as a means of gaining access to resources in labor, to the services of a woman and her children, be overlooked. (This aspect may be played down very much in modern western marriage but the freely given, home making services of a wife are still of considerable importance in a man's decision to marry.) Rivière (1971:70) may be right when, agreeing with Leach, he says that there is "no single definition of marriage;" in stating that ". . . in our discussion on marriage we have never taken our eyes off what the institution does in order to look at its composition, its constituent elements and the relationship between them" (Rivière 1971:63), he is making a valid criticism and suggesting a valuable line of approach; but he himself fails to make use of this approach when, without fully examining the evidence, he maintains that ". . . the constituent elements in marriage are men and women," that ". . . relationships in marriage are concerned with the conceptual role of male and female." Further, in trying to get marriage viewed as ". . . merely one aspect of the total possible relationship between the male and the female categories in any society" (Rivière 1971:70-71), he is limiting himself to a part only of the relationships within marriage.

CONCLUSION

What comes out clearly from this study is that woman-marriage is no aberrant, quaint custom. Nor has it any sexual connotation for the two women concerned. It forms an essential part of, and is closely integrated with, the whole social system in which it is found. It can serve a great diversity of purposes, has shown itself to be flexible in the modern situation and bears testimony to a conception of marriage among the people who practice it that is far wider, more comprehensive, less bound up with the sexual needs of the individual partners than in western society. Indeed, it may be said that in the societies under discussion marriage carries with it no necessary sexual implications for the individuals in whose names it is contracted.

NOTES

Acknowledgments. The research on which the material in this paper is based was undertaken first in 1936-38 when I held an International African Institute Fellowship and again over the period 1964-70 on a grant from the Human Sciences Research Council of South Africa. It has been of special value in my analysis of Lovedu woman-marriage to be in a position to view it in particular families over a time span of nearly forty years.

The preparation of this paper was made possible by the generosity of the National Science Foundation of the United States of America and of the University of Florida in allowing me to use a portion of the period during which I held a National Science Foundation Fellowship (1970-71) to work up my research material. I wish to express my thanks and gratitude to all these bodies. I am indebted also to Professor John Argyle of the University of Natal and Dr. G.I. Jones of Cambridge University for the care with which they read an earlier draft of this paper and for their valuable comments and criticisms; also to Professor A. Vilakazi of The American University, Washington, D.C., for permission to use some of his unpublished material on the Zulu.

1 He observes the obligations of a bridegroom and makes the usual marriage payments, all except the ritual ones, consisting of 720 cowries ("a considerable sum in the old days," [Herskovits 1938 I: 338]), a goat for the ancestral founder of the girl's family, 5.50 francs, and a raffia bag of salt. It is by virtue of these ritual gifts that rights in the children are transferred in *akwenusi*, or full marriage. The *vidotohwe* bridegroom is accepted and blessed by the oldest man of the

compound in the name of the ancestors. Other examples of marriage without transfer of rights to the children in Dahomey are the marriage of a princess (*axovivi*, prince-child-child marriage [Herskovits 1938 I: 333]) and that of female attendants to princesses. These differ widely from one another and from the *vidotohwe* form (Herskovits 1938 I: 320, 326; Bohannan 1949: 281).

2 These conditions still prevail today except that, owing to the density of population and insufficient land, families have to rely largely on migrant labor earnings to buy maize, their staple food.

3 For a fuller discussion of these points see Krige (1964: 155-195).

4 If she is a married woman with young children it might not be easy to leave her husband's *kraal* [homestead] to go and live in the *kraal* of her deceased father. Sometimes for other reasons she may prefer to be an absentee ruler, e.g., if she fears being bewitched.

5 The situation today is that the genitor or lover (and it is rare to appoint a genitor nowadays) tends to enter the woman's house openly. He is expected to give her clothes and if necessary to help her with food, repairs to her house, and so on. In one case where a female husband had been giving clothes to her "wife" she stopped doing so when this woman began going out with lovers, saying, ". . . these men can now dress her."

REFERENCES CITED

Bohannan, Laura
    1949 Dahomean Marriage: A Revaluation. Africa 19(4): 273-287.
Evans-Pritchard, E.E.
    1945 Some Aspects of Marriage and the Family among the Nuer. Rhodes-Livingstone Papers, No. 11. Northern Rhodesia: Rhodes-Livingstone Institute.
    1951 Kinship and Marriage among the Nuer. Oxford: Clarendon Press.
Herskovits, Melville J.
    1937 A Note on Woman Marriage in Dahomey. Africa 10(3): 335-341.

1938   Dahomey: An Ancient West African Kingdom. Two volumes. New York: Augustine.

Jones, Gwilyn I.
1963   The Trading States of the Oil Rivers: A Study of Political Development in Eastern Nigeria. London: Oxford University Press, for the International African Institute.

Krige, Eileen Jensen
1964   Property, Cross-Cousin Marriage and the Family Cycle among the Lovedu. *In* The Family Estate in Africa: Studies in the Role of Property in Family Structure and Lineage Continuity. Robert F. Gray and P.H. Gulliver, eds. Pp. 155-195. London: Routledge and Kegan Paul.

Krige, Eileen J., and J.D. Krige
1943   The Realm of a Rain-Queen: A Study of the Pattern of Lovedu Society. London: Oxford University Press, for the International Institute of African Language and Cultures.

Krige, J.D.
1939   The Significance of Cattle Exchanges in Lovedu Social Structure. Africa 12(4): 393-424.

Leach, E.R.
1961   Rethinking Anthropology. London School of Economics Monographs on Social Anthropology, No. 22. London: Athlone Press.

Mair, Lucy P.
1971   Marriage. Harmondsworth, England: Penguin.

Rivière, Peter G.
1971   Marriage: A Reassessment. *In* Rethinking Kinship and Marriage. Rodney Needham, ed. Pp. 57-74. A.S.A. Monographs, No. 11. London: Tavistock.

Royal Anthropological Institute of Great Britain and Ireland
1951   Notes and Queries on Anthropology. 6th ed., revised. London: Routledge and Kegan Paul.

Seligman, Charles G., and Brenda Z. Seligman
1965   Pagan Tribes of the Nilotic Sudan. London: Routledge and Kegan Paul. (First ed., 1932.)

Talbot, Percy A.
1969   The Peoples of Southern Nigeria: A Sketch of their History, Ethnology and Languages, with an Abstract of the 1921 Census. London: Cass. (First ed., 1926.)

236

Van Warmelo, Nicolaas J.
    1943/49   Venda Law. Ethnological Publications, No. 23. Part 1,
    1943; Parts 2 and 3, 1948; Part 4, 1949. Department of Native
    Affairs. Pretoria: Government Printer.
Winch, Robert F.
    1968   Marriage: Family Formation. *In* International Encyclope-
    dia of the Social Sciences. Vol. 10. Pp. 1-8. New York: Mac-
    millan.

SUGGESTIONS FOR FURTHER READING

Gough, E. Kathleen
    1959   The Nayars and the Definition of Marriage. Journal of the
    Royal Anthropological Institute of Great Britain and Ireland 89:
    23-34.
    Assesses the problems of standard anthropological definitions of
    marriage from the perspective of an 18th century caste society in
    Kerala, India. A classic essay.
Lewis, Oscar
    1941   Manly-Hearted Women among the North Piegan.
    American Anthropologist 43: 173-187.
    Describes the processes of gender transformation that enabled
    Canadian Blackfeet women to acquire masculine ("manly-
    hearted") attributes. The author states that ". . . the manly-
    hearted woman is a deviant, —a highly endowed woman who
    takes advantage of the opportunities afforded women in this
    culture" (1941: 187).
O'Brien, Denise
    1977   Female Husbands in Southern Bantu Societies. *In* Sexual
    Stratification: A Cross-Cultural View. Alice Schlegel, ed.
    Pp. 109-126. New York: Columbia University Press.
    Excellent discussion of woman-marriage institutions among
    traditional and contemporary African societies. Concludes that
    in some systems women must be sociologically converted into
    males in order to exercise or symbolize political power and
    authority.

SEX DIFFERENCES IN THE INCIDENCE OF *SUSTO* IN TWO ZAPOTEC PUEBLOS: AN ANALYSIS OF THE RELATIONSHIPS BETWEEN SEX ROLE EXPECTATIONS AND A FOLK ILLNESS

Carl W. O'Nell and Henry A. Selby

Susto is a name frequently given to an illness widely reported in Hispanic America. Because of its obvious affinity to specific cultural patterns and because the condition falls beyond the pale of orthodox medical practice, *susto* is classed as a folk illness (Rubel 1964). In dealing with the phenomenon we have chosen *susto* in preference to other terms (e.g., *espanto, miedo, pasmo, desasombro*) largely because of its rather general usage in anthropological literature. *Susto* has been richly described by numerous authors writing on Hispanic American cultures, among the more recent being Carrasco (1960), Clark (1959), Foster (1953), Gillin (1948), Guiteras Holmes (1961), and Rubel (1960).

Although widely distributed in Hispanic America, the distribution is by no means uniform, and there are local variations in assumed causalities, symptomatologies, diagnoses, and treatment processes (Kelly 1965). Nevertheless, the consistencies in ethnographic reports of this condition for various groups are strong enough to warrant the description of a basic syndrome (Gillin 1948; Rubel 1964). In wakefulness, the *susto* sufferer is listless, depressed, and timid, usually exhibiting a loss of interest in his customary affairs, and frequently complaining of poor appetite and loss of strength. In sleep, the patient is restless, often complaining of troublesome dreams or other manifestations of sleep

Reprinted by permission of the authors and publisher from *Ethnology* 7(1):95-105, 1968.

disturbance. One of the more consistently encountered folk beliefs is that the *asustado* (sufferer from *susto*) has lost his soul to a malignant spirit and that the patient's cure rests upon the recovery of the soul through specific treatments or rites performed by a curing specialist.[1]

The majority of anthropological contributions to the subject of *susto* have been descriptive. Recent work (Clark 1959; Foster 1952; Gillin 1948) suggests that the condition probably serves a psycho-social function in certain cultural settings. The contribution of Rubel (1964) is particularly valuable, not only because it attempts an orderly description of the phenomenon—its symptomatology and folk etiology—but especially because it presents an array of hypotheses which can be considered for empirical research.

Having learned in the course of our fieldwork in two Zapotec communities in Oaxaca, Mexico, that *susto* was commonly experienced in both villages, we were encouraged to undertake a collaborative study of this folk illness as a psycho-social phenomenon. Using Rubel's work as a point of departure, we developed an hypothesis linking sex role performance to the incidence of *susto*. Each of us worked independently, collecting the necessary field data in his selected village, O'Nell in San Marcos Tlapazola and Selby in Santo Tomas Mazaltepec.

THE VILLAGES

The villages are each about one hour's drive by automobile from the city of Oaxaca. San Marcos Tlapazola lies to the southeast and Santo Tomas Mazaltepec to the northwest of the capital. Both are old foundations. Santo Tomas Mazaltepec is clearly pre-Columbian in origin, and it appears in the list of towns originally allotted to Cortez (Iturribarría 1955:75). The antiquity of San Marcos Tlapazola is not as clearly documented, although Spanish archives currently stored in the local *palacio,* dealing with civil and religious administrative affairs, support the probability that it was a settled community at the time of the arrival of the Spaniards.

The preconquest histories of the two pueblos are divergent, evidenced by the fact that San Marcos Tlapazola speaks a Valley dialect, and Santo Tomas Mazaltepec a Sierra dialect. Events since the Spanish conquest have tended to produce convergence. The two villages share approximately the same ecological conditions, subsistence patterns, social organization, and general cultural form. Despite their proximity—they are about forty-two kilometers from each other—there is no direct contact between them.[2] For our purposes, then, they represent two independent cases within the same cultural area.

In describing their experiences with or knowledge of *susto*, the people in San Marcos Tlapazola and Santo Tomas Mazaltepec evidenced close agreement. Reports of symptomatology, folk etiology, and courses of treatment were essentially consistent between the two communities. Commonly reported symptoms closely approximated those making up the syndrome described by Rubel (1964).

A few variations will illustrate regional and individual differences which conceivably could be of importance in cross-regional studies of *susto*. These variations tended to be in the nature of additional symptoms, i.e., unexpected complaints offered in addition to, rather than in place of more commonly reported symptoms. Loosely ranked in order of the frequency with which they were reported, these symptoms were fever, muscular pains, complexion changes, nausea, other stomach or intestinal upsets, and vertigo. One person gave intense thirst as a *susto* symptom; another listed rectal bleeding.

There is also a widespread and interesting belief that in stubborn cases the assistance of a *medico* (orthodox medical practitioner) may be efficacious. Strongly implicit in this belief, however, is the notion that the powers of the native curer are paramount in soul recovery and that the medical doctor assists only in strengthening the body by supplying vitamins and other medicines. Also deserving of mention, because it is consistent with similar beliefs elsewhere in Hispanic America, is the belief that unless cured, *susto* culminates in death.

THE PSYCHO-SOCIAL FUNCTION OF *SUSTO*

Developing an hypothesis relating sex role expectations to the reported incidence of *susto* in each of the villages seemed the most feasible approach we could take in this study. Because of anticipated sampling difficulties and the reduced likelihood of obtaining sufficient data to specify variables, we excluded the study of age role expectations. And because of the gross social and cultural similarities between the villages, we focused the study on sex role differences rather than inter-village differences.

Following Rubel (1964), we made the basic assumption that *susto* represents an important culturally and socially sanctioned avenue of escape for an individual suffering from an intraculturally induced stress. *Susto* was assumed to be the result of an individual's self-perceived failure to meet a set of culturally established expectations in a role in which he had been socialized. Although not fundamental to the design of our study, we made the further assumption that the *susto* experience provides a person and his social group with mechanisms for the eventual social reinstatement of the individual.

Once a person is labeled *asustado,* an important shift obviously occurs in his relationship to others. Normal role expectations are relaxed to a greater or lesser extent and a new repertoire of behavior becomes appropriate. The *asustado* becomes temporarily what Goffman (1959: 95-96) would call a "non-person"—a person who by virtue of his relaxed social situation can act without reference to the detailed codes that normally bind his behavior. The disease condition provides a psychological respite—a moratorium in normal role performance. This shift in role is conceived to be the basic function of *susto* as a psychosocial phenomenon. The culture provides a channel of escape for the relief of psychological stress engendered within the cultural framework.

Of no less importance, either to the individual or society, are the processes of rehabilitation and reintegration which ultimately will reunite the individual to his group (Parsons and Fox 1952). The treatment of the sufferer involves a temporary change of status which of itself may signal the beginning of rehabilitation. By village standards, considerable time and money are expended upon the *asustado.* More importantly, perhaps, he frequently becomes the focus of a great deal of sympathetic understanding, especially within his own extended family group. The treatment thus constitutes a form of reassurance that the sufferer is, in fact, an important member of the extended family.

From Bateson's (1958) point of view, the development of *susto* constitutes a signal that schism within the extended family had gone too far for the affected individual to tolerate. Treatment is the process whereby the schism is resolved and the sufferer is reincorporated into the group.

We do not, of course, assume that *susto* represents the only mechanism of escape in the face of stress generated through self-perceived role inadequacy. General health conditions, temperamental tendencies, personality traits, situational variables, and other factors conceivably must all be assumed to have a bearing upon whether a given person develops *susto* when confronted with role stress or whether some other avenue of relief from stress becomes manifest. Our assumption is merely that, once it is developed, *susto* presents us with a measure of role stress.

Cognizant of all the preceding assumptions, but focusing upon the assumption that *susto* is the result of emotional stress engendered through a self-perceived failure to meet a set of social expectations regarding sex role performance, we have formulated the following hypothesis: *The sex which experiences the greater intracultural stress in the process of meeting sex role expectations will evidence the greater susceptibility to* susto.

SEX ROLE DIFFERENCES

Male-female sex role differences hinge fundamentally upon the differential socialization of boys and girls. Parents in the two communities often indicate that boys are more delicate than girls in infancy with the observable result that boys are more freely indulged. The factual basis for this alleged delicacy is difficult to validate with our data, but it agrees with findings in our own and other cultures that male infants are subject to higher mortality rates than are female infants (Scheinfeld 1958). It may simply reflect a prevailing tendency to prefer male off-spring to female offspring.

From some point early in childhood girls learn that they are more restricted than boys. A small sample of mothers in Santo Tomas Mazaltepec (N = 6) indicated that boys require greater indulgence than girls because they are eventually due to experience greater liberty. Although parents in San Marcos Tlapazola were less explicit on

242

this point, very young boys were more frequently observed moving about freely in the *calles* near their homes than were young girls.

In middle childhood both sexes are expected to perform certain simple duties, such as carrying small bundles and running errands. Observation seems to indicate that boys frequently escape punishment for dalliance on errands, whereas girls may be severely reprimanded or punished for similar dalliance. Responsibilities of childcare are preponderantly allotted to girls, although boys do not escape such duties, especially if there are no girls in the household.

Young boys are permitted, even encouraged under certain conditions, to manifest aggressive behavior, whereas girls rarely exhibit aggressive tendencies and run the risk of punishment if they do exhibit them. This is particularly evident in teasing behavior and the maltreatment of small animals.

Prepubescent and adolescent girls are expected to learn and master many tasks the counterparts of which occur much later for boys. At an age when a boy is just learning how to direct a plow and drive oxen, a girl may be married, pregnant, and responsible for an adult woman's tasks of food preparation.

These differences in socialization are but reflections of the differential sex role expectations of mature men and women. A woman should be constantly at work caring for her house, her children, her mother-in-law, her husband, or tending to her pottery making. In contrast, a man is expected to rest periodically because his work is deemed to be harder. If a woman appears idle she is suspected of being a gossip. Except for infidelity, this is the worst offence a woman can commit since it tends to disrupt communal harmony.

A woman is expected to control herself. In Santo Tomas Mazaltepec a woman's loss of composure is associated with temporary possession of *mal de ojo* (evil eye). In San Marcos Tlapazola it may indicate that the woman is incapable of presenting a proper spiritual defense against malignant forces which may harm her or her family. In either circumstance an angry mother is frequently held accountable for illness in her children. The ideal woman is enduring and patient. Men, too, are expected to control themselves, but if a man seriously loses his temper it is often assumed that he is justified in doing so.

A woman must be submissive and give no indication of rebelliousness (actually women learn to get their way by the practice of guile). Ideally, men do not rebel either, but they have at their disposal many more ways of making their wishes known or effecting their own plans.

The Zapotec woman in these communities is allowed virtually no freedom of sexual expression, and she must tolerate her husband's infidelities as long as he does not publicly proclaim a rupture in their marital relations. Men, on the other hand, enjoy a distinct sexual advantage in being able to exploit women other than their wives. Cognizant of the intricacies of this situation, men show extreme jealousy of their wives. The slightest suspicion of infidelity grants a man license to beat his wife. Unaccompanied women do not move about freely in either village. Men frequently say, ''Women have no vices because they do not go out in the streets.'' It would be more correct to say, ''Women do not go out in the streets so that there will be no suspicion of vice.''

Residential patterns after marriage also complicate a woman's sex role expectations as compared to those for men. In both Santo Tomas Mazaltepec and San Marcos Tlapazola it is customary for the young bride to move to her husband's family. In Santo Tomas Mazaltepec residence is 75 percent patrilocal, i.e., with the husband's parents. In San Marcos Tlapazola it is 78 percent patrilocal. [3]

Currently some girls marry as early as fourteen years of age. [4] Although the vast majority of marriages are contracted within the village, girls move into a new extended family setting. The emotional effect of changing residential patterns at marriage may be considerable. The new bride is subject to the authority not only of her husband but also of his mother and father, and in effect she may find that she has to obey many other persons as well. To be sure, the authority of her father-in-law or husband's older brother may be indirect, it is nevertheless felt and in actuality may outweigh the authority of her husband.

The mother-in-law is usually the key figure with whom the new bride has to contend. The young girl may literally be under the surveillance of her mother-in-law from dawn until dusk. The prevailing ethic brooks no disrespect or disobedience to the mother-in-law, and neither beatings, tongue lashings, nor ''sweat-shop'' work conditions constitute grounds for noncompliance. Ordinarily mothers-in-law are strict, much stricter than mothers. Boys continue to work with their fathers and brothers even after marriage. Young men, married or unmarried, have considerable freedom of movement and in their leisure meet with friends in the *calles* or the *cantinas*.

Children represent a positive value in these communities. Sterility is regarded as a very unfortunate condition and is feared by married couples since it means that in old age they will not have the assistance of adult children. The major responsibility of any married woman is the bearing and rearing of children. If the union is sterile, the onus of sterility is commonly placed on the woman, although some people realize that men as well as women can be sterile. Child mortality in the two villages is high—conservatively estimated at about 40 percent of all births. Stillbirths are frequent, and in such cases little if any public recognition is given to the fact that pregnancy has even occurred. For children who have survived the first year of life, however, death is viewed as a tragic occurrence, and someone, nearly always the mother, is held responsible for the tragedy. (In neither village did we observe the resignation to the death of young children which has been reported for other parts of Meso-America.) The grave responsibilities associated with having children and the uncertainties which surround it constitute a potential source of deep emotional stress weighing more heavily upon women that upon men.

It seems quite clear that women must conform to a tighter set of role expectations than men. Moreover, they have fewer ways of reducing anxiety over role performance. The role expectations of the male more readily allow him to shift responsibility from his shoulders than is true for the female. If his crops do poorly, he may blame the weather or a malevolent agent, but if the woman fails in her household tasks or in the care of children she alone is to blame. Similarly men are freer than women to engage in strategic retreat from uncomfortable situations. A man under emotional stress may relieve his anxieties by going to his *milpa* (corn field) for a day, on a trading expedition for a week, or, if necessary, to the *fincas* (plantations) in the hot country for a prolonged period of work. Women, with extremely few exceptions, cannot practice comparable forms of social withdrawal. Finally, men can retreat into an approved state of irresponsibility, the most frequent and obvious being that of drunkenness. The *borracho* (drunk), even when he proves to be a nuisance, is treated with exceptional tolerance. People are also willing to concede that he may have his reasons, and there are many situations in which this method of escape is socially sanctioned.

Young women are effectively barred by community pressures from using drunkenness as an escape from responsibility. And older women, who enjoy increased status and greater freedom from restraint in their use of alcohol, find the occasions which they can use alcohol with impunity fewer in number and kind than those open even to younger males. [5]

Two additional measures of differential sex role expectations support our other ethnographic observations. The first of these measures freedom of social participation; the second measures cognitive evaluation.

In Santo Tomas Mazaltepec drunken fiestas lasting three to five days are customarily celebrated in honor of a person's saint's day (called *cuelga* or *dia del onomastico*). These are socially sanctioned occasions when participants are permitted relatively free expression of aggression and affective feelings. We interpret them as opportunities for the relief of emotional stress. The frequency of *cuelga* attendance by men and women, obtained from a sample of fifty-five individuals in Santo Tomas Mazaltepec, revealed a statistically significant difference between the sexes (see Table 2).

If our assumption about the *cuelga* as a sanctioned means of stress relief is correct, it appears that men are significantly freer to avail themselves of this avenue of escape than women are. However, one must be cautious in making the broad assumption that the *cuelga* operates uniformly as a mechanism for relief from stress for the two sexes. It may be that young married women find attendance at *cuelgas* stressful. [6]

The second measure is one of the cognitive evaluation of comfort in the life situation. Fifty individuals in San Marcos Tlapazola—twenty-five men and twenty-five women—were asked which sex, in their opinion, finds life more comfortable. The results are reported in Table 3.

Both men and women agree that life is more comfortable for men than it is for women. We find the agreement between the sexes on this

Table 2. Reported Attendance at *Cuelgas* in Santo Tomas Mazaltepec: Differential Response by Sex.

	Attend	Do not attend	Total
Men	26	4	30
Women	12	13	25
Total	38	17	55

Result: $x^2 = 7.2; p < 0.01$ (1 df).

Table 3. Differential Response by Sex Concerning which Sex Experiences Greater Comfort in the Life Situation [San Marcos Tlapazola].

	Men do	Women do	Both equal	Total
Men	13	5	7	25
Women	16	2	7	25
Total	29	7	14	50

matter interesting in view of the fact that it supports descriptive ethnographic data gathered largely by observation with data of an evaluative type from a sizable sample of informants.

DIFFERENTIAL SUSCEPTIBILITY TO *SUSTO*

Since women appear to experience greater intracultural stress than do men in the process of meeting sex role expectations in both San Marcos Tlapazola and Santo Tomas Mazaltepec, our hypothesis would lead us to anticipate that they would reveal greater susceptibility to *susto* than men. Susceptibility to *susto* is defined as the relative proportions of individuals of each sex reporting *susto*.

The data were gathered first in San Marcos Tlapazola from a sample of thirty individuals—fifteen males and fifteen females. They were commonly sought in context with other data, the rationale being that people might not respond readily if confronted by direct questions regarding their experiences with *susto*. In the course of gathering other data, respondents were asked about their personal experiences with *susto* when it seemed convenient to do so. The questions followed a generalized pattern, though they were not always phrased in exactly the same terms for all respondents. They were first presented in Spanish in most cases but frequently had to be repeated in Zapotec. The respondent was first asked whether or not he had experienced *susto* at any time in his life. Then his approximate age at the time of each experience and its duration were recorded. If they wished to do so, respondents were allowed to give details of their experiences concerning symptoms, precipitating causes, etc., but such data were not actively solicited. The ethnographer indicated an equal interest in negative and positive responses to guard against bias.

It was found that most people showed no obvious reluctance to answering questions about their experiences with *susto*. Consequently some persons—both men and women—were approached directly with these questions. In such cases the investigator made it known that he was interested in various health problems in the village and would appreciate any help the respondent might give him by answering a question or two about his experiences with *susto*.

For each individual it was noted whether or not he or she had experienced *susto*. The case was considered positive if an individual reported having had such an experience, regardless of the number and intensity of the experiences reported. An individual was regarded as a negative case if he reported no such experience. The chi square (x^2) test was made of the individual responses. The x^2 difference between men and women was 2.14 (1 df.) Though not significant at the .05 level, this result was encouraging; 67 percent of the women reported some experience with *susto* as compared to 40 percent of the men (Table 4).

Two modifications were made in the method for Santo Tomas Mazaltepec. First, it was felt that a random sample was necessary to control for latent bias. Second, it was decided to take a slightly larger sample. Accordingly, a sample of forty persons—twenty males and twenty females—over twenty years of age was randomly made of the entire native population of Santo Tomas Mazaltepec. Each respondent was asked directly, i.e., not in connection with other data, whether or not he or she had ever experienced *susto*. The number of experiences, the ages at which they had occurred, and the duration of each were recorded for each respondent.

A chi square (x^2) test was run on these data, and the result $X^2 = 5.22$ (1 df) was significant, p< 0.025. In Santo Tomas Mazaltepec 55 percent of the women sampled indicated that they had experienced *susto* at some time in their lives as compared to 20 percent of the men (see Table 5).

CONCLUSIONS

We feel that these two independent tests of our hypothesis serve to support our basic assumption that *susto* represents an important culturally and socially sanctioned mechanism of escape and rehabilitation for persons suffering from intraculturally induced stress resulting from failure in sex role performance. The ethnographic evidence encountered in the two villages indicated that women stand the greater likelihood of experiencing role stress both because their sex roles are more narrowly defined than are those for men and because fewer outlets for escape from stress are open to them in this culture. Consistent with this is our evidence on differential susceptibility, indicating a markedly higher incidence of *susto* among women than among men.

Table 4. Relative Proportions of Males and Females Reporting *Susto* in San Marcos Tlapazola.

	One or more times	Never	Total
Men	6 (40%)	9 (60%)	15
Women	10 (67%)	5 (33%)	15
Total	16	14	30

Result: $x^2 = 2.14$; $p > 0.10$ (1 df).

Table 5. Relative Proportions of Males and Females Reporting *Susto* in Santo Tomas Mazaltepec.

	One or more times	Never	Total
Men	4 (20%)	16 (80%)	20
Women	11 (55%)	9 (45%)	20
Total	15	25	40

Result: $x^2 = 5.22$; $p < 0.025$ (1 df).

The fact that the percentages of men and women who experienced *susto* were greater in San Marcos Tlapazola than in Santo Tomas Mazaltepec may possibly reflect unanalyzed differences between the two communities. On the other hand, they may be only a reflection of differences in method. If this is the case, the data collected in Santo Tomas Mazaltepec, because of the use of random sampling, may be presumed to represent the situation in that community more accurately than would be true of the data collected in San Marcos Tlapazola.

Ethnographic work on *susto* has largely tended to be descriptive. Valuable as this has been for many purposes, it is limited in the understandings it provides of the cultural, social, and psychological underpinnings of folk illnesses such as *susto*. We agree with Rubel (1964:269) who writes:

> *In the absence of precise chronological, social or cultural parameters it is hazardous to attempt to infer rates of prevalence or incidence of a folk illness, much less the relationships which obtain between these rates and such demographic variables as age, sex or marital status. Yet it is precisely from such inferences and associations that we may hope to gain an understanding of the nature of folk illness.*

NOTES

Acknowledgments. We wish to express our gratitude to Robert A. Le Vine of the University of Chicago and to Arthur J. Rubel of the University of Notre Dame for their interest in and comments upon this paper, but any shortcomings it may have are our own.

[1] Either male (*curanderos*) or female (*curanderas*) curers are sought to alleviate this condition in various places in Oaxaca. However, residents of San Marcos Tlapazola insist that only women are effective as curers of *susto* in their community. This preference was not noted for Santo Tomas Mazaltepec.

[2] Estimated from a map of Oaxaca produced by Cecil R. Welte (Mapa de las localidades del Valle de Oaxaca, segun el censo de poblacion de 1960, Oaxaca, 1965).

[3] These percentages were higher in the past (cf. Murdock 1960: 13). In San Marcos Tlapazola, however, 35 percent of all households are nuclear family residential units.

[4] A small number of informants in Santo Tomas Mazaltepec reported marriages at from six to eight years of age, and the customary age for the marriage of girls in previous generations was reported to be from ten to twelve years of age. When this occurred it meant that the young girl, still immature, went to live with her husband's family. Such a girl slept with her mother-in-law until she was sufficiently developed to sleep with her husband. During this maturation period the young girl was socialized in her wifely role under the close supervision of her mother-in-law. Older informants who had experienced this pattern reported that they went to their husbands' houses ignorant of sex, nervous at leaving their family of orientation, feeling abandoned, ex-

252

ploited, and intimidated. Young husbands during the same period of maturation neither changed their residence nor were they so closely supervised. Older and freer than their wives, they were permitted the adolescent license of running with a *palomilla* (gang) and gaining such sexual experience as could be found.

5 Upon becoming a *suegra* (mother-in-law) a woman's status changes appreciably in both communities. The status of mother-in-law brings with it not only respect, deference, and obedience from daughters-in-law but also some relaxation of the disabilities and restrictions associated with the feminine role. At its fullest expression it brings with it a privilege of drunken license and ribaldry approximating that of a senior male.

6 Women who attend these fiestas in Santo Tomas Mazaltepec may actually be subjected to increased stress by the fact of their attendance. Although older women may participate rather freely in the festivities, younger women are expected to remain in the background, sitting discreetly to one side if not working in the kitchen. If a man wishes to dance with a woman other than his wife, he requests this privilege of her husband. Women fear such requests because they may raise suspicion and ire in their husbands. The wife of a jealous man is in danger of a beating on such an occasion.

REFERENCES CITED

Bateson, Gregory
    1958 Naven. 2nd ed. Stanford: Stanford University Press. (First ed., 1936.)
Carrasco, Pedro
    1960 Pagan Rituals and Beliefs Among the Chontal Indians of Oaxaca, Mexico. Anthropological Records 20(3): 87-117.
Clark, Margaret
    1959 Health in the Mexican-American Culture: A Community Study. Berkeley: University of California Press.
Foster, George M.
    1952 Relationships between Theroretical and Applied Anthropology: A Public Health Program Analysis. Human Organization

11: 5-16.
1953 Relationships between Spanish and Spanish-American Folk Medicine. Journal of American Folklore 66: 201-217.

Gillin, John
1948 Magical Fright. Psychiatry 11: 387-400.

Goffman, Erving
1959 The Presentation of Self in Everyday Life. Garden City, New York: Doubleday.

Guiteras Holmes, Calixta
1961 Perils of the Soul: The World View of a Tzotzil Indian. New York: Free Press of Glencoe.

Iturribarría, Jorge F.
1955 Oaxaca en la Historia, de la Época Precolombina a los Tiempos Actuales. Mexico City: Editorial Stylo.

Kelly, Isabel T.
1965 Folk Practices in North Mexico: Birth Customs, Folk Medicine, and Spiritualism in the Laguna Zone. Austin: University of Texas Press, for the Institute of Latin American Studies.

Murdock, George P., ed.
1960 Social Structure in South East Asia. Chicago: Quadrangle Books.

Parsons, Talcott, and Renée Fox
1952 Illness, Therapy and the Modern Urban American Family. Journal of Social Issues 8(4): 31-44.

Rubel, Arthur J.
1960 Concepts of Disease in Mexican-American Culture. American Anthropologist 62: 795-814.
1964 The Epidemiology of a Folk Illness: *Susto* in Hispanic-America. Ethnology 3: 268-283.

Scheinfeld, Amram
1958 The Mortality of Men and Women. Scientific American 198(2): 22-27.

SUGGESTIONS FOR FURTHER READING

Broverman, Inge K., Donald M. Broverman, Frank E. Clarkson, Paul S. Rosenkrantz, and Susan R. Vogel

1972   Sex-Role Stereotypes and Clinical Judgments of Mental Health. *In* Readings on the Psychology of Women. Judith M. Bardwick, ed. Pp. 320-324. New York: Harper and Row. (Originally published in the Journal of Consulting and Clinical Psychology 34[1]: 1-7, 1970.)

Suggests that clinical evaluations of mental health follow sex role stereotypes prevalent in American society. According to this study, ". . . the general standard of health is actually applied only to men, while healthy women are perceived as significantly less healthy by adult standards" (1972: 323).

Morsy, Soheir

1978   Sex Roles, Power, and Illness in an Egyptian Village. American Ethnologist 5: 137-150.

The folk illness of '*uzr*, described ". . . as an index of asymmetrical power relations and sex status," is related to stresses in sex role performance associated with different stages in the developmental cycle of the family (1978: 143). Based on a sample of a hundred households, sons' wives in extended families reported the highest incidence of affliction and mothers of married sons the lowest.

Smith-Rosenberg, Carroll

1972   The Hysterical Woman: Sex Roles and Role Conflict in 19th-Century America. Social Research 39: 652-678.

Examines female hysteria as a social role within the 19th century family. Interesting discussion of hysterical afflictions as an index of marital stress and as a tactical means of "resolving" that stress.

Spring, Anita

1978   Epidemiology of Spirit Possession among the Luvale of Zambia. *In* Women in Ritual and Symbolic Roles. Judith Hoch-Smith and Anita Spring, eds. Pp. 165-190. New York: Plenum Press.

Challenges the social conflict theory of women's spirit possession as a manifestation of intersex antagonism (see Gomm, this volume). Cites data on female natality (profile of a woman's childbearing and childrearing history) to show that Luvale women participate in possession rituals in order to cure their reproductive and other bodily afflictions, as well as the illnesses of their children.

SEXUAL ANTAGONISM IN THE NEW GUINEA HIGHLANDS: A BENA BENA EXAMPLE

L.L. Langness

Throughout the Highlands of New Guinea, with a population of approximately 750,000 people, there is remarkable homogeneity with respect to many aspects of culture. All of the Highlanders are horticulturalists and pig raisers, and hunting is a minor activity. The staple crop everywhere is the sweet potato, and the variety of supplemental food grown is similar. Material culture has only slight regional variations. The gross features of religious, political, and economic organization likewise resemble one another. The annual cycle of life is much the same, and even the major rituals are alike in their fundamentals although elaborated much more in some areas than others (they are generally larger in scale in the Western and Central Highlands than in the Eastern Highlands). Even the ecological setting, acknowledging certain rare extremes, can be considered a constant. This homogeneity seems all the more remarkable when we consider the great language diversity and the fact that the largest autonomous political units are relatively small local groups that seldom attain more than four or five hundred members.

Along with the many similarities, however, are found some important variations. There are significant differences in the genealogical depth of the ubiquitous patrilineal groups; differences in systems of land tenure; differences in residence pattern (a scattered homestead type in

Reprinted by permission of the author and publisher from *Oceania* 37(3):161-177, 1967.

the Western Highlands and a village type in the Eastern Highlands); differences with respect to change and in attitudes towards Europeans. There are also extremes of child training practices and, perhaps, in personality, although these have been little studied. There may be differences in the pattern of warfare from East to West. Probably the most remarkable variation of all can be found in courtship, marriage, and sexual behavior. Within the space of a few miles there is a range of behavior from an almost incomprehensible prudery and ignorance about sexual matters to the opposite of all-night courting parties involving intercourse with several partners, blatant adultery, wife-stealing, rape, and, perhaps, necrophilia. Homosexuality is found and openly discussed in some areas, whereas it appears to be absent in others. Even here, however, in spite of the variation, there are certain constant features. Relations between males and females are everywhere tense and hostile. There is everywhere a fear of menstrual blood, associated always with beliefs about polluting nature of women, with powerful sanctions designed to keep men and women apart. There is always residential separation of the sexes, men's cults of one kind or another, and a complex of belief and ritual expressing the antagonism between the sexes. Little has been written specifically on this subject although the broad features were well described soon after the Highlands area was opened to systematic research in the early 1950s.

In a survey article written in 1954, K.E. Read suggested that: male-female hostility would be found throughout the Highlands; part of the aggressiveness that is said to be characteristic of the Highlanders can be traced to the antagonism pervading sexual encounters; this is reflected in separate housing for males and females throughout the Highlands; connected with the aforementioned is some form of male initiation and seclusion intended to strengthen and purify the young men; but we could expect to find regional differences in the patterned relationships of men and women. Subsequent investigations in the Highlands have confirmed these points, as Meggitt (1964) has recently shown.

Meggitt (1964:221) has further demonstrated three variations on this general theme, two of which he discusses in some detail and one that, although he does not discuss it, he suggests is a combination of the other two:

257

> *I suggest that in Highlands ethnography we must discriminate between at least two kinds of inter-sexual conflict or opposition—the Mae type and the Kuma type. The one reflects the anxiety of prudes to protect themselves from contamination by women, the other the aggressive determination of lechers to assert their control over recalcitrant women . . . . Finally, I should remark that some other societies, apparently only those in the Eastern Highlands, display both sets of characteristics simultaneously or in parallel.*

He then goes on to suggest a correlation between the two general types and, ". . . presence or absence of particular kinds of men's purificatory cults, differences in the status of women in everyday life, and with the degree of hostility existing between affinally related groups." He makes no ". . . explicit assertions about the direction of causal sequences or the relative efficacy of particular factors," as these questions, ". . . cannot be taken up until many more Highlands data have been reported," (Meggitt 1964:206).

I would like in this paper to take a different, but in some ways similar, approach to the subject of male-female relationships. First, I shall restrict myself only to the Bena Bena of the Eastern Highlands. This will add to the ethnographic material on the Bena Bena and will also help to clarify the Eastern Highlands "type" implied in the quotation above. Second, I shall discuss what I think is a more fundamental proposition than has hitherto been suggested, one that asserts a genuine causal and/or functional nexus between four disparate phenomena, namely: warfare; male solidarity; sex and dependency needs; and hostility between the sexes, including the broadest expression of such hostility in daily life as well as in belief and ritual. The general proposition might be stated thus: living in an hostile environment, and faced with the almost constant threat of annihilation by enemy groups, has resulted in, or is related to, a distinctive pattern of male solidarity which offers what the Bena Bena perceive as a better chance for survival. Male solidarity involves the residential separation of the sexes and a complex of beliefs and sanctions designed to insure such separation, as well as a minimal amount of contact between males and females in general. These beliefs and sanctions that exist to buttress the social distance between males and females, although they are functional in terms of group survival in a dangerously warlike environment, are so only at some cost to the sex and dependency needs of individuals and thus ultimately promote hostility and antagonism between the sexes. This assumes, of course, that Bena Bena social structure is intimately related to the exigencies of warfare, a point I have discussed elsewhere (Langness 1964b, 1965), and that there are certain basic human sexual and dependency needs that must be met at some minimal level of satisfaction, which I am simply taking as given. It is not necessary to assume that the sexual and dependency needs of New Guinea natives are precisely the same as those of western Europeans, nor is it necessary to assume that Bena Bena social organization is the only type that could have evolved for coping with warfare.

I shall attempt to show: (1) that sex and dependency needs of both males and females are affected, but in different ways and for different reasons; (2) that legitimate and/or satisfactory outlets for the expression of sexual and dependency needs either do not exist or do not entirely suffice; (3) that this results in or is related to antagonism and hostility between the sexes; and (4) that various Bena Bena attitudes, beliefs, and rituals express and attempt to control this hostility. I hope that discussion along these broad lines will shed further light on the propositions suggested by Meggitt, will introduce as relevant certain psychological considerations which, to date, have not been considered in discussions of New Guinea Highlanders, and will, at the same time, define new lines for investigation.

The name "Bena Bena" originally referred to one relatively small local group ("tribe") that inhabited the ground upon which the first airstrip was built in the Highlands. It has subsequently been extended by the [Australian] Administration to include all people who speak the same language. Thus Bena Bena now applies to a census division of about 14,000 persons divided into approximately 65 "tribes" that were aboriginally, and continue to be, independent groups. Each of these is composed of from two to five patrilineal exogamous clans. This group is by far the most important political entity and is almost totally autonomous. Each clan inhabits a ridge top, usually surrounded by its gardens, and controls a limited amount of territory. There are, nowadays, from one to three villages in each clan territory. Clans of the same tribe usually help each other in warfare, sometimes initiate their young men at the same time, and sometimes participate jointly in the annual pig exchanges with other tribes. There is, however, some suspicion of sorcery between clans, and an individual's ultimate loyalty is always to his own clan rather than to any larger political or social unit.

Prior to European contact, villages were fortified, and there were elaborate precautions and strategies for defence. [1] Men and women slept apart; the men in the men's house, and each married woman had a house of her own for herself, her children, and the pigs. Because the men's house was the prime target for a raid, it was sometimes fitted with a false door that could be easily kicked out to allow the men to escape. In other instances there was a tunnel leading from the floor to some point outside, and in still other cases an imitation menstrual hut was built forty or fifty yards distant, where a selected number of men slept each night. The rationale in the last case was that in the event of an attack, they could help their clansmen escape. Boys were not taken to sleep in the men's house until they were from ten to twelve years old; the men say, "... if there was a raid they were too small to understand and get away." [2]

Prior to European contact the men, heavily armed, would leave the village first and take up positions around the gardens where they could watch while the women came out to work. In the afternoon or evening the women, followed by the ever watchful men, would return to the village through the one small opening in the stockade. It seems difficult to believe that such a system could have evolved in the absence of the threat of serious warfare. Korofeigu, the tribe with which I worked, was successful in this pattern of warfare and raiding. At the time of European contact it dominated the entire Bena Bena Valley.

Nupasafa clan, with which I lived, consisted of 232 persons and was the second largest of the four Korofeigu clans. Like all clans, it is further subdivided into a number of subclans, each of which traces its ancestry (not without a great deal of difficulty) back to one of the sons of the clan founder, always a named individual. There are five such subclans in Nupasafa which operate towards one another as discrete units, mostly for the purpose of arranging funerals. There is a tendency for subclan members to help one another more than others, but there are myriad exceptions. Each subclan is divided into lineages, little more than extended families, in which there is a more marked degree of internal co-operation. But here, again, there are many exceptions.

260

When boys are about five years of age they are taken from their mothers for a day to participate in a dramatic ritual in which their ears are pierced. They are feasted with pork. When they are approximately eight years old they go through a similar ritual in which the septum is pierced. A final initiation is held when they are about fourteen to eighteen. It is a violent month-long event, during which the boys are kept in seclusion by the adult males. At various stages sharp leaves are rolled pencil thin and thrust repeatedly into the nostrils to cause bleeding. The urethra is pierced with a miniature bow and arrow until blood is drawn. This is mixed with soot in a secret magical ritual and used to paint the carved wooden butterfly-shaped pieces that hold together the men's short bark *pul-puls*. The tongue is pierced in the same manner as the urethra, and the ceremony also involves the swallowing of bent lengths of supple cane, which induces vomiting. The cane swallowing is repeated seven times during the initiation, and at the end of this period the initiates are supposed to be able to practice it by themselves.

The initiation ceremony is clearly designed to impress upon youths the importance of male solidarity and the evils of associating too much with women. This theme can be seen in the ceremonial acts themselves. The purpose of the blood-letting and vomiting is to cleanse the youths from the contaminating influence of women, and as adults, the males continue periodically to cleanse themselves in this way. No adult male can participate in the initiation ceremonies if he has recently had intercourse. Food is cooked for the initiates exclusively by men during their seclusion. The initiates are shown the sacred flutes, which are carefully concealed from the women and kept in the men's house. The youths are told the secrets of *nama,* a mythical bird-like demon whose voice is explained by the flutes. The flutes are also identified with the ancestors and are passed on from generation to generation within subclans. The polluting and dangerous nature of menstrual blood is impressed upon the initiates repeatedly. There are many taboos they must learn if they have not already done so. Women cannot step over a man, touch his hair, climb on the roof of a house, or walk on certain paths near the men's house. Men cannot accept food cooked by a menstruating woman; and women, while menstruating, must live in their separate huts and are forbidden to enter the gardens for any purpose. Boys are repeatedly cautioned not to spend too much time with women; if they do, "their skins will be no good," "their work will go wrong," "they will die young," and so on. Male superiority and solidarity are concepts constantly reinforced during the initiations and continue to be reinforced during the entire cycle of a man's life. Men believe it is their responsibility to keep women in line. Men make all major decisions as to when and where to garden, when and where to move, when to hold pig exchanges, when to buy brides, when to fight, etc. Women have nothing to do with decisions about major activities, whether they be ritual, social, religious, or political; and they have only slight direct influence on economic tasks. The initiates also learn the methods and strategies of warfare, the importance of clan and age mate solidarity, and various clan traditions. [3]

Even so, there is a curious contradiction involved in male initiation. Though warned about women, the initiates also learn that the highest good is having many children, particularly male children, who will grow up to be warriors and stay home, protect, and care for the others in their old age. They are taught to be attractive to women and how to use love magic and encouraged to have many wives, something that brings renown not only to individuals but to the clan itself. Furthermore, unlike the neighboring Gahuka-Gama (Read 1952, 1955) or the Enga (Meggitt 1964), they are not warned about sorcery emanating from or through their wives. Bena Bena men categorically deny that such sorcery could happen. It is also possible to exaggerate the fear of menstrual blood, which, although clearly believed to be polluting, is also joked about between men and women, just as there is also much joking about sexual matters in general.

In any event, after initiation, the young men spend most of their time together, venturing off to court, to raid and fight, to steal pigs and, if possible to steal women. These youngsters have virtually no responsibilities and do little work. Men continue courting until as late as twenty-five to thirty, even though they are married and have children. It is during the period subsequent to the initiation that the fathers begin to buy brides. Before discussing marriage, however, let us turn to girls.

The Bena Bena used to practice female infanticide, which, again, emphasizes the difference in status between males and females. Not all female children were killed, of course; but if a woman already had a small child to look after, she might well strangle her new female offspring and bury it in the floor of the menstrual hut, where she retires to give birth. The people explain this custom in terms of practical neces-

262

sity. They say, for example, "Girls don't stay with us when they grow up. They marry and go to other places. They don't become warriors, and they don't stay to look after us in our old age." Or, "Before, we fought all the time. We had to take our children and pigs and run, and we can't carry too many children." One sees here, again, the importance of warfare in shaping life.

For obvious reasons, all female children could not be destroyed. In order to buy brides for sons there must be daughters for whom to receive bridewealth. There is an unusual situation in the Bena Bena, however, in which a father is not permitted to receive brideprice for his daughter. The explanation offered for this is simply, "It is wrong to accept pay for your own semen." Thus all female children are legally adopted shortly after birth by a clansman of the father, who becomes their legal guardian and ultimately collects the bulk of the brideprice. This man is responsible for furnishing pigs and paraphernalia for the girl's initiation, including a large and expensive ceremony at the first menstruation. Girls are usually well treated by their guardian, who becomes like a second father, giving them choice titbits of pork from time to time, presents of shell, and, in general, being kind.

Girls do much more work and have many more responsibilities than boys. Even small girls follow their mothers to the gardens and learn by watching them at work. They are given small net bags to carry suspended from their foreheads in emulation of the adults and soon are carrying small loads of sweet potatoes and firewood. They fetch water, run errands, tend smaller children, and are, in fact, relatively important adjuncts to female economic activities. It is only subsequent to their first menstruation that they enjoy a period of freedom, and at this time they begin to pal around together in an informal age grade. The teen-age girls do virtually no work and spend their time in courting.

Courting is elaborate, time-consuming, and uninhibited. Formal parties are held once or twice a month in the men's houses. The unmarried girls and both married and unmarried young males from one clan go in the evening to another clan's men's house for an all-night session. There is much singing, joking, and excitement on the way. The interior of the circular men's house is swept clean, and fresh banana leaves are spread on the floor along the walls. A fire is built in the center. The girls lie down, girls of one clan along one wall and girls of the other opposite. They then call for partners, usually young men they particularly fancy. The men lie down alongside, and they all begin to sing. This lasts for an hour or two, continually mounting in intensity. The fire dies, and the behavior, which up to this point has consisted mostly of the girls kissing or bussing the young men around the neck and lower jaw, can, and often does, change in more ardent love-making that results in intercourse. The fire is then rekindled, the girls call out for new partners, and the behavior repeats itself. A girl is expected to change partners three or four times, but in some cases, if they particularly favor one, they do not. They do not believe that one act of intercourse with any given partner is sufficient to cause pregnancy. Therefore keeping the same partner is discouraged. Surprisingly few girls actually become pregnant, and if one does, the child is taken by her parents and raised as her sibling. The girl subsequently marries as if nothing happened. Prepubertal girls occasionally attend the courting ceremonies to learn the songs and watch. [4]

Marriages are arranged by adult males for their sons. This is always a clan-wide enterprise as no one man ever has enough wealth in the form of pigs, shells, and (nowadays) money for the purpose. The youths are married following the system of age grading. When the father of the eldest member of a newly-initiated age grade decides he has enough pigs to instigate proceedings, and provided he believes the time to be propitious (often determined by divination), he consults with other adult males and begins to accumulate the brideprice. [5] He usually calls out in the morning that he is buying a bride for his son, so that any clan member who wishes can come to his assistance. In most cases every adult male in the clan contributes something, and it is not uncommon for older women, also, to contribute a pig, or a string of shell, or a few shillings or pounds. After a sufficient amount is accumulated, three or four men, usually close relatives of the groom-to-be, begin carrying it to other clans where they know there are eligible girls. It is displayed in front of the man who is the legal guardian of the girl they particularly fancy. This is a very time-consuming and difficult process, because the brideprice is never accepted immediately. Usually weeks are spent before anyone takes it, and the final negotiations begin.

Once a bride is found, there is an elaborate wedding ceremony. A long path of flowers and brightly colored leaves is laid the length of the groom's village. Pigs are cooked for the exchange of pork, and all is in

264

readiness for the appearance of the bride's clan. [6] When they arrive they stand massed at one end of the village with the bride hidden within. She is dressed in a new bark-cloth skirt with an elaborate headdress borrowed from her guardian or father, has her face painted, is heavily smeared with pig grease, and has pieces of cooked pig suspended from her shoulders and waist. A man of her clan, usually her legal guardian or a close relative of his, steps forward and delivers a speech emphasizing the ties being formed between the two groups, their future peaceful intentions, and the fact that the groom's clan should treat the bride kindly and take good care of her. This speech is reciprocated by the groom's father or some close relative of the groom, and then suddenly the bride's clan opens rank and the bride dramatically appears. A man from the groom's clan, usually the groom's father's brother, walks forward to the bride, picks her up, and symbolically carries her the length of the path of flowers where she is placed near a gift of pork for herself, her mother, and any other woman of her clan who may be wearing mourning for her wedding. The pork is removed from the bride by female members of the groom's clan and all people sit down to eat. The groom's clan along with the bride and her attendants keep to one end of the village, the bride's clan to the other. At one point during the feasting the bride must present each female member of the groom's clan with a portion of pork. She is usually assisted in this by her brothers, who carry a net bag full of the portions to be distributed. The bride's clan then departs, leaving the bride. Her mother or legal guardian, or both, also stay behind for a few days. This is to help insure that she will not run away and will "settle down."

The following morning there is a gathering that might well be described as a kind of "welcome wagon" ceremony. The members of the groom's clan congregate and present the new bride with gifts of various kinds. Her father-in-law invariably gives her one or more sows, others bean seed, bamboo tubes of pig grease, bark cloth, cooking utensils, and, today, tobacco and newspaper. She becomes acquainted with the members of her new clan. She is urged to be content and told that she will be respected. Brides are, in fact, well treated and do little or no work for about a month—"until her new skirt gets dirty." At the end of approximately the first month she begins to go with the other women to the gardens and to take an active part in the various tasks that make up the daily round.

While arrangements for this marriage are well under way, or reaching finality, the men begin negotiations for the next bride, because no youth can be truly married until all his age mates are wed. Indeed, the groom is not in attendance at the above-mentioned ceremony and even seeing his bride is taboo to him and all of his age mates until they all have brides. If any of the age mates should accidentally see the bride (or she one of them), they are required to run and hide.

Neither the young men nor women have any choice. And, after the period of unbridled liberty, girls are, understandably, not eager to marry; indeed, they actively resist. They are dressed and readied for the ceremony only after temper tantrums, running away, arguments, and, not infrequently, physical attacks on their legal guardian. What often happens after the ceremony, and what one might expect to happen given the fact that all sexual relations are forbidden to the brides, is that many of them run away. As there is no point in trying to return to their natal group (which has just "betrayed" them), they usually go to the village of some young man to whom they were attracted during courting. Invariably they are located and brought back, often by violent means. Some new brides get involved in sexual relations with their father-in-law, or an elder brother of the groom, or some other clansman of the groom. When this happens the girl is invariably blamed and sent home and the price refunded. [7] Thus, even from the beginning, women cause trouble and hostility within the clan—but not as much as one might suppose, because women tend, ideologically, to be valueless, and none is ultimately worth serious dissention between males of the same clan.

Some girls, of course, settle down immediately; some are brought back often enough so that they eventually give up; and finally all of the youths have brides. There is, at this point, a ceremony in which many pigs are killed, the youths come forward and symbolically take food from the hands of their wives, and they are all then formally, and finally, wed. But the young men continue to court whether married or not. Their wives are supported out of their father's gardens and live with their father's wives. Bena husbands, being juvenile and not very responsible at this time, ignore their new responsibilities. [8] Sometimes they abuse their wives by ignoring them, and sometimes the bride and groom find that they do not like one another. There is a strong possibility that even after the final ceremony the wife will desert her husband or the husband continue to ignore his wife, or both.

The above description applies to the more usual mode of marriage. About 30 percent of brides fall into a different category and are purchased in marriage prior to first menstruation. Because of female infanticide and polygyny, there is a shortage of eligible girls, and it is difficult to contract marriages for an entire age grade. Therefore it is not uncommon for a man to purchase a young girl prior to her first menstruation. In some cases she may not even speak Bena. She is then raised by the groom-to-be's parents until she menstruates, at which time she is married. There are still other ways to get brides. Prior to contact it is possible to obtain a wife by capture. After a woman is married, has children and divorces, she is more or less free to remarry. Men, if they are strong enough, can "steal" wives without paying for them, or at least can get a wife or second wife by paying only a relatively small amount. Or, if a man works hard and is successful he can sometimes accumulate enough to buy a second bride. Between 25 and 30 percent of Nupasafa males have more than one wife at any given time. 9

What happens eventually to marriage? Everyone must marry, and a single person is a rarity, usually someone who has some serious deformity or handicap. Divorce is common and, if the union has produced no children, very troublesome because of the brideprice that must be returned. "Divorce" in these circumstances is difficult to define. What I mean by it here is any marriage that is dissolved either by the return of the brideprice or, after children are born and brideprice need not be returned, any marriage that is dissolved by the permanent separation of the partners for any reason other than death. With this as a definition it is possible to say that virtually all adult males and females, by the time they reach middle age, have had more than one and usually several spouses. Many married couples do settle down. But even in the best marriages there are continuing tensions having to do with attitudes towards women, rules regarding sexual behavior, and the amount of time a man can comfortably spend with a woman.

Sexual relations between husband and wife are difficult to investigate, but certain facts seem to be clear. Intercourse between a husband and wife occurs probably on an average of once a week. There is no foreplay before the act itself, nor do people remove their modest garments. Intercourse most usually takes place in the privacy of the woman's house and in the evening. The only time it occurs with greater frequency is when a man and wife are attempting to conceive. In this case a man copulates with his wife several evenings in a row and then stops for a time. Once a woman is known to be pregnant all sexual relations are discontinued and are not resumed until after the child has cut its second tooth—a considerably long period. Furthermore, when female visitors come from other places to stay with a man's wife (and this is not uncommon) privacy, which is essential for the act, is disturbed.

If a man has more than one wife, he still has intercourse approximately once a week, going to one wife one week and the next week to another. If relations are in any way strained between a man and one of his two or more wives, that wife may be ignored for long periods. Also, if a man is trying to woo a woman away from another place he devotes much of his time to her, leaving his wife or wives without attention. This can create much ill will.

Needless to say, this system leads to many fights between co-wives and not infrequent fights between husband and wife. Quarrels between co-wives occur in Nupasafa clan at the rate of about one per week and are often violent. The women attempt to tear off one another's clothing, bite, strike each other with fists and clubs, sometimes enlist the aid of their friends, and so on. They rarely kill one another but are often painfully injured. Men usually stand around laughing, unless the struggle becomes too violent, when they intervene. Fights between co-wives are disruptive, and even though the men profess to be indifferent, they are concerned, as the trouble affects the well being of the clan, pig raising, gardening, and other economic pursuits, all of the things that must be tended to if men are to gain prestige and be successful. The men must have domestic peace—they need children, gardens, pigs, and so on— but they also recognize the nature of women and the feelings of animosity between co-wives. Thus a man with more than one wife is careful to build their houses in different villages or at least at opposite ends of a village. He is careful not to intervene between co-wives unless it appears necessary. Men also tolerate a great deal of nagging, and it is not unusual to see a woman following her husband scolding him for the greater part of a day.

Squabbles between co-wives, especially if the man has to intervene, lead to fights between husband and wife or wives. But women fear childbirth and sometimes resort to contraception and attempt to abort (or they say they do), and this, too, leads to trouble. It is commonly believed by men that women grow secret plants for this purpose. The fact that barrenness is common reinforces these beliefs and makes the men suspicious and angry.[10] Women are, I think, sexually frustrated, and resentful of their inferior status. This leads to further hostility and antagonism. In so far as religious beliefs stress fertility, success, and abundance, women's actions tend to go against the expressed intentions of the religious ceremonies. Significantly, religion is strictly a male activity.

What about the situation, sexual and otherwise, for men? How might men be similarly frustrated? Men are actually ambivalent towards women. They tell you that women are no good, are unclean, are less intelligent, untrustworthy in certain ways, and so on. But simultaneously they recognize their dependence. "Women are our tractors," one of my more preceptive informants remarked one day. Furthermore, men complain when their wives are in menstrual seclusion. They complain about having to dig and cook their own sweet potatoes, about the care of the pigs, and about not being able to find things kept in the women's houses. A man would not think of killing a pig or arranging a marriage for his son or adopted daughter without consulting his wife. He needs her co-operation for a number of very important reasons, and women can hold things up and make it very uncomfortable if they choose. Ultimately, of course, in a battle of wills, a husband wins out, but it is not as simple a matter as one might suppose.

If a man has a good wife, one who works hard and co-operates with him, does not run away or have affairs with other men or cause trouble and so on, he wants to keep her happy. This entails maintaining adequate sexual contact with her as well as doing the various jobs he is obliged to do, such as building and repairing her garden fences, fetching firewood, and helping with the feeding and care of pigs. But this can entail spending considerable time in her company, and the other men, especially older men, continually warn against too much feminine contact. They repeat to him what he already knows—that he will sicken and die, his skin will be no good, he will not be strong, etc. A man, then, is caught between the demands of his wife and the demands of his peers and elders. This can be frustrating—the more attached to his wife he is, the more frustrating it becomes. A man who prefers the company of women in general, or his wife in particular, can be subjected to

269

powerful sanctions, and other men make it obvious to him they do not approve and make fun of him and insult him. In one extreme case of which I have first-hand knowledge, a man who had been to the coast working for Europeans, and then returned, attempted to emulate a more European type of marriage. He spent much of his day with his one wife, openly expressed a desire to sleep in the same house with her, and in general treated her with more respect and kindness than would usually have been the case. Within the space of a few days he was virtually a social outcast and could expect no help from other men, who went out of their way to make him miserable.

If a man does not like his wife, he has different problems. If he is to have prestige and a "name" he must have many pigs and gardens. He can only have them if he gets along well with his wife or wives and has their co-operation. If, for some reason, he is not temperamentally suited to a wife or vice versa, he can be in trouble. Even sexually he can suffer, because in fact sexual outlets for men are not as easy as one might think. Although married men continue to attend courting parties until, perhaps, thirty years of age, men must be asked by girls. There are always many more men than girls at the courting parties, and generally speaking, a married man, or an older man, is not quite as popular as one who is unmarried. Homosexuality is unknown in the Bena, so it cannot be considered an alternative. There are cases of adultery, of course; but adultery with a clansman's wife causes friction within the clan (the clan must maintain its solidarity if it is to compete adequately in warfare). There are, therefore, strong sanctions against interclan friction of any kind. Even if one wishes to commit adultery, there are sizeable stumbling blocks. In the first place, people who walk about alone are immediately suspect. Both men and women for the most part work communally and are seldom alone. A woman does work in her garden by herself for a time in the afternoons, but even then there is usually a child with her or at least someone nearby. Villages are deserted during the day except for old people and children, who would see anyone who returned there. Villages are completely surrounded by gardens, and sexual intercourse in a garden, although it happens, is believed to have a deleterious effect on the crops. It is also likely to be seen. Women from other clans are not easy to find alone, and travelling, although it occurs, is always dangerous, since one might become a victim of sorcery or physical attack. Furthermore, although Bena men deny that their wives would work sorcery against them, this denial does not extend to strange women from other places.

Thus, although men might want women for sexual reasons, they want multiple wives for material and prestige reasons, and probably want the company of at least one wife for dependency needs, there are many sanctions, frustrations, and obstacles placed in their way. The system, although it insures male solidarity and may be satisfactory for coping with warfare and raiding, makes little allowance for what one might consider other basic human needs, or even for the "animal" needs, if you prefer, of men. And because men's needs cannot be satisfied, women's needs can also not be satisfied. In this case one finds neither the "anxiety of prudes" not the "determination of lechers" but, rather, as Meggitt (1964) has suggested, a combination in which there is a highly ambivalent relationship between males and females. This situation is the result of conditions largely outside their control but which, from necessity, have been buttressed by strong sanctions, religious and otherwise, designed to ensure survival.

The ambivalent attitudes of males towards females is reflected in ritual and in the religious sytem itself; for example, when a group of men are returning home with the pigs received for a bride, a party of women and children waylay them, attack them with sticks and stones, and attempt to kill one or more of the pigs. This the men expect, and provided no one is seriously injured, they do not defend themselves or retaliate. This indicates, I believe, recognition that it would somehow be better if girls did not have to marry against their will and leave their own people who genuinely grieve for them. The mourning of the mother at weddings expresses the same feeling.

The custom of having a legal guardian for each girl is also an acknowledgement of the trauma of marriage. When a girls learns she is to be wedded she invariably goes to her parents to complain, only to be told that it is "out of their hands." She may then go to her legal guardian with her complaints (she may, indeed, attack him), but to no avail. The guardian can be seen as a kind of scapegoat, and it is significant that of women I interviewed, although most continued to see their real parents occasionally after marriage, only in very rare cases did they visit their guardian. The relationship is dropped once it is known the girl has settled down.

Furthermore, as Read (1952, 1955) has shown for the Gahuku-Gama, and as is also generally true for the Bena, there is a paradox in the religious system which also reveals an ambivalence on the part of males towards females. Although religious activities are performed exclusively by males and are supposed to be closely guarded male secrets, women and even children know the secrets. They are aware of what the sacred flutes really are, they say the *nama* is a myth, and they can tell, in general what takes place at male initiations. But, even so, both men and women accept the situation for what it is—a ritual expression of the relations that obtain between males and females, a means whereby males can exert their dominance over, and solidarity against, females. It is an expression of clan strength and unity, and an attempt to gain the favor of the (patrilineal) ancestors so that life will continue and people will be fertile and successful. It is difficult to understand how the farce can perpetuate itself, and why women in particular continue to accept it, if there is not some felt realization on the part of all people that things must be the way they are, that male solidarity is a necessity.

What is the evidence that might support the view I have presented? First, it would seem that the "divorce" rate and extramarital activities indicate fairly clearly the discontent of sexually frustrated and inferior women. The amount of fighting between co-wives is another indication. It is significant here that no matter what the precipitating cause of the fight (that is, whether it be because a husband did not repair a fence for one wife, or did not come to receive food she had cooked for him, etc.) the woman at some point in the argument says specifically that her husband does not have intercourse with her. This appears to be a factor of great importance and occurs with such regularity that it cannot be overlooked. I have heard it brought up in general meetings of the clan as part of the business, and the people recognize that problems between husbands and wives result in the breaking off of sexual relations.

There are indications that men are more sensitive to "femininity" than is apparent on the surface. For example, if you ask what constitutes a good wife, or the best wife, the emphasis is always on hard work and knowledge of pig tending and gardening. Eventually, however, you find that there are standards of beauty as well, and men prefer women with acquiline noses and firm breasts. They also like women with lighter skins. They condemn women who have "sharp tongues" and those who are large. Large women are said to be inferior workers, though in part this is nonsense. One young man spent months trying to persuade his companions to help him to buy a new wife although he had only recently been married, and this first wife worked hard and was successful at both gardening and pig tending. She was the largest Bena woman I have ever seen and, as he and I were of roughly the same age, and "friends," it eventually came out that she was simply too strong and domineering for him. He was uncomfortable with her. He had difficulty in trying to manage her, and this expressed itself in the marital bed as well as elsewhere.

Sometimes women freely admit their discontent. They agree that men are superior to women and know more. They attribute male superiority largely to the fact that men do not menstruate or bear children. They are ashamed of menstruation and wish to be men. Their resentment comes out in more indirect ways—in attempts to abort, unco-operativeness, nagging, delight over incidents that frustrate men (such as a woman becoming illegitimately pregnant), and so on. At the same time, women encourage dependency in men, especially if they can do it at the expense of a co-wife. First wives are always angry when a man attempts to take a second wife, and wives are commonly believed to use magical means to bring a co-wife into disfavor or make the husband forget her.

Probably the most important single reason for accepting the argument presented here is the fact that now warfare has been effectively suppressed by the Australian administration, the relations between men and women are rapidly changing. Indeed, the Gahuku-Gama, who are similar to the Bena in most respects, gave up the pattern soon after contact. Men began sleeping with their wives, the sacred flutes were burned after a public display, and the men's houses and associated activities were largely abandoned. The men's cult constitutes the religious system, which operates on the principle of male superiority. In terms of most anthropological experience, this should therefore constitute a core value and be resistant to change. Yet it appears that the freedom from the threat of warfare allowed the men to do something they had really wanted to do always.

The same process is now occurring in the Bena, immediately to the east of the Gahuku, although the Bena are more conservative and go about it in a compromise fashion. The people believe that the Administration has asked them to build new houses and to sleep with their wives. [11]

As warfare no longer occurs their reasons for resisting this request are questionable. For example, men say they do not want their wives to see them naked. This is probably not valid as men are not really modest and strip themselves to ford rivers with little regard to the presence of women. Men say their work will be unsatisfactory if they do not have the men's house in which to discuss it. This also is unlikely, for they now have regular meetings of the clan, sometimes as often as every morning. In any case, men sit around and chat much of the day. The main stumbling block, although it is seldom mentioned, is the continued existence of the flutes (although these are no longer played) and the persistence of religious beliefs themselves in the process of change.

Some of the men are cleverly compromising by building their own private houses next door to the wife's dwelling. Furthermore, they rationalize spending a night with her by using arguments that are transparently feeble; for example, "If it rains I'll stay with my wife as I don't want to walk back to the men's house." This was told to me by a man whose wife's house was less than fifty yards from the men's house where he still slept in spite of the fact he commonly walked in the rain without discomfort.

Men are also now building menstrual huts for their wives, something they would never have done formerly. This is a result of the fact that the new houses are constructed of hollow flattened woven cane, and women have never learned how to use this type of construction. It disturbs the men to think of the old style (round and squat) menstrual huts alongside the new rectangular higher houses (I suspect this also has a great deal to do with the fact that they think the Administration will disapprove).

Finally, women no longer commit suicide when a man dies or is killed. Formerly if the husband perished the wife (or even wives) might hang herself. She was not required to do this: in fact, the act would seem to do violence to leviritic privilege; moreover, women are considered to be clan, not individual, property. Nevertheless, suicide occurred, apparently because the woman was apprehensive about how a new husband would treat her. She could not easily escape, by running away, for her natal group would not necessarily take her back even if the deceased's clan permitted her to go. Bena men are disturbed and recognize that a woman has certain rights and freedoms now that she did not possess before (guaranteed by the Administration). They say women do not care about their husbands any more, that nowadays widows are eager to go to another man or to return home. All of these things, it seems to me, are difficult to comprehend unless the underlying needs mentioned are conceded.

I have attempted to show that the exigencies of warfare have made it necessary to sacrifice the satisfaction of certain individual needs. This affects males differently from females but results in mutual hostility and antagonism. The Eastern Highlands "type" is, as Meggitt (1964) has suggested, a combination of the Mae and Kuma types. It is related to warfare but not to hostility existing between affinally related groups, as in the Bena groups do not "marry those they fight" but fight, in fact, with all groups. There is no highly elaborated men's purificatory cult as Meggitt describes for Enga, though the religious activities and male initiations have this function. There are differences in status between Bena women and Enga women, and it would appear that, in general, Bena women enjoy a higher status. Although menstruation and female contact are not as strongly abhorred as in Enga, there is not the blatant violation of these proscriptions that is apparently found in Kuma groups. Bena Bena beliefs and rituals appear to attempt to control the expression of hostility between the sexes but simultaneously to betray an understanding of the necessity for it.

NOTES

Acknowledgments. The research on which this paper is based was carried out during the period January 1, 1961 to May 15, 1962, at which time I held a Predoctoral Fellowship and Supplemental Research Grant (No. M-4377) from the National Institute of Mental Health, United States Public Health Service. Their generosity is gratefully acknowledged. An original version of this paper was presented at the Northwest Anthropological Conference, Banff, Alberta, April, 1966. I am grateful to Sterling Robbins for reading and commenting on the revised version.

[1] It is likely that prior to contact there was only one village per clan, the current multiplicity being a result of the forced suppression of hostility between groups.

[2] This age is not typical for all the Highlanders. In Enga, for example, according to Meggitt (1964: 207), boys begin sleeping in the men's house at about five years of age.

[3] For a more adequate account of similar initiation ceremonies see Read (1952, 1955, 1965) and Langness (1964a).

[4] Little can be seen, however, even when the fire is burning brightly.

[5] It is not always the father of the eldest youth in the age grade. Sometimes another father is in a more advantageous position to start the proceedings. Ideally, however, it is the father of the eldest.

[6] This is in addition to the brideprice (paid in live pigs) but is different in that there is an equal exchange of pork between the clans.

[7] I do not know exactly what the frequency of this is, but it is apparently not uncommon in that there are several cases of it within living memory of the members of Nupasafa clan.

8 For a more thorough discussion of men of this age see Langness (1965).

9 This relatively high incidence of polygyny is due, I think, to the fact that the Nupasafans have a large number of pigs. This, in turn, is probably due to the ecological setting.

10 There are no good figures available on the percentage of barren women in the Highlands. Out of seventy-three married women known to have been married for three years or longer, eleven were barren in the area in which I worked. Interestingly enough, none of the twenty wives married prior to their first menstruation were barren. The eleven were of the other fifty-three.

11 The Administration actually has not suggested this. It was, in fact, the suggestion of the Bena councillors when this body was first formed in 1960. They appear to have assumed that it was something the Administration would favor and began to implement the policy. For details see Langness (1963).

REFERENCES CITED

Langness, L.L.
1963   Notes on the Bena Council, Eastern Highlands. Oceania 33: 151-170.
1964a   Bena Bena Social Structure. Ph.D. dissertation, Anthropology Department, University of Washington, Seattle.
1964b   Some Problems in the Conceptualization of Highlands Social Structures. In New Guinea: The Central Highlands. J.B. Watson, ed. American Anthropologist 66: 162-182, Part 2.
1965   Hysterical Psychosis in the New Guinea Highlands: A Bena Bena Example. Psychiatry 28: 258-277.
Meggitt, M.J.
1964   Male-Female Relationships in the Highlands of Australian New Guinea. In New Guinea: The Central Highlands. J.B. Watson, ed. American Anthropologist 66: 204-224, Part 2.
Read, Kenneth E.
1952   Nama Cult of the Central Highlands, New Guinea. Oceania 23: 1-5.
1954   Cultures of the Central Highlands, New Guinea. Southwestern Journal of Antrhopology 10: 1-43.

1955   Morality and the Concept of the Person among the Gahuku-Gama. Oceania 25: 233-282.
1965   The High Valley. New York: Scribner.

SUGGESTIONS FOR FURTHER READING

Ahern, Emily M.
   1975   The Power and Pollution of Chinese Women. *In* Women in Chinese Society. Margery Wolf and Roxane Witke, eds. Pp. 193-214. Stanford: Stanford University Press.
   Explores the question of why Chinese women are considered unclean from three different perspectives: birth and death as sources of pollution; women's social roles and pollution; and the Chinese ideological system concerning ritual defilement. Material in this essay is based on fieldwork in Taiwan.
Brown, Paula, and Georgeda Buchbinder, eds.
   1976   Man and Woman in the New Guinea Highlands. Washington, D.C.: American Anthropological Association.
   A short collection of essays that address the diversity of female-male relations in the Highlands of New Guinea. An excellent supplement to the discussion of patterns of sexual antagonism among the Bena Bena (Langness, this volume).
Douglas, Mary
   1966   Purity and Danger: An Analysis of Concepts of Pollution and Taboo. Harmondsworth, England: Penguin.
   An important analysis of the relationships between purity and defilement. Chapter 9 discusses the concept of sexual pollution.
Harper, Edward B.
   1969   Fear and the Status of Women. Southwestern Journal of Anthropology 25: 81-95.
   Discusses cultural conceptions of the dangerous mystical powers of women among Havik Bramins of South India. Relates beliefs of the especially malevolent attributes of widows to their low status position within the caste.

278

Meggitt, M.J.

1964 Male-Female Relationships in the Highlands of Australian New Guinea. *In* New Guinea: The Central Highlands. J.B. Watson, ed. American Anthropologist 66: 204-224, Part 2. Describes the organization of female-male relations and bachelors' rituals among the Mae Enga. Compares the Enga with patterns of intersex opposition reported from other societies in the Highlands.

MALE AND FEMALE IN TOKELAU CULTURE

Judith Huntsman and Antony Hooper

On the sporadic but entirely predictable occasions when some special
public contest or undertaking quickens the Oceanic calm of Tokelau
village life, the local clowns or *fāluma* are inevitably thrown up in the
mounting wave of public excitement. Seemingly *ad hoc*, chaotic, and
disorderly, their performances are always incidental to the task or
activity at hand, yet they briefly pre-empt the center of attention by
their sheer vitality and exuberant obscenity.

The clowns are invariably women—the best of them middle-aged or
elderly—and in their most developed and sustained performances they
are dressed as men in European shirts, ties, coats, trousers, and shoes,
the garments crumpled and filthy, trouser flies gaping open and shoes
odd and ill-fitting. Trailing behind them a swarm of delighted, shriek-
ing children, the clowns appear with dramatic suddenness in the open,
public places of the village, strutting and shoving, yelling commands
and directives, cursing and fighting. A favorite performance (derived
from tragic real-enough incidents of little over a century ago) is that of a
group of foreign sailors ashore from a "blackbirding" ship with swords
and guns, dragging their struggling victims from among the onlookers
into supposed captivity and exile. Another uses a "stethoscope" made
from a piece of rope as an effective prop, with the actors rushing
quickly beyond the stylized decorum of a medical examination to
explore one another's every orifice with exclamations of amazement,

Reprinted by permission of the authors and the Polynesian Society from *The Journal of
the Polynesian Society* 84(4):415-430, 1975.

envy, or disgust. Inevitably, there are bouts of wrestling, with the contestants piled upon one another, yelling curses. In half an hour or so it is all over, leaving only the young children to carry on an excited mimicry of all that they have seen. The clowns retire to ease their bruised bodies, put on once again their flowing dresses and *lāvalava* and disappear into their houses. Order is restored.

To anyone seeing one of these rollicking performances for the first time, the element of mockery, of the somewhat deferential Tokelau women putting down males, seems paramount. This impression is heightened by the marked contrast in the very physical appearance of the two sexes; the men lean and taut, bare from the waist up, hair close-cropped and bodies burnt dark from exposure to sea and sun; the women lighter-skinned and soft, tending strongly to obesity, their long hair caught up on their heads, and dressed always with sleeves to cover their upper arms and skirts falling thickly to below their knees. And the impression would be further confirmed by the fact that on public occasions it is always men who have authority, and display it; it is men who sit in council, orate, judge, and decide, while women sit on the sidelines or are absent altogether. However, this is not what Tokelauans themselves, both men and women, see in the performances. To them they are *tafaoga*, "games" and *mea tauanoa*, "things of no account." No man feels humiliated by them. The women do not see themselves as taunting, or as settling scores by their displays.

Yet even if the clowning is mere "games" and "things of no account," it is hardly arbitrary, haphazard, or fortuitous. The form of the performances is in fact stylized; the themes are both predictable and repetitious, although the people's enjoyment of them is undiminished by constant repetition. And since the clowning never occurs as part of the formal, ceremonious, and slightly solemn rituals by which the villagers welcome strangers or the rare visiting parties, it remains a rather private thing—a game, with many slight variations on a constant theme that the village plays for itself alone.

Another, equally repetitious and stylized but even more intensively private play upon a related theme, occurs in the brief *faleaitu*, "skits," which are performed by both men and women in the course of evening dances that are a part of nearly all village-wide occasions, such as weddings, feasts, and cricket matches. These skits are much less boisterous, less slapstick and obviously lewd than the performances by the *fāluma,* "clowns," although the same women are often leading actors in them. The "skits" commonly involve only two performers, often playing out a mock quarrel or dispute of a minor domestic nature, with little apparent wit or inventiveness. The humor, in fact, remains totally obscure to anyone (who would have to be a stranger to Tokelau and the village) who did not know that the players were, in real life, related to one another as "brother" and "sister."

These then are two favorite Tokelau "games," whose appeal is undulled by constant repetition and which depend for their impact and meaning on the themes of relations between male and female. Both involve inversion, but what is inverted is not the same in each case. The spontaneous clown performances always involve only women dressed as men. The "game" in this case plays on the culturally ascribed attributes of the sexes. The skits done at evening dances involve both men and women acting in their proper sexes; what is inverted is their real relationship. As "siblings" they are playing as spouses, and the "game" in this case is concerned with relationships.

Some 1,700 Tokelau Islanders live on the three atolls of the group, which lies about 300 miles north of Western Samoa.[1] Although the group is constitutionally "a part of New Zealand" it has a separate administration and each atoll is a relatively independent social and political unit, with a high degree of island endogamy and strong feelings of local loyalty and identity. This parochial character of Tokelau society is due in part to difficulties of movement within the group; a few ancient rivalries between the atolls still survive, exacerbated in some cases by differences of religious affiliation.

In setting and scale as well as in certain pervasive themes of social organization, the islands resemble three large efficient ships moored eternally in the central Pacific, capable of a hard-won self-sufficiency, though replenished from time to time through brief contacts with the outside world. On each island settlement is confined to a single village, and movements outside these village areas are rather strictly controlled by regulations and edicts of the village councils. Authority in the local village organization is tied closely to the unequivocal principle of relative age. Everyday life is routinized, punctuated by bells and by *kalaga,* "calls," for prayers, assemblies, distributions, and meetings

282

of one sort or another. Weekly schedules of activities and events for each village are discussed and planned in detail fine enough to allow most things to be done with a deceptively casual efficiency. Even the unplanned events, such as storms, deaths, or the sudden, unexpected appearance of schooling fish have their well-known organizational routines.

Co-operative enterprise, the authority of elders, and *māopoopo*, a unity of purpose and of action, are key cultural values. Roles are relatively clearly defined, areas of responsibility finely marked, and duties explicitly allocated. The frequent community gatherings provide the venue for statements and admonitions about obligations and relationships between people as fellow villagers and as kin. Deviations from the well-known expectations rapidly become public knowledge and are frequently dealt with in a public setting. There is little which is vague, equivocal, or left unexplicit about the principles of Tokelau social organization.

In this paper we discuss the Tokelau cultural concepts of male and female, and the manner in which these are expressed in both everyday social behavior and "inverted" in the skits and *fāluma* performances. [2] We are concerned with the following questions:

What are the culturally ascribed attributes and the domains of activity which are considered appropriate to males and females?

How do these attributes and domains relate to one another and to the more general Tokelau concepts of "maleness" and "femaleness?"

How are these ideas made manifest in the system of sex-linked roles — husband and wife, brother and sister, and so on?

What is so humorous in the "games" and "things of no account," and why is it mainly females who are involved in them?

We describe first the attributes and the domains of activity which are linked with the sexes, generalizing about males and females as the *fāluma* do in their exaggerated portrayals of "maleness" to contrast with their normal "femaleness." We then consider the separate dyadic role relationships based on a sex distinction, and show how these follow, in different ways, from the more general concepts of male and female.[3]

MALENESS AND FEMALENESS

There is a widely known Tokelauan adage—*Ko te fafine e nofo: ko te tagata e fano i te auala* "The woman stays: the man goes on the path"—which expresses a basic principle of Tokelau thought, and which is used by Tokelauans, quite explicitly, to point up the rationale for various diverse customs and aspects of Tokelau life. In general, female activity is on land, within the village, and in the domestic sphere of house and cookhouse, while male activity is at sea, on the outlying plantation islets of the atoll and in the public places of the village, known figuratively as "the path." Thus land and sea, village and outlying islets, domestic and public areas of the village are contrasted as complementary domains of the sexes. In each contrast set, it is the female who is more confined, more restricted in both social and spatial terms.

The complementary nature of the two domains is neatly expressed by various common usages and transactions. While a man is fishing at sea a woman should prepare food for his return, which should, properly, be cooked and garnished with coconut cream. This food prepared especially for a fisherman's return is known as the *ipu lolo*, literally "a drinking vessel of coconut cream" is seen as being given in exchange for the fish, which it is the woman's duty to divide and distribute. Again, men do not ordinarily gather the octopus which is used as bait in sea-fishing, but will ask kinswomen to get it for them; or women gathering on the reef may hail fishing canoes, offering octopus in exchange for fish. Many women do go fishing but they do not leave the reef and lagoon shores, where they can join in fish-drives, do line-fishing for the small reef and lagoon fish, and gather clams and octopus. The offshore waters are the exclusive domain of men.

Men regularly journey to the outlying islets to harvest plantations, returning to hand over what they have harvested to women, for them to distribute and cook. Occasionally, women accompany men to the plantations to cut pandanus, assist with clearing and collecting, and to search for landcrabs. For women these trips are a refreshing change from routine normal village tasks, though this is hardly so for their male companions. Within the village, women normally stay within their houses and cookhouses engaged in the domestic tasks of childcare, food preparation, and mat plaiting. Men gather in the public places of the village—the meeting house, canoe slips, cricket pitch, and "the path." Even with regard to the house itself, men are responsible for the structure, the outside, and women for the furnishings, the inside.

In short, a man's life is outside and active while a woman's life is inside and largely sedentary.

Another common Tokelau saying is that men are the *itū mālohi*, "strong side," while women are the *itū vāivāi*, "weak side." This contrast does not refer solely to physical capabilities; it also applies to the culturally ascribed character traits of the two sexes. *Mālohi*, "strength," implies that men are dignified and controlled and are thereby qualified to make decisions and exercise authority. At public gatherings and at meetings of decision-making bodies it is men who make formal and measured speeches, with frequent repetition of familiar phrases and homilies. The more adept speech-makers, usually elder men, show a certain erudite cleverness by coining new adages, using clever turns of phrase, and making appropriate references to fragments of esoterica. When disagreements arise male councils should conduct their arguments logically and unemotionally, and the outcome should be a wise resolution of the conflict. Feminine *vāivāi*, "weakness," implies that women are emotional, vulnerable, and erratic, that they are unable to control their feelings and are prone to express themselves without caution. Female gatherings do not in fact maintain the decorum of their male counterparts. Inevitably bickering breaks out, tempers flare, quarrels erupt, and tears flow. The only really effective means of dealing with these situations is for the accomplished "clown" to take center stage. Dancing, mimicking, grimacing, she quickly diverts attention from the issue at hand. Shrieks of laughter drown out the vituperations and eventually the combatants join in the general hilarity and the dispute is forgotten, at least for the moment. The "clowns" intervene to pacify the situation by substituting laughter for hostility. Their erratic behavior is the very antithesis of that of the dignified male orator and conciliator, and their actions do not resolve the issue at hand, which, inevitably, will come up again.

Women are also referred to as *manu hā*, "sacred beings," and it is

285

through this quality that they have power to halt conflicts between men. A woman may simply place herself in the midst of a situation of confrontation, and the matter will be abruptly dropped. In the frequent Tokelau cricket competitions, the winning side customarily hazes the losers, who are expected to respond good-naturedly; on occasion, however, the winners get over-enthusiastic and strain the losers' sense of good-natured fun. At times such as this the interposition of a woman will quickly restore a sense of proper proportion and decorum.

Naturally, not all individuals conform to their proper sex stereotypes. Effeminate men are neither shunned nor stigmatized, but rather pitied and treated with affection by both men and women. There is, however, strong disapproval of males who behave "like women" by gossiping, squabbling, and being unable to control their emotions; and a forceful, domineering woman may be castigated as *tagatā*, "manly."

We have thus far considered only those qualities of maleness and femaleness which are summarized in common Tokelau sayings which contrast "staying" with "going" and "strength" with "weakness." There is, however, another dimension of contrast which, though not explicitly stated, is none the less apparent in folktales and ideas about sickness, and which is thoroughly congruent with the other, more explicit oppositions.

Men, as we have shown, are supposed to be in control of themselves, of their society, and of the immediate surroundings of sea and outlying plantations, whereas women are not. Yet women seem to be seen as having close links with beings inhabiting other worlds, that is, with *aitu*, "spirits" or "ghosts" of the generally unseen world, and with animals (fish, including turtles, and birds) of the natural world. [4] These creatures are attracted to women, who are both vulnerable to their malicious acts and can enlist their aid to accomplish their own desires.

In Tokelau folktales women become wives of birds, give birth to children who are transformed into fish, are transported to distant lands by birds and fish, and are pursued by impassioned fish, whereas men marry or are pursued by human women and always transport themselves by canoe. Males, unless they have a "spirit side" due to the strange circumstances of their birth, regard natural creatures as their prey; they exploit the natural world. Women's relations with *aitu* in the tales are both positive and negative; on the one hand, they are carried off or killed or replaced (as when an *aitu* assumes the guise of a pregnant wife) by them, and on the other hand, they revive the dead or rescue men in danger with the aid of *aitu*. As in their relationships with animals, men confront *aitu* and defeat them by trickery and guile. With few exceptions male *aitu* in stories are either abductors or parents ("fathers from the sky" who have been attracted to earthly women), but animals, if they are given sexual attributes, are invariably male. Women *aitu* are malicious, often cannibalistic, demons, or ghosts avenging undeniable wrongs, and in two well-known tales half-human, half-animal females manage by ingenious means to become pregnant by human men and bear human children. By the evidence of Tokelau folktales, it is clearly women who are in league with or who are victims of the creatures of the animal and spirit worlds, while men oppose, prey upon, and outwit animals and spirits. Males not only control their immediate personal, social, and natural surroundings; they can by their innate human skills also effectively deal with *aitu*. The women, though vulnerable, can often do miraculous things by their potentially dangerous links with animals and *aitu,* whom they clearly do not fully control.

Again Tokelau beliefs about sickness involve the notion that women are especially vulnerable to the influence of *aitu,* and they are more commonly the victims of sickness which are believed to be supernaturally caused. In the most dramatic instances they are *ulufia,* "possessed" by *aitu* which enter into their bodies. Furthermore, men are believed to be on occasions punished by their own kinswomen, who inflict reproductive disorders and inexplicable sicknesses, not on them, but on their wives. Wherever these *aitu* powers lie, whether in ghosts of the deceased, connections of the living, or in unrelated malicious beings, they seem to be channelled through women, manifest in women, but not under the control of women.

As far as we can determine, all the most renowned Tokelau curers, those who deal with sickness attributed to *aitu,* are or have been men. They are relatively few in number, but the significant point is that it is male curers who are able to control *aitu* whereas their patients, predominantly females, cannot.

These qualities of male and female implied in tale and belief appear to corroborate the explicit qualities Tokelauans talk about. Women, weak and vulnerable, "stay inside" protected from *aitu* attack, away from contact with those creatures of the natural and unseen world with whom they are linked; yet despite these precautions, the erratic, emotional women show their *aitu* links. In other words, women have *mamana* or "mystical power" which is imperfectly controlled. Men, by contrast, are strong and in control, able to handle the oustide social or natural world, or even that of the *aitu*. They have no connections with animals or spirits; they encounter them and defeat them. In the stories, however, the encounters they are not able to cope with are those in which women are in league with *aitu* to harm them. In this aspect, women can be dangerous.

HUSBANDS AND WIVES

It is unacceptable, and virtually impossible in fact, for a Tokelau couple to live openly together in the atolls outside of marriage. When any clandestine sexual relationship is exposed, the partners to it are publicly castigated and punished by village courts.

At marriage celebrations, the major participants are divided into those of the groom's side and those of the bride's side, each contributing large quantities of food to be consumed by the whole village, and pandanus mats and new clothes for the newlyweds. Their contributions are approximately equal and of like nature, except for the *kahoa*, "pearlshell lure" given to the bride by her male kinsmen and the *malo*, "fine pandanus kilt" given to the groom by his female kinsmen. Both these items are highly valued goods, symbolic of the continuing concern of kinsmen for the recipients.

Postmarital residence is ideally in the wife's natal home, at least initially; the woman thus "stays" with her family while the man "goes" from his. [5] From strictly practical considerations, Tokelau women try to avoid moving into a house full of female affines with whom they necessarily have intense daily interaction while their husbands are away, and which is full of female property (weaving materials, cooking equipment) to which they have no rights. Those few women who do reside virilocally are always liable to criticism for daring to treat property in and around the house as if it were their own.

More pertinent to our present concerns is the belief that a newly married woman is particularly attractive to malevolent *aitu* and vulnerable to their attack until she has successfully delivered a child. Within her own home she is protected by the good will of kin, both living and dead, who will comfort, assist, and support her during a dangerous and trying period of her life. A husband, by contrast, is "outside" during the day fulfilling his responsibilities to his own family and to the village, and the fact that he is an outsider in the household where he sleeps and normally eats may be slightly uncomfortable for him, but this is not a matter of major concern.

Tokelauans recognize physiological paternity and affirm that one act of intercourse is adequate for conception. They deny that the contribution of each parent to the physical makeup of their child is in any way different; they insist that each parent contributes the same substance in equal amounts and that this accounts for the resemblance of children to their parents and siblings to one another. When a woman delivers, her husband should be on hand. Though he takes no part in the actual delivery, a matter for women, he should be near by to "acknowledge the agony" of his wife, to bury the afterbirth, and then to bring food, specifically coconuts, for his wife and those who assisted her.

With the arrival of a child, the unity of a couple, socially recognized at the wedding celebration, is confirmed. They had been enjoined to live in peaceful unity, the wife to obey and the husband to "rule with compassion," and to "make" their family. The beginning of their family is now "made" and their unity has borne fruit in a being that partakes of them both. They now begin to contribute to the care and nourishment of their child, by virtue of their separate rights to property derived from their respective families. Tokelauans draw a parallel between the physical substance and nourishment of children. Both are drawn from separate sources and united in them. They are seen as things of the same sort, although they are of different origin.[6]

Couples are expected to be close, to treat one another as near if not absolute equals, to help one another in everyday tasks (whether these be regarded as male or female ones), to share a sleeping mat, and to eat together. Spouses may be substituted for one another in certain social contexts, the participation of the wife, for example, fulfilling the obligations of her husband; and spouses are preferably on the same "side" and in the same clubs within the village. In church and village organizations, the status of a wife is derived from that of her husband. This caused no little concern when one church congregation decided to appoint female deacons. The problem lay in the fact that their husbands had not yet achieved positions of authority within the church, and was only solved by appointing the husbands as lay preachers.

Although it may be stated as a general Tokelau rule that husbands direct and wives obey, the domineering husband and submissive wife are not a feature of Tokelau society. Rather banter, teasing, joking, and an easy-going companionship is characteristic of Tokelau couples, as well as forthright criticism and thoughtful counsel. While verbal and occasionally physical abuse is frowned upon, it is considered to be a natural consequence of married life and not a matter for public censure. Major marital upheavals, usually precipitated by acts or suspicions of infidelity, will result in one partner, usually the husband, packing up and going back to the natal home. But such ruptures are rarely permanent, especially when the couple have children. [7]

In summary, marriage is a socially created and usually permanent union of two people stemming from different origins (in terms of substance and property). This new couple is expected to live together, sleep together, eat together, work and play together, and in due course produce children as physical representations of their combined selves who will be nourished from their combined resources.

Romantic love is not a significant theme of Tokelau culture. The attraction of a man and a woman to one another is expressed in the term *fofou*, "desire" and not by the term *alofa*, "affection," and simple "desire" is considered to be neither sufficient nor particularly important grounds for marriage. More crucial is the acceptability of the union to the families involved, the proven abilities and character of the proposed spouse, and the existing relationships among the involved families. [8] Couples are urged to live in peace and to diligently carry out their duties to each other, their respective families, and their own children. The issue of "affection" is rarely raised, although it is frequently present. Tokelauans compose no love songs; they dance no erotic dances, and it is only parents and children who make public demonstrations of affection for one another. Nor do their folktales take as important themes romance and love. Sometimes proposals of marriage are made, or suitors court village maidens, but these are stories that the Tokelauans claim came from Samoa. Tinilau, the Polynesian womanizer, is a secondary character in a number of Tokelau tales, but he is always said to live in Tonga or Samoa; although not Tokelauan, he may be attracted to Tokelau women who eventually suffer from his fickleheartedness. In the majority of the episodes involving couples a similar pattern is followed: they meet and *nonofo*, "stay together;" the woman becomes pregnant and delivers, the child is cared for and grows up. [9] However, unlike present-day Tokelauans, the characters in folktales abandon or drive away their spouses with hardly a care; but then they have not been "married" as Christians.

BROTHERS AND SISTERS

Tokelauans claim that full siblings are identical beings, *tutuha*, "the same." This sameness comes from the substance contributed by their common parents, from the food provided by the property in which they have a common share via their parents, and from their ancestry, the ultimate source of both physical substance and property. Despite this physical "sameness," brothers and sisters are socially set apart, their attributes culturally differentiated. They are assigned different domains of activity and their relationship is strictly circumscribed. The relationship is described as a *feagaiga*, "covenant," and involves a number of explicit rights and obligations.

Mamana, "mystical power" is attributed to sisters. From this is derived their ability to curse and their designation as *mātua hā*, "sacred mother" or *mātua tauaitu*, "spirit-holding mother" by their brothers' children. Although anthropologists in Polynesia have tended to emphasize the cursing aspect of the sister's power, her capacity to bring harm to her brother, his wife, and children, this "mystical power" also enables her to bless and assist. [10] Customarily, a sister cares for the newborn children of her brother and assumes a prominent role in any major event of their childhood. A sister should plait the fine mat for her brother's son at his marriage, as a token of her blessing of the union. Prohibited from close contact with her brother, a sister should send her son to look after him when he engages in a potentially dangerous enterprise, delegate a daughter to care for him if he is seriously ill, and dispatch her children to comfort him if he is bereaved.

291

Pule, "secular authority" is attributed to brothers, who are enjoined to provide for and protect their sisters and sisters' children. They should look after and defend the rights of their sisters against outsiders, decide what is in their sisters' best interests, and implement such decisions. It is by their physical strength, their ability to control any situation, their wisdom, and cleverness that they are supposed to keep their sisters safe and, if necessary, rescue them from adversity.

At maturity sisters remain within the natal family while brothers depart. Men often stop sleeping in their parents' houses before they are married, particularly if a sister is living there with her husband, though they will continue to keep their personal belongings there and will continue to eat there. Even after he is married and living in his wife's home a brother should bring his catches of fish and harvests from the plantations to his sister. These expectations apply particularly when the produce comes from property such as canoes and plantations, to which both have rights. In any case, a brother should regularly contribute something to his sister's larder. Upon receiving this produce, a sister should then divide it and return a portion to her brother. On occasion, and almost invariably on Sunday, a sister sends a portion of cooked food to her brother. Other items are irregularly transferred between brother and sister as tokens of their *alofa,* "affection" for one another, yet they remain at the distance required by the cultural demands of deference, respect, and avoidance.

It is repugnant to Tokelauans for mature brothers and sisters to live in the same dwelling. If by force of circumstances such a situation arises, it is the brother who should move out as soon as he can find an alternative. Eating together is something that many brothers and sisters find most discomforting, except when they are attending a large gathering where people sit side by side around the edges of a building, women separated from men, and therefore sisters from brothers. It is the intimacy of sharing a meal, of sitting opposite one another, that is avoided. Sisters regularly offer food to their brothers, but they always eat at a distance and sometimes with their back turned to where sisters are sitting.

The degree of restraint in verbal communication varies between individual brothers and sisters. Some, particularly those close in age and of the elder generation, hardly speak to one another at all, transmitting messages and requests through others, usually their children. Others converse directly but in a formal and restrained manner. Some even indulge in mild banter and innocuous gossip. But in no case should brothers and sisters tease or joke obscenely, criticize, or quarrel. Furthermore, it is poor taste for others to gossip or joke about one in the presence of the other. Convivial men's banter may suddenly turn to embarrassed silence when someone realizes that he has inadvertently referred to the sister of a man present. This reserve in the relationships of brothers and sisters conditions relationships with their respective spouses and, to a lesser extent, their children. There is a strong pro-hibition on sexual joking between a man and his wife's brothers and sisters' husbands, and between a woman and her husband's sisters and brothers' wives.

Despite the distance they keep from one another, the affective ties of brother and sister are usually strong and positive, summed up in the word *alofa* which designates the emotion most often attributed to ties of kinship. When on occasion brothers and sisters do not fulfil their *feagaiga*, "covenant," they are in effect denying their common origin by not demonstrating *alofa*.

Tokelau folktales, as might be expected, place considerable emphasis on the bonds between brothers and sisters. Conforming with the Tokelau ideology, brothers rescue sisters stolen by *aitu*, enthusias-tically respond to requests of sisters (usually to aid sisters' children), and return sisters who have journeyed afar, to their natal homes. Sisters assist brothers in impossible tasks, revive dead brothers, while sisters' children, as companions of their mothers' brothers, often subtly make amends for their mothers' brothers' ill-considered behavior. More dramatic, however, are the stories in which brothers either violate their sisters or deny their requests. Minor violations impel sisters to depart for far-off lands. Major violations provoke sisters to employ their mystical powers against their unloving brothers. The most extreme story of violation tells of how a brother, goaded by his wife, kills and cooks his sister for the wife to eat during pregnancy. Their child is born without limbs, but the sister's spirit later provides them. In the end, the sister's spirit confronts the couple, invokes horrible demons, kills the wife, and promises a like end for her brother in the near future. She says: ". . . what you did is not the act of a human . . . you have more love for your wife than you do for me, though we descended both of us, from a single belly."

293

Following from the social and cultural separation of brother and sister is the distinction between *tamatāne,* "the descendants of brothers" and *tamafafine,* "the descendants of sisters" with reference to a particular pair or group of siblings. These categories, though derived from sexual criteria, do not necessarily classify people by their own sex, for *all* descendants of brothers are *tamatāne* in relationship to *all* descendants of their sisters who are *tamafafine.*

Within the *kāiga,* "cognatic stocks" which are the major property-holding units in Tokelau, status as *tamatāne* or *tamafafine* usually determines the allocation of leadership positions and of rights and obligations among members. *Tamatāne,* like brothers, represent the *kāiga* in village affairs, protect its interests, and manage its property, but reside "outside." *Tamafafine,* like sisters, stay "inside," receiving and dividing harvests, managing the day-to-day internal affairs of the *kāiga,* and deferring to the authority of *tamatane.*

Not all *tamatāne* and *tamafafine* can actually exercise their ascribed rights and fulfil their ascribed obligations in any particular *kāiga,* since they have similar (or complementary) duties in others. Nevertheless, positions are allocated in this way so that the *fatupaepae,* literally, "the foundation stone" is a senior female *tamafafine* who resides within the *kāiga* home, receives and distributes food and goods, and cares for the immediate needs of the members; whereas, the *pule,* "ruler" is a senior male *tamatāne* who resides elsewhere, controls and directs the exploitation of productive property, and represents the *kāiga* in village government.

The *tamatāne: tamafafine* contrast is also appropriate in various other Tokelau domains. Within the village context, the men chosen to be responsible for managing feasts and for supervising the village-wide distributions of food which are made from time to time, may be referred to as the *tamafafine.* In a similarly figurative vein the *pulenuku* or elected "mayor," who is responsible for the management of the internal affairs of a village, may be seen as *tamafafine* to the *faipule* who is responsible for links with the external Administration, and who is thus *tamatāne.* These are casual, almost whimsical elaborations of the contrast which has real effectiveness and meaning only within the *kāiga* context. There are strong indications, however, that the *tamatāne: tamafafine* contrast had a wider application in village structure and ideology in pre-European times, when the *aliki,* "king" stood in a *tamatāne* relationship to the *vakaatua,* "vessels of the gods" and *taulaaitu,* "priests" as *tamafafine.* [11]

In Tokelau ideology, the *kāiga,* "cognatic stock" takes precedence over the nuclear family, and the brother-sister relationship over the relationship of husband and wife. The doctrine is expressed in terms of brother and sister being "from the same belly" and "irreplaceable," by contrast to spouses, whom it is possible to replace. Nevertheless, obligations to spouses should be fulfilled, and this gives rise to a characteristic dilemma, since most adults have spouses as well as siblings of the opposite sex. The demands of one relationship may conflict with those of the other, and it takes both patience and judgement to balance the two.

For Tokelau men, the attributes of generalized maleness seem to be consistently and equally manifest in both consanguine and conjugal roles. In each they are "outside," "strong," and exercise "controlled authority." However, Tokelau women's attributes do not appear to be so congruent. This is where Leach's (1961: 22) distinction between "uncontrolled" and "controlled" influence or power appears to be analytically useful. Whether consanguines or affines, women are "inside" and either attract *aitu* or are in touch with them. As wives, women are vulnerable to *aitu* attack and do not employ *aitu*—they are subject to powers which they cannot control. Sisters, however, especially on the evidence of folktales, appear to exercise control over *aitu* and to actively invoke mystical forces. Females, then, are both users of mystical power and victims of it—ambiguous beings who are both vulnerable and powerful in their different aspects.

"THINGS OF NO ACCOUNT"

Now, to return briefly to where we began, to the "games" and "things of no account" which Tokelauans play and relish. What motivates them and why are they so hilarious? [12]

In the "clown" performances the players are women, who are normally deferential and absent from public areas and who have the attribute of *mamana* or mystical power. Furthermore, the clowns are usually older women, secure in their roles as wives, mothers, and sisters. They act as men, not as their Tokelau brothers and husbands, but rather as foreigners—marauding seamen, doctors, even western brawlers (inspired by old movies shown in the islands)—dressed in European male clothing. Their performances not only exaggerate male authority but also invert its normal expression so that it is uncontrolled. The pun is on the juxtaposition of male and female attributes which are normally separated. Female lack of control is combined with male authority and strength resulting in uncontrolled authority or aggressiveness. The accepted pattern of male and female attributes is briefly challenged by drawing together aspects of each to present a logical alternative. But as is obvious to all, this pattern is impossible because chaos ensues and so there is no real challenge.

The performances therefore present two linked confrontations to normal order: women playing that they are men, and the miscombining of male and female attributes. The enjoyment of the audience arises as much from these women playing at what they are not, as from the plot and action displaying behavior that cannot be—at least in a Tokelau village. Perhaps they even point the lesson of what it would be like if women had authority, or if men could not control themselves. Seen in this light, the performances are clearly not a challenge to Tokelau men; rather the men are being flattered because they are dignified and controlled, unlike the men being played. Alternatively, are men being warned of the chaos that would ensue if they did not temper their strength and authority with dignity and control? Perhaps all these messages, and others beside, are involved.

We have mentioned that these performances are stylized and of a highly conventionalized form. They also escalate to a certain level of boisterousness and then abruptly end, as though they reach a limit which cannot be crossed, at least in the public arena, the domain of men inside the village. Female clowns do perform on other occasions, in other contexts. We have mentioned how they may relieve the tension of dispute at more or less formal gatherings of women by *ad hoc* clowning. They also perform whenever women work together on village projects, providing a diversion from the normally tedious task at hand. However, their most exuberant performances are reserved for the rare occasions when women take a holiday of a day or two outside the village. These are strictly female affairs and strictly recreational.

Moving outside the village, they separate themselves from their normal domestic duties and from men. The accomplished clowns lead the games, but others join in. Any pretext initiates the play and the comedy escalates from one plateau to the next in an unplanned manner—each episode becoming more obscene, the general hilarity inspiring ever greater licence. It is said of these affairs, *hē ai he tuakoi* "there are no limits." But note, they are private to women and outside the confines of the village.

There are also male comedians in Tokelau, but they are "stand-up comics" relying on verbal virtuosity and ingenuity to make people laugh. Their inspiration is real comic incidents involving their fellow villagers, which are embellished for the enjoyment of all. The performances are controlled and clever and the comedians do not clown or make themselves ridiculous.

Turning now to the *faleaitu* or skits.[13] The classic performance is the real "brother" and "sister" playing husband and wife, never the reverse. Husband-wife relationships, intimate and occasionally uncontrolled, are the logical skit plots, not the controlled, formal behavior of brother and sister. But the source of the comedy is in the relationship that really underlies the one being played, which is, of course, immediately recognized by the audience. A trivial domestic quarrel is at least slightly funny in its own right; but much funnier is inversion of the normal situation in the play situation—a man and woman who are normally reserved as "brother" and "sister" berating one another as husbands and wives are apt to do. The content of the skit soon becomes swamped by the hilarity of the audience each feeding upon the other. In a sense, perhaps, people are laughing at themselves and some of the complicatons (and tensions?) of their society. For Tokelauans, as for other people, their ultimate joke is themselves.

NOTES

Acknowledgments. At the annual meetings of the Association of Social Anthropology in Oceania in 1972 and 1973, Jane Goodale and Martin Silverman convened symposia on the topic "Male-Female in Oceania." We were invited by Jane Goodale to contribute a chapter to a proposed volume on the subject. After some hesitation, because neither of us had participated in the earlier discussions, we accepted her invitation. Unfortunately, enthusiasm for the project waned and plans for the volume were abandoned. Nevertheless, we are grateful to Dr. Goodale for encouraging us to confront the subject and hope that some of the other contributions prepared for the volume will be published in the near future.

During the past year or so, we have discussed this paper with a number of our colleagues. Julia Hecht has commented helpfully in the light of the contrasts with her Pakapuka data. We have, however, made only passing references to her material, anticipating that she will publish it soon. Bradd Shore has commented from a Samoan perspective and Garth Rogers from a Tongan one. The paper was formally presented at the ANZAAS Congress 1975 where a number of participants offered helpful ideas and suggestions.

We have done field research in the Tokelau islands, and with Tokelau migrants in New Zealand, at various times over the past eight years, and have incurred many debts to the people for their patience and tolerant understanding. Financial assistance from many sources enabled us to initiate, continue, and expand our Tokelau work. Hooper has been aided by grants from the New Zealand University Grants Committee and the Nuffield Foundation; Huntsman has been supported by grants from the United States Institutes of Health, the Society of

Sigma Xi, the Wenner-Gren Foundation for Anthropological Research, and the New Zealand University Grants Committee. Our continuing association with the Epidemiology Unit at Wellington Hospital in the Tokelau Migrant Study has been stimulating as well as financially helpful, and we are most appreciative of the generous support given our research by Dr. I.A.M. Prior, Director of the Epidemiology Unit.

[1] General ethnographic background on the Tokelau Islands may be found in Huntsman (1971), Hooper (1968, 1969), and Hooper and Huntsman (1973). For an extended discussion of one atoll, see Huntsman (1969).

[2] Kinship, sex, and age are the basic building blocks of Tokelau social organization. Here we emphasize sex, but the other bases of discrimination—age and particularly kinship—must be considered. An earlier article (Huntsman 1971), which focused on kinship, should be considered as a companion piece.

[3] We have attempted to use a wide variety of Tokelau statements on these topics, drawn from both *muāgagana*, "common sayings" and *kakai*, "folktales," to supplement our own observations and understandings. Although we worked in different atolls, we found that we had made similar observations and heard the same statements, and we arrived independently at some broadly similar interpretations.

[4] To separate the unseen or "spirit" world from the "natural" or animal world may do some violence to Tokelau concepts. *Aitu* may have human or animal manifestations; animals may have spirit "sides," just as humans may have spirit "sides." In the folktales, clear distinctions are not necessarily made between *aitu*, animals, and people; to ask what a particular character *is*, seems to be an irrelevant question.

[5] In each of the three atolls, some two-thirds of the married couples reside uxorilocally, if not in the wife's natal household, then in a house belonging to one of the wife's kin groups.

[6] These beliefs are congruent with the thorough-going cognatic nature of Tokelau social organization. They are to be contrasted with those held by Pukapukans (Hecht 1974) that different types of substances are contributed by the separate parents who likewise transfer different kinds of rights to their children.

[7] In 1971, of the 718 Tokelauans 20 years and older, only 14 (less than 2 percent) had been permanently separated or ever divorced. At

least a quarter of this small number were separated or divorced from Samoan spouses.

8 This touches upon the issue of marriage prohibitions which will be explored in a forthcoming paper.

9 Again, a Pukapukan contrast is illuminating. Hecht (1974) writes: ". . . Pukapukan love stories and chants are highly explicit [about sexual topics]." She relates this to the Pukapukan emphasis on the husband-wife relationship in contrast with the Tokelau emphasis on the brother-sister relationship. This then relates to Burrows' ([1938] 1970) Western versus Central Polynesia distinctions: "The western center has richer terminology for collateral relatives. . . . The central center has richer terminology for affinal relatives."

10 The sacredness of the sister (or father's sister) in Western Polynesian societies is well documented, but the beliefs (or interpretation of these beliefs) which give rise to her sacred qualities may vary. Firth (1957: 197), following Radcliffe-Brown, attributes the father's sister's sacredness in Tikopia to her association with the father and denies that she is invested with any particular spiritual power, at least while living (Firth 1957: 210). For Tonga, the position of father's sister is usually viewed as derived from rank: "A woman is always superior in rank to her brother . . ." (Gifford 1929: 17). From this superior rank stems the respect and privilege accorded her as a sister and father's sister, and to her children as sister's children. Rogers (1975) connects this superior rank to spiritual power, thus bringing the Tongan situation into line with the Samoan (Mead 1930) and Tokelauan ones.

The special position of the sister is documented for other Oceanic societies (see particularly Mead [1934]). Mabuchi (1960, 1964) writes of an "Oceanic type" of interpersonal relationship pattern ". . . characterized by the spiritual superiority of the sister . . ." (1964: 88), which assumes different manifestations in powers to bless and/or curse brothers and descendants of brothers, as well as the extent and way it is transferred to sisters' descendants, and in its association with special privileges and/or duties of sisters' children to mother's brothers and their children, etc.

A detailed investigation, expanding on Mabuchi's work, would seem to have merit, but is not appropriate here. In the meantime, we only point out that Tokelau represents yet another manifestation of the "Oceanic type" with some interesting characteristics, most importantly its association with a thoroughly cognatic society rather than patrilineal societies (Leach 1961: 22).

11 Newell ([1895], cited in Macgregor 1937: 51) writes: ". . . the son of the *Ariki* became king, but the son of his sister became priest." He gives the Tokelauan statement about this in a footnote: *"O tamafafine na fai ma vakatua; o tamatane na fai ma ariki,"* in which he mistranslates *tamafafine* as daughter and *tamatane* as son. Macgregor (1937) confuses the issue further by translating the Tokelau phrases as "the children of a sister" and "the sons of a father." We suggest that the Tokelauan should be translated: "Priests are selected from children of daughters; chiefs are selected from children of sons," which still, however, begs the question of *whose* daughters and sons.

12 The following interpretation of Tokelau comedy owes much to Douglas (1968), which illuminated for us certain features of these performances.

13 Shore (n.d.) writes that the male actors in Samoan *faleaitu* are seen as "ghosts," thus explaining the etymology of *faleaitu,* "ghost house." The Tokelau term may well be a Samoan borrowing; however, the comedy form is not a close borrowing.

REFERENCES CITED

Burrows, Edwin G.
    1938   Western Polynesia: A Study of Cultural Differentiation. (Reprinted Dunedin: University Book Shop, 1970.)
Douglas, Mary
    1968   The Social Control of Cognition: Some Factors in Joke Perception. Man (n.s.) 3: 361-376.
Firth, Raymond
    1957   We, the Tikopia: A Sociological Study of Kinship in Primitive Polynesia. Boston: Beacon Press. (First ed., 1936.)
Gifford, Edward W.
    1929   Tongan Society. Bernice P. Bishop Museum Bulletin, No. 61. Honolulu: Bernice P. Bishop Museum Press.
Hecht, Julia
    1974   From Conception to the Grave: Double Descent in Puka-

puka. Paper presented at the American Anthropological Association meetings, Mexico City.

Hooper, Antony
1968 Socio-Economic Organization of the Tokelau Islands. Proceedings, Eighth International Congress of Anthropological and Ethnological Sciences. Vol. 2. Pp. 238-240. Tokyo: Science Council of Japan.
1969 Land Tenure in the Tokelau Islands. *In* Symposium on Land Tenure in Relation to Economic Development. Working Paper, No. 11. Suva, Fiji: South Pacific Commission.

Hooper, Antony, and Judith Huntsman
1973 A Demographic History of the Tokelau Islands. Journal of the Polynesian Society 82: 366-411.

Huntsman, Judith W.
1969 Kin and Coconuts on a Polynesian Atoll: Socioeconomic Organization of Nukunonu, Tokelau Islands. Ph.D. dissertation, Anthropology Department, Bryn Mawr College.
1971 Concepts of Kinship and Categories of Kinsmen in the Tokelau Islands. Journal of the Polynesian Society 80: 317-354.

Leach, E.R.
1961 Rethinking Anthropology. London School of Economics Monographs on Social Anthropology, No. 22. London: Athlone Press.

Mabuchi, Toichi
1960 The Two Types of Kinship Ritual among Malayo-Polynesian Peoples. Proceedings, Ninth International Congress for the History of Religions. Pp. 51-62. Tokyo: Maruzen.
1964 Spiritual Predominance of the Sister. *In* Ryukyuan Culture and Society: A Survey. Alan H. Smith, ed. Pp. 79-91. Tenth Pacific Science Congress Series. Honolulu: University Press of Hawaii.

Macgregor, Gordon
1937 Ethnology of Tokelau Islands. Bernice P. Bishop Museum Bulletin, No. 146. Honolulu: Bernice P. Bishop Museum Press.

Mead, Margaret
1930 Social Organization of Manu'a. Bernice P. Bishop Museum Bulletin, No. 76. 1st ed. Honolulu: Bernice P. Bishop Museum Press. (Second ed., 1969.)
1934 Kinship in the Admiralty Islands. Anthropological Papers of the American Museum of Natural History. Vol. 34, Part 2.

302

Pp. 180-358. New York: American Museum of Natural History.
Rogers, Garth
    1975 *Kai* and *Kava* in Niuatoputapu: Social Relations, Ideologies and Contexts in a Rural Tongan Community. Ph.D. dissertation, Department of Anthropology, Auckland University.
Shore, Bradd
    n.d. Ideas of Order: Covert and Formal Conflict Management in Samoa. Unpublished manuscript.

SUGGESTIONS FOR FURTHER READING

Dwyer, Daisy Hilse
    1978 Images and Self-Images: Male and Female in Morocco. New York: Columbia University Press.
    Analyzes sexual stereotypes in thirty-five Moroccan folktales. Considers how images of femaleness and maleness ". . . buttress, and occasionally undermine, existing power relations between men and women" (1978: 5).
Hecht, Julia
    1977 The Culture of Gender in Pukapuka: Male, Female and the *Mayakitanga* "Sacred Maid." Journal of the Polynesian Society 86(2): 183-206.
    Detailed discussion of male-female symbolism and gender statuses in a Polynesian society. Provides a useful comparison with Tokelauan conceptions of the sexes (Huntsman and Hooper, this volume).
Schlegel, Alice
    1977 Male and Female in Hopi Thought and Action. *In* Sexual Stratification: A Cross-Cultural View. Alice Schlegel, ed. Pp. 245-269. New York: Columbia University Press.
    Assertions of universal female subordination are contradicted by the high status of Hopi Indian women. Describes the balance and interdependence that characterize intersex relations among the Hopi.

GLOSSARY

Acculturation
Cultural changes resulting from extended contact between two or more previously autonomous groups or societies.

Adelphic Polyandry
A form of polyandry in which a wife has two or more co-husbands who are brothers; fraternal polyandry.

Affine
Relative by marriage; an in-law.

Age Grade
An association of persons of the same sex and approximately the same age; by cross-cutting lineage, clan, or other groupings in society, age grades join together individuals of similar status for common action.

Age-Set
A group of individuals of the same sex and similar age, who maintain close ties throughout their lives and pass together through age-related roles and statuses.

Agnates
Persons related to each other through common ties of patrilineal descent.

Agnatic Descent
See patrilineal descent.

Avunculate
Relationship between a nephew and his maternal uncle in which the nephew is subject to the authority of, and is likely to inherit the possessions or position of, the uncle. See avunculocal residence.

Avunculocal Residence
Pattern of residence found in certain matrilineal societies specifying that the newly married couple lives with or near the brother of the husband's mother.

Brideprice
See bridewealth.

Bride Service
Labor or other work performed by a husband for his wife's kin, either before the marriage or after. It may take the place of, or supplement, the brideprice.

Bridewealth
Payment of goods or money prior to marriage by a prospective husband and/or his kin to his bride's kin; brideprice.

Chiefdom
A form of sociopolitical organization consisting of hierarchic rankings of status positions and a specialized system of production in which the chief acts as a central coordinator of religious, social, and economic activities.

Clan
A kinship group consisting of a number of lineages whose members believe they are descendants of a common ancestor, even though they may not be able to demonstrate exact genealogical links.

Cognate
A person related to another by common ancestry.

Cognatic Descent
Rule of descent that affiliates an individual with groups of kin related to him or her through males or females, depending on circumstances and choice; ambilineal descent.

Cognatic Stock
A kindred consisting of all the descendents of a person or a married pair traced through either the male or female line, depending on circumstances and choice.

Consanguineal Relations
Relatives by birth.

Cross-Cousins
The offspring of siblings of the opposite sex; for example, the children of a mother's brother or a father's sister.

Endogamy
A cultural practice requiring marriage within one's social group.

Ethnography
Descriptive study of a particular culture.

Exogamy
A cultural practice requiring marriage outside one's kin group or community.

Extended Family
A social group composed of a monogomous, polygynous, or polyandrous conjugal unit, plus offspring, and containing at least three generations of blood relations.

Family of Orientation
The family into which an individual (ego) is born and in which he or she is reared and considered a child in relation to the parents.

Family of Procreation
The family formed by marriage of an individual (ego) and in which he or she is a parent.

Foraging
See gathering and hunting.

Gathering and Hunting
A foraging economy based on simple tools for collecting and hunting wild foods and animals.

306

Genitor
A person's biological father.

Ghost Marriage
The institution whereby a woman is married to the name of a kinsman who died without male children to sacrifice to him.

Hoe Agriculture
See horticulture.

Horticulture
A simple form of cultivation using hand held tools without the assistance of plows, draft animals, and irrigation.

Kindred
A personal kin group that is ego-focused rather than ancestor-focused, as in lineages.

Levirate
The practice whereby a man may marry his deceased's brother's widow (or demand a brideprice from any other man she marries) and has an obligation to provide for her. The term comes from the Latin *levir*, brother-in-law.

Lineage
A unilineal descent group (either matrilineal or patrilineal) whose members reckon descent from a common ancestor through known genealogical links.

Marriage
A socially recognized relationship between two or more persons of the same or opposite sex which serves to legitimize their offspring and establish reciprocal rights and obligations between or among spouses.

Matriarchy
The legitimate exercise of political power and authority by women; commonly contrasted in feminist writings with patriarchy, the rule by men.

Matriclan
A kin group consisting of a number of matrilineages whose members believe they are descendants of a common female ancestor.

Matrikin
Matrilineal relatives.

Matrilateral
Relationships traced through the mother in a patrilineal descent system.

Matrilineage
A unilineal descent group whose members reckon matrilineal descent from a common female ancestor through known genealogical links traced solely through females.

Matrilineal Descent
Ancestry reckoned exclusively through the maternal (female) line; defines children as members of their mother's descent group.

Matrilocal Residence
Pattern of residence specifying that a newly married couple lives with or near the wife's kin.

Monogamy
Marriage with only one man or one woman at a time.

Neolocal Residence
Pattern of residence whereby a newly married couple lives separately from the kin of both spouses.

Nuclear Family
A social group consisting of a husband and wife and their young children; elementary family.

Pastoralism
A specialized form of animal husbandry based on maintaining herds of grazing animals such as goats, cattle, or camels.

Pater
A person's socially recognized father, who is not necessarily his or her genitor.

Patriclan
A kin group consisting of a number of patrilineages whose members believe they are descendants of a common male ancestor.

Patrikin
Patrilineal relatives.

Patrilateral
A kinship system where descent is only traced through males; or, relationships traced through the father in a matrilineal descent system.

Patrilineage
A unilineal descent group whose members reckon patrilineal descent from a common male ancestor through known genealogical links traced solely through males.

Patrilineal Descent
Ancestry reckoned exclusively through the paternal (male) line; defines children as members of their father's descent group.

Patrilocal Residence
Pattern of residence specifying that a newly married couple lives with or near the husband's kin.

Peasants
Small scale rural agriculturalists who are part of complex state societies and market systems over which they have little or no control.

Polyandry
Marriage between one woman and two or more men at the same time.

Polygyny
Marriage of one man to two or more women at the same time.

Rights in Genetricem
A husband's rights over the children his wife may bear him.

Rights in Uxorem
A husband's sexual and domestic rights over his wife.

Siblings
Persons born of the same mother; brothers and sisters.

Subsistence
The means by which people obtain resources in order to make a living.

Transhumance
A form of pastoralism characterized by seasonal movements in which the community splits up into sedentary base and migratory camps.

Tribe
An egalitarian social group which lacks specialized political roles and formal positions of leadership; it is characterized by internal mechanisms that serve to integrate local segments into a large whole.

Unilineal Descent Group
A kin group based on reckoning descent through one line only, either the paternal or maternal. See lineage.

Uterine
Having the same mother but a different father; for example, uterine sisters.

Uxorilocal Residence
See matrilocal residence.

Virilocal Residence
See patrilocal residence.

Woman-Marriage
The institution whereby a woman gives bridewealth for and marries another woman, thus acquiring rights over the latter and her children, with the duties of procreation delegated to a male genitor.

SELECTED BIBLIOGRAPHY FOR FURTHER READING

Ardener, Shirley, ed.
    1975   Perceiving Women. New York: Halsted Press.
    1978   Defining Females: The Nature of Women in Society. New York: John Wiley, Halsted Press.

Beck, Lois, and Nikki Keddie, eds.
    1978   Women in the Muslim World. Cambridge: Harvard University Press.

Boulding, Elise
    1977   Women in the Twentieth Century World. New York: Sage Publications.

Bricker, Victoria Reifler, ed.
    1975   Special Issue: Sex Roles in Cross-Cultural Perspective. American Ethnologist 2: 587-776.

Bridenthal, Renate, and Claudia Koonz, eds.
    1977   Becoming Visible: Women in European History. Boston: Houghton Mifflin.

Burstyn, Joan N., ed.
    1978   Special Issue: Women, Science, and Society. Signs: Journal of Women in Culture and Society 4(1): 1-216.

Chiñas, Beverly L.
    1973   The Isthmus Zapotecs: Women's Roles in Cultural Context. New York: Holt, Rinehart and Winston.

Croll, Elisabeth
    1978   Feminism and Socialism in China. London: Routledge and Kegan Paul.

Delamont, Sara, and Lorna Duffin, eds.
    1978   The Nineteenth-Century Woman: Her Cultural and Physical World. London: Croom Helm.

Elmendorf, Mary Lindsay
    1976   Nine Mayan Women: A Village Faces change. Cambridge, Massachusetts: Schenkman.
Fernea, Elizabeth Warnock
    1965   Guests of the Sheik: An Ethnography of an Iraqi Village. Garden City, New York: Doubleday, Anchor Books.
Fernea, Elizabeth Warnock, and Basima Qattan Berzirgan, eds.
    1977   Middle Eastern Muslim Women Speak. Austin: University of Texas Press.
Friedl, Ernestine
    1975   Women and Men: An Anthropologist's View. New York: Holt, Rinehart and Winston.
Gale, Fay, ed.
    1974   Woman's Role in Aboriginal Society. Australian Aboriginal Studies, No. 36. Social Anthropology Series, No. 6. 2nd ed. Canberra: Australian Institute of Aboriginal Studies.
Giele, Janet Zollinger, and Audrey Chapman Smock, eds.
    1977   Women: Roles and Status in Eight Countries. New York: John Wiley, Wiley Inter-Science.
Gornick, Vivian, and Barbara K. Moran, eds.
    1971   Women in Sexist Society: Studies in Power and Powerlessness. New York: Basic Books.
Hafkin, Nancy J., and Edna G. Bay, eds.
    1976   Women in Africa: Studies in Social and Economic Change. Stanford: Stanford University Press.
Iglitzin, Lynne B., and Ruth Ross, eds.
    1976   Women in the World: A Comparative Study. Studies in Comparative Politics, No. 6. Santa Barbara, California: American Bibliographic Center, Clio Press.
Jacobs, Sue-Ellen
    1974   Women in Perspective: A Guide for Cross-Cultural Studies. Urbana: University of Illinois Press.
Jaquette, Jane S., ed.
    1974   Women in Politics. New York: John Wiley.
Jones, Rex L., and Shirley Kurz Jones
    1976   The Himalayan Woman: A Study of Limbu Women in Marriage and Divorce. Palo Alto, California: Mayfield.
Jordan, Brigitte
    1978   Birth in Four Cultures: A Cross-Cultural Investigation of Childbirth in Yucatan, Holland, Sweden, and the United States.

Monographs in Women's Studies. Montreal: Eden Press Women's Publications.

Lebra, Joyce, Joy Paulson, and Elizabeth Powers, eds.
1976   Women in Changing Japan. Stanford: Stanford University Press.

McCormack, Patricia A.
1976   Special Issue. Cross-Sex Relations: Native Peoples. Western Canadian Journal of Anthropology 6(3): 1-288.

Martin, M. Kay, and Barbara Voorhies
1975   Female of the Species. New York: Columbia University Press.

Matthiasson, Carolyn J., ed.
1974   Many Sisters: Women in Cross-Cultural Perspective. New York: Free Press.

Raphael, Dana, ed.
1975   Being Female: Reproduction, Power, and Change. The Hague: Mouton.

Rohrlich-Leavitt, Ruby, ed.
1975   Women Cross-Culturally: Change and Challenge. The Hague: Mouton.

Rossi, Alice S., ed.
1973   The Feminist Papers: From Adams to De Beauvoir. New York: Bantam.

Saffioti, Heleieth I.B.
1978   Women in Class Society. Michael Vale, trans. New York: Monthly Review Press.

Schneir, Miriam, ed.
1972   Feminism: The Essential Historical Writings. New York: Vintage Books.

Schuster, Ilsa M. Glazer
1979   New Women of Lusaka. Palo Alto, California: Mayfield.

Smuts, Robert W.
1959   Women and Work in America. New York: Columbia University Press. (Reprinted New York: Schocken Books, 1971.)

Stromberg, Ann H., and Shirley Harkness, eds.
1978   Women Working: Theories and Facts in Perspective. Palo Alto, California: Mayfield.

Tinker, Irene, Michèle Bo Bramsen, and Mayra Buvinić, eds.
1976   Women and World Development. New York: Praeger.

Vicinus, Martha, ed.

1972 Suffer and Be Still: Women in the Victorian Age. Bloomington: Indiana University Press.

Whyte, Martin King

1978 The Status of Women in Preindustrial Societies. Princeton, New Jersey: Princeton University Press.

Youssef, Nadia Haggag

1974 Women and Work in Developing Societies. Westport, Connecticut: Greenwood Press.

INDEX

Aba Riots. *See* Women's War
Abortion, 268-69, 273
Abuse: Barabaig, 154-55;
    Digo, 125; Navaho, 78, 85;
    sanctions against, 169,
    177-78; Tokelau, 290;
    Zapotec, 244, 253n.6
Adelphic polyandry, 209
Adultery: Bena Bena, 270;
    Digo, 127-28; Navaho, 85;
    Tokelau, 290
Afigbo, A.E.: quoted, 176
Afikpo Ibo, 11
Age grades, 263-67
Age-sets: Igbo women's,
    167-68
Agnatic descent. *See* Patri-
    lineal descent
Ancient Society (Morgan), 52
Androcentrism: and research,
    5-6; and women's roles, 7
Anorexia, 18
Antagonism. *See* Sexual
    antagonism
Australian Aborigines: and
    anthropological models, 7;
    division of labor among,
    42, 48
Azande, 41

Barabaig, 14, 145ff.; bride-
    wealth in, 147, 151-52; kin-
    ship organization of,
    146-47; legal status of
    women in, 150-51, 160;
    pastoral economy of,
    146-47; political organiza-
    tion of, 147-50; women's
    councils in, 14, 146,
    149-50, 152ff.; women's
    ritual status in, 151
Barrenness. *See* Infertility
Ba Venda, 134, 227-29
Beauvoir, Simone de: quoted, 1
Bemba, 10, 56ff.; division of
    labor in, 59-60; female
    production in, 63; and food
    distribution in, 66-67;
    women's status compared
    with Iroquois, 56, 67-68
Bena Bena, 21, 256ff.; contra-
    ception in, 268-69; court-
    ing in, 263-64, 270; co-wife
    relations in, 268, 273;
    divorce in, 267; fear of
    female contact in, 269-70;
    female age grades of, 263;
    female initiation in, 263;
    female socialization in,
    263; incidence of female
    infertility in, 269, 277n.10;

315

kinship organization of, 259-60; male dominance in, 261-62; male initiation in, 261-62; marriage in, 264ff.; menstrual taboos of, 261; premarital pregnancy in, 264; sexual antagonism in, 258-59; treatment of brides in, 265-66; warfare and male solidarity in, 258-60; wedding ceremony in, 264-65; women's fear of childbirth in, 268-69

Bernard, Jessie, 94, 96

Birth spacing, 9, 54

Blackfoot Indians, 17

Bogoras, Waldemar: quoted, 40

Bohannan, Laura: quoted, 229-30

Bonding, male, 2. *See also* Male dominance

Boserup, Ester, 103-4; quoted, 99, 101-2

Bossen, Laurel, 11; quoted, 12

Brideprice. *See* Bridewealth

Bride service, 194

Bridewealth, 166, 215-18; Barabaig, 147, 151-52; Bena Bena, 264; definition, 3; Digo, 125-26; Nuer, 210; and transfer rights over children, 210, 214; used by women to acquire wives, 17, 212-19, 221-22, 226-27

Brown, Judith K., 9-10, 98

Chiefs: Barabaig, 147; Warrant, 171-74, 176; women as, 8

Childbirth: and definition of women's roles, 2, 5; male offenses against, 154-55; Tokelau, 289; women's fear of, 268-69. *See also* Childcare; Premarital pregnancy

Childcare: Iroquois, 58; Navaho, 78, 82, 89; as primary responsibility of women, 9, 78; as source of stress, 245; and women's work, 9, 38. *See also* Childbirth

Chukchee, 40

Clan: Barabaig, 150; Bena Bena, 259-60; defined, 10; Navaho, 79

Clowns. *See* Female clowns

Coastal Digo. *See* Digo

Colonialism: and women's political roles, 163-64, 170-78; and women's status, 7, 11. *See also* Development; Modernization

Concubinage: definition, 210

Contraception, 268-69. *See also* Abortion

Cornell University Southwest Project, 76

Council of women. *See* Women's councils

Courts, Native, 176-78

Cults, possession, 19, 134; and Digo women, 134; and social status of members,

139-40n.11; and *zar* spirits, 134, 139n.11. *See also* Exorcism; Possession

Culture, Man and Nature (Harris), 25n.

Curers: as chronically possessed women, 134-35; as diagnosticians, 203-5; Digo, 122, 132-33; Irigwe, 193, 204-5; Lovedu, 220; Nuer, 210-11; as possession specialists, 203ff.; and *susto*, 239, 252n.1; Tokelau, 287; Zapotec, 252n.1; Zulu, 227. *See also* Cults; Exorcism; Possession

Dahomey, 212-14, 226-27, 229; woman-marriage in, 227, 229-30

Dakar, 105

Depression: and women, 18

Desertion, 78, 124-25, 266. *See also* Divorce

Development: and studies of women, 93-100

Development programs: and underdevelopment of women, 12, 112-14

Development theory: criticisms of, 96-98. *See also* Colonialism; Underemployment; Women and work

Digo, 14, 19, 120ff.; female sexuality in, 123, 127-28; male dominance in, 135; male view of female psychology in, 125, 127-28; women's work in, 123

Dinka, 210-11

Disorders, female, 18. *See also* Illness; Possession; *Susto*

Diviners. *See* Curers

Division of labor, sexual, 9-10; Bemba, 59-60; Chukchee, 40-41; Digo, 123; Guatemala, 108-12; Igbo, 166; Iroquois, 57-59; Iroquois and Bemba compared, 60-62; Navaho, 76-77; physiological theories of, 36-38; and suitability of women for dull work, 37-38; Tokelau, 284-85. *See also* Women and work

Divorce: Bemba, 56; Bena Bena, 267, 272; consequences of for women, 11-12, 78, 86-87; Digo, 14, 124-25; Irigwe, 16, 197; Navaho, 11-12, 78, 86-87; Tokelau, 290, 299-300n.7; Toro, 11. *See also* Desertion

Domesticity. *See* Women and domesticity

Domestic organization: Iroquois, 54-55, 64-68; Navaho, 11-12, 77-78, 82, 89. *See also* Women and domesticity

Dowry: and economic status of Barabaig women, 14, 147, 151-52

Dual-sex system, 14, 146

Durkheim, Émile: quoted, 36

Dwyer, Daisy Hilse: quoted, 6

Dyk, Walter: quoted, 78

317

East Africa, 14
Education: and illiteracy of
Indian women, 113; and
Navaho women, 84
Education, mission, 113,
178-79, 182n.7
Employment. *See* Division of
labor; Labor; Under-
employment; Women and
work
Enga, 258, 262, 275-76n.2
Engels, Friedrick, 99
Eskimo, 40
Ethiopia, 134
Ethnocentrism: and research,
5-6
Ethnographic Atlas (Murdock),
49
Ethnography: definition, 5
Evans-Pritchard, E.E., 100,
208-11, 225, 230; quoted,
101
Exorcism: demands of posses-
sing spirit during, 125-26,
139n.7; diagnosis, 127-29,
133-35; expenses of, 204;
and possessed women,
122, 132-35, 203-4. *See
also* Cults; Possession
Exorcism ceremonies. *See*
Exorcism

Fāluma, 280, 282-83. *See also*
Female clowns
Family, extended: Irigwe, 188,
191-92; Navaho, 11, 76-77,
81; Zapotec, 241-42
Family, nuclear, 37, 81; defini-
tion, 12
Family, of orientation: Lovedu,

219, 221, 227; Navaho, 77
Family, of procreation: Lovedu,
227; Navaho, 77
Farming. *See* Female farming;
Horticulture
Feil, D.K., 20
Female clowns, 22, 280-81,
295ff.; as mediators, 285;
middle-aged women as,
280, 295-96; and sex role
inversion, 281-83, 295ff.
Female farming, 101-4. *See
also* Horticulture
Female husband: infertility of,
211-12; Lovedu queen as,
222-23; "male" roles
stressed, 231ff.; political
roles of, 219-20, 231; rights
of in woman-marriage,
213-14. *See also* Lovedu;
Nuer; Woman-marriage
Female infanticide. *See* Infanticide
Female infertility. *See* Infertility
Femaleness: androcentric
views of, 6, 20-21; cultural
concepts of, Tokelau,
284-88; male views of,
Bena Bena, 20, 269;
Zapotec ideal of, 243-46.
See also Femininity;
Women
Female sexuality: Digo, 127-28;
Igbo, 169-70; Irigwe, 198;
Morocco, 6; Mundurucú,
20; Zapotec, 244
Femininity: cultural attributes
of, Tokelau, 285-86; male
ideal of, Bena Bena,

318

272-73; male stereotypes of, 20-21. *See also* Female-ness

Fenton, William N.: quoted, 51

Folk illness. *See Susto*

Foraging. *See* Hunting-gathering

Friedl, Ernestine, 2

Frieze, Irene H.: quoted, 18

Fruitland Irrigation Project, 75

Gahuka-Gama, 262, 271, 273, 275

Gardening. *See* Female farm-ing; Horticulture

Gathering. *See* Hunting-gathering

Gender: and woman-marriage, 17-18, 230-32; and women's status, 4

Genitor, 210, 228; legal rights of in woman-marriage, 218, 225-26, 228-30, 235n.5. *See also* Woman-marriage

Gerlach, L.P., 126

Ghost-marriage, 210-12, 225; definition, 210. *See also* Marriage; Woman-marriage

Gifford, Edward W.: quoted, 300n.10

Girgwaged gademg, 150, 156, 160. *See also* Barabaig; Women's councils

Giriama, 139-40n.11

Goldenweiser, Alexander A.: quoted, 51-52, 60

Gomm, Roger, 13-14

Goodale, Jane C., 7

Goode, William J., 94-96

Gouldner, Alvin W., 130, 132, 137; quoted, 131

Government policies: and effect on Navaho women's pro-ductive roles, 12, 79-80, 88

Green; Margaret M., 176, 181n.1; quoted, 165

Guatemala, 11-12, 93, 107ff.; division of labor in, 108-12

Gusii, 39

Gusinde, Martin: quoted, 42-43

Haiti, 105

Hamamsy, Laila Shukry, 11; quoted, 12, 106-7

Handsome Lake, 63-64

Harris, Jack: quoted, 170, 182n.4

Harris, Marvin, 25

Hart, C.W.M., 7

Herding, 14, 146. *See also* Transhumant pastoralism

Herskovits, Melville J., 209, 213, 229; quoted, 208, 214

Highland Guatemala. *See* Guatemala

Highland New Guinea. *See* New Guinea

Hoe agriculture. *See* Horti-culture

Hooper, Antony: quoted, 21-22

Horticulture, 188, 256; and compatibility with child-care, 41-42; definition, 10; women and, 41-42, 101-4. *See also* Female farming

Hostility. *See* Sexual antago-nism

Hunting-gathering, 6-7

Huntsman, Judith: quoted, 21-22

Ibo. *See* Igbo
Ideology. *See* Sexual ideology
Igbo, 15, 102, 104, 163ff., 212-13, 227; division of labor in, 166; political organization of, 164-70, 182n.5; women's councils in, 167-70, 176-78, 182n.4; and Women's War, 171-76
Ijo, 212, 214
Illness: sex typing of, 18-19. *See also* Possession; *Susto*
Industrialization: consequences of for women, 7-8, 94. *See also* Colonialism; Development; Modernization
Infanticide, 262-63, 267
Infertility, 199, 245; and gender conversion, 210; incidence of, 269, 277n.10; and Nuer women, 210-11
Initiation: female, 263; male, 261-62
International Encyclopedia of the Social Sciences, 209
Irigwe, 16, 188ff.; kinship organization of, 189-92; marriage system of, 193ff.
Iroquois, 9-10, 41-42, 48ff.; compared to Bemba, 10, 49; division of labor in, 41-42, 54-55, 57-59, 62, 64-68; kinship organization of, 9-10, 54, 60-61; marriage in, 54; tribal organization of, 10

Jemison, Mary, 69n.; quoted, 41, 58-59
Jenness, Diamond: quoted, 48
Jesuit Relations (Lafitau), 50, 64, 70n.
Judicial councils. *See* Women's councils. *See also* Barabaig; Dual-sex system; Igbo

Kaberry, Phyllis: quoted, 42
Kenya, 14, 120ff.
Klima, George, 13-14
Knowledge: and women, 14-15, 151, 178-79. *See also* Education
Kon, 102
Krige, Eileen Jensen, 17
Kuma, 258, 275

Labor, division of. *See* Division of labor
Labor, wage: and changes in family structure, 93; and Guatemalan women, 12, 111-12; as index of modernization, 94, 98-100; and Navaho women, 12, 79-83, 106-7; women as exploitable surplus, 99-100. *See also* Division of labor; Modernization; Women and work
Lafitau, Joseph F., 64-65; quoted, 50-51
Lambert, William: quoted, 39
Langness, L.L.: quoted, 21
Law: and Barabaig women, 150-51, 160; and Digo women, 123; and Igbo

women, 15, 167-70; and Toro women, 11. *See also* Barabaig; Igbo; Women's councils

Leach, E.R.: quoted, 209

League of the Ho-De'-No-Sau-Nee, Iroquois (Morgan), 52

Leavitt, Ruby Rohrlich. *See* Rohrlich-Leavitt, Ruby

Leith-Ross, Sylvia, 176, 181n.1; quoted, 182n.7

Lévi, Claude Strauss. *See* Lévi-Strauss, Claude

Levirate, 225

Lévi-Strauss, Claude: quoted, 37

Lewis, I.M., 18-19, 134, 139n.11; quoted, 120-21, 127

Life of Mary Jemison (Seaver), 69n.

Life of Mary Kingsley, The (Gwynn), 182-83n.9

Lobedu. *See* Lovedu

Logoli, 37

Loskiel, George H.: quoted, 59, 66

Lovedu, 145, 208ff.; woman-marriage in, 216-24; political roles of women in, 215-16, 231. *See also* Woman-marriage

Lowie, Robert H., 48

Lunga, 42. *See also* Australian Aborigines

Mabuchi, Toichi: quoted, 300n.10

Mafia Island, 134

Mair, Lucy P.: quoted, 208

Male dominance: and anthropological bias, 22-23; assumptions of, 8; Bena Bena, 261-62, 273; Digo, 14, 135-36; Mundurucú, 20; universality of, 1; and warfare, 2. *See also* Sexual dominance

Maleness: cultural concepts of, 284-88

Malinowski, Bronislaw, 22-23, 48; quoted, 37

"Man the Hunter", 6-7. *See also* Hunting-gathering

Marketing. *See* Trading

Marriage: and age grade membership, 264-67; age of, 244, 252n.4; anthropological studies of, 15-16; Bena Bena, 264ff.; and bride purchase, 267; bride's relationships in, 78, 151, 244-45, 265-66; conflict between spouses in, 78, 84-87, 124-25, 267-73; conjugal rights in, 16, 78, 150-52, 169-70, 198-99; and co-wife conflict, 124, 268-69, 273; cross-cousin, 214, 223; definition, 15, 209; and dowry, 152; as exchange of women, 3, 16; frequency of, 199-200; functions of, 15, 232-33; Iroquois, 54; primary, in Irigwe, 16, 193-95; resistance to, 266, 271; rights over children in, 16, 198-199, 212-14, 234-35n.; secondary, in

Irigwe, 16, 195-200; and
spirit possession, 123-25,
202ff.; stress in, 16, 202-5,
245; Tokelau, 288-90. *See
also* Bridewealth; Woman-
marriage
Matriarchy, 25n.; Iroquois, 50,
52-53
Matriclan. *See* Clan; Matrilineal descent. *See also*
Iroquois; Navaho
Matrilineage. *See* Matrilineal
descent
Matrilineal descent: contrasted
with matriarchy, 25n.;
definition, 9-10; European
misconceptions of, 98, 145;
Iroquois, 9-10, 49; Navaho,
11-12, 77
Matriliny. *See* Matrilineal
descent
Matrilocal residence: Iroquois,
49; Navaho, 76, 81, 86,
106-7; Tokelau, 288-89,
299n.5
Matrons. *See* Middle-aged
women
Maya-Quiché Indians, 108
Mead, Margaret: quoted, 37-38
Mediumship, 134, 204-5. *See
also* Possession
Meggitt, M.J., 257, 271, 275;
quoted, 257-58
Melville Island, 7
Menopause, 4
Menstruation: male fear of,
257, 261-62, 275; women's
shame of, 273. *See also*
Pollution
Mexico, 19, 238ff.

Middle-aged women: Bemba,
56, 66-67; Bena Bena, 264;
as clowns, 280; depictions
of, 7, 20; domestic authority of, 55-59, 78; Irigwe,
16, 199, 201; and medium-
ship, 204-5; and political
power, 10, 51-52; poverty
of, 83, 88; religious roles
of, 53-54; ritual status of,
16, 203-5; status of, 246;
stereotypes of, 20; Tiwi, 7;
Zapotec, 246, 253n.5
Middle Eastern women, 6
Mikiri, 15, 163, 168-70, 172-74,
177-78. *See also* Igbo;
Women's councils
Milliken, Charles: quoted,
69-70n.
Minturn, Leigh: quoted, 39
Mintz, Sidney W.: quoted,
104-5
Missionization: consequences
of for women, 7-8, 163-64,
178-79. *See also* Colonialism; Modernization
Models, anthropological, 5. *See
also* Androcentrism,
Ethnocentrism
Modernization: criticism of,
94-100, 114-15; definition,
93; and Igbo women,
163-64; and Navaho
women, 106-7; and sexual
equality, 95, 114-15; and
women's trading, 104-5.
See also Colonialism;
Development
Monogamy, 209
Moots, 14, 124, 128, 152,

154-59; definition, 150. *See also* Women's councils

Morgan, Lewis Henry: quoted, 50, 52-55, 57-58, 64-65

Morocco, 4, 6

Motherhood. *See* Childbirth; Childcare

Mundurucú Indians, 20

Munroe, Robert L., 37

Munroe, Ruth H., 37

Murdock, George Peter, 51, 55; quoted, 36-37, 50

Murphy, Robert F.: quoted, 20

Murphy, Yolanda: quoted, 20

Mystical powers: of women, 286-88, 291, 295

Navaho, 11-12, 75ff., 106-7; division of labor in, 76-79; domestic organization of, 77-78, 82, 89; economic dependence of women in, 82-83, 88-90, 106-7; extended family in, 76, 81; kinship organization of, 76-79; marriage, 78, 84-87; matrilocal residence in, 76, 81, 107

Neighborhood councils, 149-50. *See also* Barabaig; Igbo; Women's councils

Neolocal residence, 87, 107

New Guinea, 20-21, 256ff.; and sexual antagonism in, 20-21, 257-59

New Mexico, 75

Nigeria, 11, 15-16, 102, 105, 163ff., 188ff., 212, 227

Nonindustrial societies. *See* Development; Industrialization

Northeastern Rhodesia. *See* Rhodesia

Notes and Queries on Anthropology, 209

Nsaw, 38

Nuer, 208-12, 225-27, 231

Oaxaca, 19, 239

Older women. *See* Middle-aged women

O'Nell, Carl W., 19, 239

Ownership, land, 60-62

Papua New Guinea. *See* New Guinea

Parker, Arthur C.: quoted, 62

Pastoralism. *See* Herding; Transhumant pastoralism

Patai, Raphael, 96; quoted, 94-95

Patriarchy, 25n.

Patriclan. *See* Clan; Patrilineal descent

Patrilineage. *See* Patrilineal descent

Patrilineal descent, 17, 147, 176, 178-79; associated with woman-marriage, 226; Barabaig, 147; definition, 17; Highland New Guinea, 256; Igbo, 166-67

Patriliny. *See* Patrilineal descent

Patrilocal residence: Barabaig, 151-53; Igbo, 167-68; Navaho, 81, 86, 107; Zapotec, 244

323

Sexual antagonism, 20-21;
Barabaig, 153, 159-60;
Bena Bena, 258-59,
267-73; Highland New
Guinea, 20-21, 257-59;
Lowland South America,
20-21. *See also* Sexual
ideology; Sexual inequal-
ity; Sexual segregation
Sexual asymmetry. *See* Sexual
inequality
Sexual dominance: Mun-
durucú, 20. *See also* Male
dominance; Sexual in-
equality
Sexual equality: and modernization, 95-100
Sexual ideology, 8, 19-22. *See
also* Femaleness; Sexual
antagonism
Sexual inequality, 1, 11. *See
also* Male dominance;
Sexual antagonism; Sexual
dominance; Women's
status
Sexual segregation: Highland
New Guinea, 20-21,
257-58; Iroquois, 57-58.
See also Pollution; Sexual
antagonism; Sexual
ideology
Siblings: avoidance of opposite
sex, Tokelau, 292-93;
importance of in woman-
marriage, 215-16
Sick roles. *See* Illness. *See also*
Possession
Sister: obligations of to brother,
Tokelau, 291-93; sacred-
ness of in Oceania, 300n.10

"Sitting on a man", 15, 168-69,
173-75, 177-78
Skits: husband-wife relation-
ship as theme, 297; and
sex role inversion, 281-83.
See also Female clowns
Slessor, Mary: quoted, 179
Snyderman, George S.: quoted,
61
Socialization: and sex roles, 78,
82, 242-45, 263
Society of Jesus, 50
South America, 20
South East Asia, 101, 104
Spirit possession. *See* Posses-
sion. *See also* Cults;
Exorcism
State bias, 6, 13
Status of women. *See* Women's
status
Sterility. *See* Infertility
Stites, Sara H., 64; quoted,
65-66
Stress: and sex role expecta-
tions, 19, 245, 248-51; and
susceptibility to *susto*,
240-42. *See also* Illness;
Susto
Subsistence activities. *See*
Division of Labor; Women
and work
Suicide: women and, 13, 18,
124, 274
Susto: and curers, 239, 252n.1;
diagnosis and treatment
of, 238-39; as folk illness,
19, 238, 251; geographic
distribution of, 19, 238;
incidence of among
women, 19, 248-51; as

measure of role stress, 241-42; psycho-social function of, 239-42, 249, 251; and soul loss, 239-40; symptoms of, 238-40. *See also* Illness; Possession; Sex roles

Taboos: menstrual, 261-62; sexual, 268. *See also* Menstruation; Pollution
Tanganyika. *See* Tanzania
Tanzania, 14, 145ff.
Technology: and alteration of women's work roles, Guatemala, 12, 108, 111, 113-14; women's access to, 102-3. *See also* Development; Labor; Women and work
Textbooks: exclusion of women from, 25n.
Third World societies: and women's status in, 8. *See also* Colonialism; Development; Modernization
Tiwi, 7. *See also* Australian Aborigines
Tokelau Islands, 21-22, 280ff.; attributes of females in, 21-22, 285-288; division of labor in, 284-85; and female clowns in, 22, 280-81, 295ff.; kinship organization of, 294-95; marriage in, 288; mystical powers of women in, 286-88; and relations between opposite sex siblings in, 291-95; social

organization of, 282-83; and spirit possession among women in, 287-88; women's mediating roles in, 22, 285-86
Tombema Enga, 20-21
Toro, 11
Trading: Afikpo Ibo women, 11; Caribbean women, 104-5; Digo women, 123; Igbo women, 15, 166, 168-69; Irigwe women, 189; West African women, 3, 104-5, 212
Transhumant pastoralism, 146-47. *See also* Herding
Transvaal, 145
Tribe: definition, 10
Trobriand Islands, 22-23
Tungus, 40

Uganda, 11
Underemployment: and women, 12, 112. *See also* Development; Division of labor; Labor; Women and work
Unmarried mothers. *See* Premarital pregnancy
Uxorilocal residence. *See* Matrilocal residence

Van Allen, Judith, 13; quoted, 15
Venda, 227-29
Village councils: Igbo, 165, 167, 176-77. *See also* Neighborhood councils; Women's councils